# A POPULIST
# READER

# A POPULIST READER

## Selections from the Works of American Populist Leaders

*Edited by*
GEORGE BROWN TINDALL

GLOUCESTER, MASS.

PETER SMITH

1976

A POPULIST READER

Introduction, compilation and headnotes copyright © 1966
by George Brown Tindall

Printed in the United States of America.

All rights reserved.

First Edition: HARPER TORCHBOOKS, 1966
Harper & Row, Publishers, Incorporated,
49 East 33rd Street, New York, N.Y. 10016

Library of Congress Catalog Card Number: 66–10531

Reprinted, 1976, by Permission of
George B. Tindall

ISBN 0-8446-3075-6

# CONTENTS

## IV—THE POPULIST SPIRIT

## V—TWO OPPOSITION VIEWS

# INTRODUCTION TO THE
# TORCHBOOK EDITION

by

**George Brown Tindall**

In recent years the musty documents of Populism have supplied ammunition for one of the most spirited battles in American historiography. Long-established interpretations have put the movement in the broad tradition of American democratic reform, linked on the one hand to Jeffersonian and Jacksonian democracy and on the other to Progressivism and the New Deal. These judgments are now under attack by critics who locate in Populism a seedbed of nativism, anti-Semitism, jingoism, paranoid delusions of conspiracy, and other malignities. In some cases these critics picture the movement as a prototype if not the source of the new radical right of the mid-twentieth century.

The controversy over the significance of Populism has raised serious questions of interpretation.[1] Was Populism on the whole a rational and forward-looking response to the end of the frontier and the rise of industrialism, thrusting crucial issues upon the reluctant major parties and advancing remedies that for the most part eventually won acceptance? Or was it a preposterous rustic mutiny infested with cranks and visionaries, looking back to a mythical golden (or silver) age of the Jackson era and offering only wild monetary schemes or scapegoats as the response to exaggerated evils? Did Populism mark the final defeat in a long agrarian struggle against domination by commerce and industry? Or did it mark the beginning of a new era in which agriculture learned to gear the power of government to its own purposes, as business had long since learned to do?

These and other questions raised by recent critics have introduced new quantities into the scales of judgment. One can no longer evaluate Populism without weighing certain components

[1] A convenient introduction to the literature of the controversy is the summary and analysis in Walter T. K. Nugent's *The Tolerant Populists: Kansas Populism and Nativism* (Univ. of Chicago Press, 1962), pp. 3–32.

that its earlier historians neglected: the provincial insularity, the evidences of xenophobia and anti-Semitism, the feverish visions of conspiracy and cataclysm. Yet one need not conclude that Populism bore a unique burden of these elements nor that it was the supreme force in disseminating them. Sympathetic historians ask whether provincialism and nativism did not characterize American society at large in the 1890s as much as or even more than they characterized the Populists; whether the Populists' resort to the image of Shylock represented anti-Semitism or a folk stereotype of avarice (it was most often associated with gentile plutocrats); whether the attacks on Baron Rothschild, allegedly the gray eminence behind currency deflation, represented anti-Semitism or Anglophobia; whether in any case these factors loomed large enough to make Populism a special source of anti-Semitism; and whether Populist assumptions of a conspiracy behind currency deflation were any more illusory or virulent than conspiracy theories harbored by other groups, such as the "goldbugs," who equated Populism with anarchism.

Some critics view Populism as an example of "status politics," as a movement derived largely from "status anxieties," feeding upon irrational fears and setting up bogeymen on which to vent its frustrations. The view has merit, for the Populist at least in one part of his mind believed that new and frightening forces were destroying an old and stable agrarian society. He still thought of himself as the sturdy yeoman idealized by Thomas Jefferson, and he resented the growing urban ridicule of "hicks" and "hayseeds."

But his anxieties derived also from grievances deeper and more material than fancied slights or declining status. For three decades after the Civil War the dramatic tides of industrial and political change swept agriculture into the economic backwaters. From 1870 to 1897 commodity prices declined persistently as a consequence of overproduction and deflation. Moreover, farmers sold in competitive world markets and bought their manufactured goods in domestic markets protected by tariff barriers. Geography and climate conspired to complicate their problems with soil depletion, drought, floods, blizzards, and insects. The existing tax structure bore disproportionately on land. Consequently many, enmeshed as never before in the toils of debt, sometimes because of unwise expansion or speculation, lost their farms by foreclosure or sale.

Little wonder, in the circumstances, that farmers should blame some malevolent force: the railroads that levied heavy and discriminatory rates while they enjoyed governmental favoritism and largesse; the middlemen who prospered by handling commodities and "gambling" on the exchanges; the monopolists who cut production and kept their prices up behind tariff barriers; the mysterious "money power" that deliberately created a scarcity of its own stock-in-trade in order to force up its value, a power symbolized by Wall and Lombard Streets, by Morgan and Rothschild.

The wonder is not so much that farmers, steeped in a provincial culture and viewing life in personal and individualistic terms, should seek villains or find the source of their woes in human greed and wickedness. The wonder is the degree to which their leaders analyzed American society and proposed reforms in the political and economic system. Most surprising of all, perhaps, was that farmers should abandon to such a degree the tradition of *laissez-faire* and turn to government as an active agent to right wrongs. But they turned to the central government only after voluntary measures of cooperation had failed and after observing the many examples of governmental intervention in economic life in the post-Civil War years: in the tariff, in currency, Civil War pensions, internal improvements, and disposition of the public domain.

In the light of subsequent agricultural history the Populists suffered from one critical blind spot, one fatal naïveté. They were unwilling to face the fact of agricultural overproduction and unable to impose the cutbacks in production with which manufacturers so often responded to restricted markets. But voluntary crop limitation was impossible, and the use of government for the purpose would have imposed an intolerable strain upon the administrative machinery of that day. Moreover, in rejecting the overproduction theory the Populists raised a troubling question that still echoes in a hungry world. How could one speak of over-production, they asked, when so many people remained in want? Instead, they suggested, in the words of L. L. Polk's *Progressive Farmer* of North Carolina, "there is something radically wrong in our industrial system. There is a screw loose. The wheels have dropped out of balance."[2]

The problem, they believed, was simply that the producing classes of society were being denied the opportunity to enjoy the fruits of their labor, that they were too often victimized, too often underfed and poorly clad while the plutocrats led a sybaritic existence founded on human misery. Populist writers represented the extravagant life of the wealthy in the most lurid terms. Using a labor theory of value, often argued moralistically, they described a fundamental antagonism in society between producers and parasites, workers and predators, "the robbers and the robbed." In this conception farmers, urban workers, and small businessmen fell on the one side, bankers, middlemen, and monopolists on the other.

This "producer rhetoric" too glibly assumed a natural harmony of interests among the different types of producing classes and anticipated too optimistically a political alliance among them. Populism did attract some support from industrial labor, urban reformers, and intellectuals. It even inspired the only serious effort in Southern history to effectuate a political alliance of white and Negro voters on the basis of common economic grievances. But it never built an effective coalition with any of these groups. Some reformers, such as Henry Demarest Lloyd of Chicago, thought the movement afforded an opportunity for a mass farmer-labor party of the left. But it remained chiefly an agrarian movement, devoted to alleviating the farmers' ills, and primarily sectional, allying parts of the agricultural South and West against the imperialistic East.

Whatever naïve illusions it may have generated, Populism remained pragmatic rather than doctrinaire in its remedies for the evils of its day, expedient rather than theoretical in its program. Populists trenchantly criticized the dehumanizing tendencies of

[2] April 28, 1887.

industrial society and what more recent writers would label "alienation." They spoke and wrote on occasion of socialism, of production for use, of public ownership, but they never formulated a program on the basis of socialist theory or, for that matter, on any comprehensive ideology other than democracy. In this sense they moved in the main stream of American political history. They spoke of "impending revolution," but they proposed practical remedies for tangible problems within a framework of democratic capitalism. Problems of land monopoly, transportation, finance, and the plutocratic control of government were seen as the core of the farmers' grievances, and proposals for their correction were the core of the Alliance and Populist platforms. The rest was peripheral.

The Populists viewed land, the ultimate source of all wealth, as a heritage of all the people. Every man deserved to have as much as he needed to insure a living. And simple remedies for the spoliation of the public domain were available. The government should hold lands for the use of actual settlers only. It should recover lands acquired by railroads and other corporations "in excess of their actual needs" and should forbid alien ownership.

In transportation the remedy seemed equally simple. Since regulation had proved inadequate to the problems of overcapitalization and high rates, let the government run the railroad (and telegraph) systems just as it did the post offices. Since the trusts were built largely on transportation monopolies, the change would in turn remove one of the most important causes of industrial monopoly.

The financial proposals, however, were the fundamental reforms. The Populist program for the currency was much broader and more sophisticated than it seemed to those bemused by the silverite panacea. It rested upon the argument that population and economic activity had been growing at a faster rate than the volume of money. The money shortage in turn placed the producers at a disadvantage by forcing their interest rates up and their prices down. The solution was a flexible currency, geared to the needs of exchange and issued by the general government only. It should be distributed directly to the people, the Populists argued, in loans either on farmlands or on nonperishable crops such as cotton or wheat. More money, the farmers contended, would raise their prices, lower their interest rates, make possible the payment of their debts, provide employment, afford a more equitable distribution of goods, and restore prosperity.

The financial program further demanded an income tax to tap the more intangible forms of wealth and relieve the pressure of taxation on land and farm property. And finally it proposed a postal savings system as protection for depositors who ran the risk of disastrous losses in small-town banks hit by agricultural depression. Financial reforms were the key to all others. First stop the money power, said Populist Senator William A. Peffer of Kansas, and the lesser spoilsmen could be conquered easily.[3]

Yet something even further was necessary to purify American society and politics. The government must be brought more fully and closely under the control of the people, which was to say the "producers." To that end the Populists supported "a free ballot and a fair count" in all elections, the secret ballot, registration laws, direct primaries, the initiative and referendum, woman suffrage, the popular election of senators, and limitations on the terms of the president and vice-president. Other demands—the eight-hour day, the restriction of immigration, and expressions of sympathy for organized labor—were directed in large measure toward the urban workers. They brought little support from that quarter, but they reflected a genuine feeling of Populist identification with all "producers."

Populism flourished in a time of momentous political upheaval, and the seismic disturbances of the 1890s left the political landscape permanently altered. In 1896, when the silverites captured the Democratic party in the name of William Jennings Bryan, they undermined the People's party as an effective political force, but the "Bryanization" of the Democrats swept both major parties out of the ruts in which they had moved for a generation. Increasingly they came face to face with the problems of reform in

---

[3] William A. Peffer, *The Farmer's Side, His Troubles and Their Remedy* (New York: D. Appleton and Co., 1891), p. 273.

political institutions, currency, business regulation, and other fields thrust upon them by the Populists. The most profound change was in the view that government should play a more positive role in social and economic life, and the Populists did much to shatter the encrusted theories that had prevented new governmental responsibilities.

That today the Populist demands seem rather limited and scarcely radical is one measure of their success. The People's party itself rose and declined quickly. Its effective existence was limited to the period 1890–1896, and even then it carried few elections and never completely controlled a single state government. But its demands anticipated many changes to come in the twentieth century. If the demands for the recovery of public lands were never met, they anticipated the rationale of the conservation movement, the land as a public heritage. If the railroads were never nationalized, they experienced more effective state and federal regulation. And if the Populists never elaborated a program for controlling the trusts, their condemnation of abuses in business helped advance corporate regulation and antitrust measures. Their demands for changes in political and electoral practices read almost like a catalog of twentieth-century reforms in that field.

The silver panacea was not adopted, but the soundness of the Populist analysis was demonstrated by an unexpected development, the sudden increase of gold production in the late 1890s that brought inflation from an unexpected quarter, raised prices, and helped to restore farm prosperity. Moreover, their critique of a limited and inelastic currency was akin to the reasoning that underlay the Federal Reserve System, established in 1913, and their demands for inflation were still seriously advanced as late as 1934. The income tax was adopted as early as 1894; ruled unconstitutional the following year, it was re-enacted in 1913 under the Sixteenth Amendment. Rural credits did not come in precisely the form demanded by the Populists, but they came in generous measure under the Warehouse and Farm Loan Acts of 1916 and subsequent enactments.

In less tangible ways the Populist spirit lived on after the

People's party. Just as the producer rhetoric echoed Jacksonian slogans, it continued to reverberate in the progressive and New Deal eras. The idea of natural harmony among the producers was transmitted through various movements for farmer-labor coalitions, which were most successfully effected by Woodrow Wilson and Franklin D. Roosevelt. It is less easy to trace any direct line of descent from Populism to later right-wing movements. Populism is an ancestry that the radical right itself has not acknowledged, and history so far has produced only one example of a Populist leader who turned fascist.[4] A fairly direct genealogical connection does exist in the Populist legacy of the Southern demagogue, however, in the line running from such figures as Tom Watson to latter-day tribunes of the people like Huey Long, who grew up in one of Louisiana's Populist parishes. Watson himself stands as the classic figure of the Populist who "turned sour." He later led the movement for the disfranchisement of Negroes in Georgia, was the father of that state's notorious county-unit system, and launched scurrilous attacks on Catholics and Jews. But the Populist heritage also strengthened the cause of Southern and Western agrarians who helped develop the progressive programs of the twentieth century—and even "demagogues" like Huey Long often delivered tangible reforms.

The Populist heritage, like that of all great political movements, is not all of one piece, but it remains by and large in the tradition of democratic reform. Populists were the harbingers of progressivism. They provided a dispensary of ideas from which the progressives of a later day drew many of their remedies. If that dispensary is now about depleted, if it offers few specifics for the new ailments of the 1960s, an understanding of the Populists' stock of ideas is still essential to a comprehension of modern America.

The selections included in this volume were chosen with an eye to presenting the mind of the Populist, a kind of Populist world view, together with characteristic examples of contrary

[4] Milford W. Howard, former Populist congressman from Alabama, wrote a book in praise of Mussolini: *Fascism: A Challenge to Democracy* (New York: Fleming H. Revell Co., 1928). This was called to my attention by D. Alan Harris.

opinion. The readings are all contemporaneous with the farmers' movement, and most are the expressions of acknowledged Populists. They are not intended to afford a running narrative of the movement's historical evolution. That and a variety of interpretations may be traced in the works given in the selected reading list, among which John D. Hicks' *The Populist Revolt* remains the indispensable introduction.

# SELECTED READING LIST

ARNETT, Alex Mathews. *The Populist Movement in Georgia*. New York: Columbia Univ. Press, 1922.

BELL, Daniel, ed. *The New American Right*. New York: Criterion Books, 1955. rev. ed., *The Radical Right*. Garden City, N. Y.: Doubleday, 1963.

BOGUE, Allan G. *Money at Interest: The Farm Mortgage on the Middle Border*. Ithaca, N. Y.: Cornell Univ. Press, 1955.

BUCK, Solon Justus. *The Agrarian Crusade*. New Haven: Yale Univ. Press, 1920.

CLARK, John Bunyan. *Populism in Alabama*. Auburn, Ala.: Auburn Printing Co., 1927.

COLETTA, Paola E. *William Jennings Bryan: II. Political Evangelist, 1860–1908*. Lincoln: Univ. of Nebraska Press, 1965.

DESTLER, Chester MacArthur. *American Radicalism, 1865–1901*. New London: Connecticut College, 1946.

DURDEN, Robert Franklin. *The Climax of Populism*. Lexington: Univ. of Kentucky Press, 1965.

EDMONDS, Helen Grey. *The Negro and Fusion Politics in North Carolina, 1894–1901*. Chapel Hill: Univ. of North Carolina Press, 1951.

GATES, Paul, Wallace. *Fifty Million Acres: Conflicts over Kansas Land Policy, 1854–1890*. Ithaca: Cornell Univ. Press, 1954.

GOLDMAN, Eric Frederick. *Rendezvous with Destiny: A History of Modern American Reform*. New York: Alfred A. Knopf, 1953.

HAYNES, Frederick Emory. *James Baird Weaver*. Iowa City: State Historical Society, 1919.

——. *Third Party Movements since the Civil War, with Special Reference to Iowa*. Iowa City: State Historical Society, 1916.

HICKS, John Donald. *The Populist Revolt*. Minneapolis: Univ. of Minnesota Press, 1931.

HOFSTADTER, Richard. *The Age of Reform: From Bryan to F.D.R.* New York: Alfred A. Knopf, 1955.

JONES, Stanley Llewellyn. *The Presidential Election of 1896*. Madison: Univ. of Wisconsin Press, 1964.

MARTIN, Roscoe Coleman. *The People's Party in Texas*. Austin: Univ. [of Texas], 1933.

NOBLIN, Stuart. *Leonidas LaFayette Polk: Agrarian Crusader*. Chapel Hill: Univ. of North Carolina Press, 1949.

NUGENT, Walter T. K. *The Tolerant Populists: Kansas Populism and Nativism*. Chicago: Univ. of Chicago Press, 1963.

POLLACK, Norman. *The Populist Response to Industrial America: Midwestern Populist Thought*. Cambridge, Mass.: Harvard Univ. Press, 1962.

RIDGE, Martin. *Ignatius Donnelly: The Portrait of a Politician*. Chicago: Univ. of Chicago Press, 1962.

ROBISON, Dan Merritt. *Bob Taylor and the Agrarian Revolt in Tennessee*. Chapel Hill: Univ. of North Carolina Press, 1935.

SALOUTOS, Theodore. *Farmer Movements in the South, 1865–1933*. Berkeley and Los Angeles: Univ. of California Press, 1960.

—— and John Donald HICKS. *Agricultural Discontent in the Middle West, 1900–1939*. Madison: Univ. of Wisconsin Press, 1951.

SCOTT, Roy Vernon. *The Agrarian Movement in Illinois*. Urbana: Univ. of Illinois Press, 1962.

SHANNON, Fred Albert. *The Farmers' Last Frontier: Agriculture, 1860–1897*. New York: Farrar & Rinehart, 1945.

SHELDON, William Dubose. *Populism in the Old Dominion*. Princeton: Princeton Univ. Press, 1935.

WOODWARD, Comer Vann. *Origins of the New South, 1877–1913*. Baton Rouge: Louisiana State Univ. Press, 1951.

——. *Tom Watson: Agrarian Rebel*. New York: The Macmillan Co., 1938.

# A POPULIST
# READER

# I
# FARM CONDITIONS

## TOWN AND COUNTRY

*A son of the Middle Border, Hamlin Garland wrote out of intimate acquaintance with the region and with perceptions heightened by his departure and return. During the 1890s he actively supported the People's party as a writer and speaker. "If any one is still at a loss to account for that uprising of the farmers in the West which is the translation of the Peasants' War into modern and republican terms,"* *William Dean Howells wrote in an introduction to the book that first established Garland's literary reputation, "let him read* Main-Travelled Roads, *and he will begin to understand. . . ." At the beginning of the story reprinted in part here, Howard McLane, a successful dramatic author and actor, has returned to the old farmstead and a surly welcome from his brother Grant.*

## –1–
## UP THE COOLLY
### by Hamlin Garland

The next day was a rainy day; not a shower, but a steady rain— an unusual thing in midsummer in the West. A cold, dismal day in the fireless, colorless farmhouses. It came to Howard in that peculiar reaction which surely comes during a visit of this character, when thought is a weariness, when the visitor longs for his own familiar walls and pictures and books, and longs to meet his friends, feeling at the same time the tragedy of life which makes friends nearer and more congenial than blood-relations.

Howard ate his breakfast alone, save Baby and Laura its

SOURCE: Hamlin Garland, *Main-Travelled Roads* (New York: The Macmillan Company, 1899; first publ. 1891), pp. 117–129.

mother going about the room. Baby and mother alike insisted on feeding him to death. Already dyspeptic pangs were setting in.

"Now ain't there something more I can—"

"Good heavens! No!" he cried in dismay. "I'm likely to die of dyspepsia now. This honey and milk, and these delicious hot biscuits—"

"I'm afraid it ain't much like the breakfasts you have in the city."

"Well, no, it ain't," he confessed. "But this is the kind a man needs when he lives in the open air."

She sat down opposite him, with her elbows on the table, her chin in her palm, her eyes full of shadows.

"I'd like to go to a city once. I never saw a town bigger'n La Crosse. I've never seen a play, but I've read of 'em in the magazines. It must be wonderful; they say they have wharves and real ships coming up to the wharf, and people getting off and on. How do they do it?"

"Oh, that's too long a story to tell. It's a lot of machinery and paint and canvas. If I told you how it was done, you wouldn't enjoy it so well when you come on and see it."

"Do you ever expect to see *me* in New York?"

"Why, yes. Why not? I expect Grant to come on and bring you all some day, especially Tonikins here. Tonikins, you hear, sir? I expect you to come on you' forf birfday, sure." He tried thus to stop the woman's gloomy confidence.

"I hate farm-life," she went on with a bitter inflection. "It's nothing but fret, fret, and work the whole time, never going any place, never seeing anybody but a lot of neighbors just as big fools as you are. I spend my time fighting flies and washing dishes and churning. I'm sick of it all."

Howard was silent. What could he say to such an indictment? The ceiling swarmed with flies which the cold rain had driven to seek the warmth of the kitchen. The gray rain was falling with a dreary sound outside, and down the kitchen stove-pipe an occasional drop fell on the stove with a hissing, angry sound.

The young wife went on with a deeper note:

"I lived in La Crosse two years, going to school, and I know a little something of what city life is. If I was a man, I bet I wouldn't wear my life out on a farm, as Grant does. I'd get away and I'd do something. I wouldn't care what, but I'd get away."

There was a certain volcanic energy back of all the woman said, that made Howard feel she would make the attempt. She did not know that the struggle for a place to stand on this planet was eating the heart and soul out of men and women in the city, just as in the country. But he could say nothing. If he had said in conventional phrase, sitting there in his soft clothing, "We must make the best of it all," the woman could justly have thrown the dish-cloth in his face. He could say nothing.

"I was a fool for ever marrying," she went on, while the baby pushed a chair across the room. "I made a decent living teaching, I was free to come and go, my money was my own. Now I'm tied right down to a churn or a dish-pan, I never have a cent of my own. *He's* growlin' 'round half the time, and there's no chance of his ever being different."

She stopped with a bitter sob in her throat. She forgot she was talking to her husband's brother. She was conscious only of his sympathy.

As if a great black cloud had settled down upon him, Howard felt it all—the horror, hopelessness, imminent tragedy of it all. The glory of nature, the bounty and splendor of the sky, only made it the more benumbing. He thought of a sentence Millet once wrote:

"I see very well the aureole of the dandelions, and the sun also, far down there behind the hills, flinging his glory upon the clouds. But not alone that—I see in the plains the smoke of the tired horses at the plough, or, on a stony-hearted spot of ground, a back-broken man trying to raise himself upright for a moment to breathe. The tragedy is surrounded by glories—that is no invention of mine."

Howard arose abruptly and went back to his little bedroom, where he walked up and down the floor till he was calm enough to write, and then he sat down and poured it all out to "Dearest Margaret," and his first sentence was this:

"If it were not for you (just to let you know the mood I'm

in)—if it were not *for* you, and I had the world in my hands, I'd crush it like a puff-ball; evil so predominates, suffering is so universal and persistent, happiness so fleeting and so infrequent."

He wrote on for two hours, and by the time he had sealed and directed several letters he felt calmer, but still terribly depressed. The rain was still falling, sweeping down from the half-seen hills, wreathing the wooded peaks with a gray garment of mist, and filling the valley with a whitish cloud.

It fell around the house drearily. It ran down into the tubs placed to catch it, dripped from the mossy pump, and drummed on the upturned milk-pails, and upon the brown and yellow beehives under the maple trees. The chickens seemed depressed, but the irrepressible bluejay screamed amid it all, with the same insolent spirit, his plumage untarnished by the wet. The barnyard showed a horrible mixture of mud and mire, through which Howard caught glimpses of the men, slumping to and fro without more additional protection than a ragged coat and a shapeless felt hat.

In the sitting room where his mother sat sewing there was not an ornament, save the etching he had brought. The clock stood on a small shelf, its dial so much defaced that one could not tell the time of day; and when it struck, it was with noticeably disproportionate deliberation, as if it wished to correct any mistake into which the family might have fallen by reason of its illegible dial.

The paper on the walls showed the first concession of the Puritans to the Spirit of Beauty, and was made up of a heterogeneous mixture of flowers of unheard-of shapes and colors, arranged in four different ways along the wall. There were no books, no music, and only a few newspapers in sight—a bare, blank, cold, drab-colored shelter from the rain, not a home. Nothing cosey, nothing heart-warming; a grim and horrible shed.

"What are they doing? It can't be they're at work such a day as this," Howard said, standing at the window.

"They find plenty to do, even on rainy days," answered his mother. "Grant always has some job to set the men at. It's the only way to live."

"I'll go out and see them." He turned suddenly. "Mother, why should Grant treat me so? Have I deserved it?"

Mrs. McLane sighed in pathetic hopelessness. "I don't know, Howard. I'm worried about Grant. He gets more an' more down hearted an' gloomy every day. Seems if he'd go crazy. He don't care how he looks any more, won't dress up on Sunday. Days an' days he'll go aroun' not sayin' a word. I was in hopes you could help him, Howard."

"My coming seems to have had an opposite effect. He hasn't spoken a word to me, except when he had to, since I came. Mother, what do you say to going home with me to New York?"

"Oh, I couldn't do that!" she cried in terror. "I couldn't live in a big city—never!"

"There speaks the truly rural mind," smiled Howard at his mother, who was looking up at him through her glasses with a pathetic forlornness which sobered him again. "Why, mother, you could live in Orange, New Jersey, or out in Connecticut, and be just as lonesome as you are here. You wouldn't need to live in the city. I could see you then every day or two."

"Well, I couldn't leave Grant and the baby, anyway," she replied, not realizing how one could live in New Jersey and do business daily in New York.

"Well, then, how would you like to go back into the old house?"

The patient hands fell to the lap, the dim eyes fixed in searching glance on his face. There was a wistful cry in the voice.

"Oh, Howard! Do you mean—"

He came and sat down by her, and put his arm about her and hugged her hard. "I mean, you dear, good, patient, work-weary old mother, I'm going to buy back the old farm and put you in it."

There was no refuge for her now except in tears, and she put up her thin, trembling old hands about his neck, and cried in that easy, placid, restful way age has.

Howard could not speak. His throat ached with remorse and pity. He saw his forgetfulness of them all once more without relief,—the black thing it was!

"There, there, mother, don't cry!" he said, torn with anguish by her tears. Measured by man's tearlessness, her weeping seemed terrible to him. "I didn't realize how things were going here. It was all my fault—or, at least, most of it. Grant's letter didn't reach me. I thought you were still on the old farm. But no matter; it's all over now. Come, don't cry any more, mother dear. I'm going to take care of you now."

It had been years since the poor, lonely woman had felt such warmth of love. Her sons had been like her husband, chary of expressing their affection; and like most Puritan families, there was little of caressing among them. Sitting there with the rain on the roof and driving through the trees, they planned getting back into the old house. Howard's plan seemed to her full of splendor and audacity. She began to understand his power and wealth now, as he put it into concrete form before her.

"I wish I could eat Thanksgiving dinner there with you," he said at last, "but it can't be thought of. However, I'll have you all in there before I go home. I'm going out now and tell Grant. Now don't worry any more; I'm going to fix it all up with him, sure." He gave her a parting hug.

Laura advised him not to attempt to get to the barn; but as he persisted in going, she hunted up an old rubber coat for him. "You'll mire down and spoil your shoes," she said, glancing at his neat calf gaiters.

"Darn the difference!" he laughed in his old way. "Besides, I've got rubbers."

"Better go round by the fence," she advised, as he stepped out into the pouring rain.

How wretchedly familiar it all was! The miry cowyard, with the hollow trampled out around the horse-trough, the disconsolate hens standing under the wagons and sheds, a pig wallowing across its sty, and for atmosphere the desolate, falling rain. It was so familiar he felt a pang of the old rebellious despair which seized him on such days in his boyhood.

Catching up courage, he stepped out on the grass, opened the gate and entered the barn-yard. A narrow ribbon of turf ran around the fence, on which he could walk by clinging with one hand to the rough boards. In this way he slowly made his way around the periphery, and came at last to the open barn-door without much harm.

It was a desolate interior. In the open floor-way Grant, seated upon a half-bushel, was mending a harness. The old man was holding the trace in his hard brown hands; the boy was lying on a wisp of hay. It was a small barn, and poor at that. There was a bad smell, as of dead rats, about it, and the rain fell through the shingles here and there. To the right, and below, the horses stood, looking up with their calm and beautiful eyes, in which the whole scene was idealized.

Grant looked up an instant, and then went on with his work.

"Did yeh wade through?" grinned Lewis, exposing his broken teeth.

"No, I kinder circumambiated the pond." He sat down on the little tool-box near Grant. "Your barn is a good deal like that in 'The Arkansaw Traveller.' Needs a new roof, Grant." His voice had a pleasant sound, full of the tenderness of the scene through which he had just been. "In fact, you need a new barn."

"I need a good many things more'n I'll ever get," Grant replied shortly.

"How long did you say you'd been on this farm?"

"Three years this fall."

"I don't s'pose you've been able to think of buying—Now hold on, Grant," he cried, as Grant threw his head back. "For God's sake, don't get mad again! Wait till you see what I'm driving at."

"I don't see what you're drivin' at, and I don't care. All I want you to do is to let us alone. That ought to be easy enough for you."

"I tell you, I didn't get your letter. I didn't know you'd lost the old farm." Howard was determined not to quarrel. "I didn't suppose—"

"You might 'a' come to see."

"Well, I'll admit that. All I can say in excuse is that since I got to managing plays I've kept looking ahead to making a big hit and getting a barrel of money—just as the old miners used to hope and watch. Besides, you don't understand how much pressure there is on me. A hundred different people pulling and hauling to have me go here or go there, or do this or do that. When it isn't yachting, it's canoeing, or—"

He stopped. His heart gave a painful throb, and a shiver ran through him. Again he saw his life, so rich, so bright, so free, set over against the routine life in the little low kitchen, the barren sitting room, and this still more horrible barn. Why should his brother sit there in wet and grimy clothing, mending a broken trace, while he enjoyed all the light and civilization of the age?

He looked at Grant's fine figure, his great, strong face; recalled his deep, stern, masterful voice. "Am I so much superior to him? Have not circumstances made me and destroyed him?"

"Grant, for God's sake, don't sit there like that! I'll admit I've been negligent and careless. I can't understand it all myself. But let me do something for you now. I've sent to New York for five thousand dollars. I've got terms on the old farm. Let me see you all back there once more before I return."

"I don't want any of your charity."

"It ain't charity. It's only justice to you." He rose. "Come, now, let's get at an understanding, Grant. I can't go on this way. I can't go back to New York and leave you here like this."

Grant rose too. "I tell you, I don't ask your help. You can't fix this thing up with money. If you've got more brains'n I have, why, it's all right. I ain't got any right to take anything that I don't earn."

"But you don't get what you do earn. It ain't your fault. I begin to see it now. Being the oldest, I had the best chance. I was going to town to school while you were ploughing and husking corn. Of course I thought you'd be going soon yourself. I had three years the start of you. If you'd been in my place, *you* might have met a man like Cook, *you* might have gone to New York and have been where I am."

"Well, it can't be helped now. So drop it."

"But it must be helped!" Howard said, pacing about, his hands in his coat-pockets. Grant had stopped work, and was gloomily looking out of the door at a pig nosing in the mud for stray grains of wheat at the granary door. The old man and the boy quietly withdrew.

"Good God! I see it all now," Howard burst out in an impassioned tone. "I went ahead with *my* education, got *my* start in life, then father died, and you took up his burdens. Circumstances made me and crushed you. That's all there is about that. Luck made me and cheated you. It ain't right."

His voice faltered. Both men were now oblivious of their companions and of the scene. Both were thinking of the days when they both planned great things in the way of education, two ambitious, dreamful boys.

"I used to think of you, Grant, when I pulled out Monday morning in my best suit—cost fifteen dollars in those days." He smiled a little at the recollection. "While you in overalls and an old 'wammus' were going out into the field to plough, or husk corn in the mud. It made me feel uneasy, but, as I said, I kept saying to myself, 'His turn'll come in a year or two.' But it didn't."

His voice choked. He walked to the door, stood a moment, came back. His eyes were full of tears.

"I tell you, old man, many a time in my boardinghouse down to the city, when I thought of the jolly times I was having, my heart hurt me. But I said, 'It's no use to cry. Better go on and do the best you can, and then help them afterward. There'll only be one more miserable member of the family if you stay at home.' Besides, it seemed right to me to have first chance. But I never thought you'd be shut off, Grant. If I had, I never would have gone on. Come, old man, I want you to believe that." His voice was very tender now and almost humble.

"I don't know as I blame you for that, How.," said Grant, slowly. It was the first time he had called Howard by his boyish nickname. His voice was softer, too, and higher in key. But he looked steadily away.

"I went to New York. People liked my work. I was very successful, Grant; more successful than you realize. I could have helped you at any time. There's no use lying about it. And I ought to have done it; but some way—it's no excuse, I don't mean it for an excuse, only an explanation—some way I got in with the boys. I don't mean I was a drinker and all that. But I bought pictures and kept a horse and a yacht, and of course I had to pay my share of all expeditions, and—oh, what's the use!"

He broke off, turned, and threw his open palms out toward his brother, as if throwing aside the last attempt at an excuse.

"I *did* neglect you, and it's a damned shame! and I ask your forgiveness. Come, old man!"

He held out his hand, and Grant slowly approached and took it. There was a little silence. Then Howard went on, his voice trembling, the tears on his face.

"I want you to let me help you, old man. That's the way to forgive me. Will you?"

"Yes, if you can help me."

Howard squeezed his hand. "That's all right, old man. Now you make me a boy again. Course I can help you. I've got ten—"

"I don't mean that, How." Grant's voice was very grave. "Money can't give me a chance now."

"What do you mean?"

"I mean life ain't worth very much to me. I'm too old to take a new start. I'm a dead failure. I've come to the conclusion that life's a failure for ninety-nine per cent of us. You can't help me now. It's too late."

The two men stood there, face to face, hands clasped, the one fair-skinned, full-lipped, handsome in his neat suit; the other tragic, sombre in his softened mood, his large, long, rugged Scotch face bronzed with sun and scarred with wrinkles that had histories, like sabre-cuts on a veteran, the record of his battles.

# II
# POPULIST GRIEVANCES

---

**OVERPRODUCTION
OR UNDERCONSUMPTION?**

*W. Scott Morgan, of Prairie County, Arkansas, was one of the
founders in 1882 of the Agricultural Wheel, a group later absorbed
into the Southern Farmers' Alliance. The following selection, taken
from a book endorsed as the "official history" of the Alliance, illustrates Populist distrust of the widely prevalent theory that attributed
the farmers' woes to overproduction.*

## –2–

# OVER-PRODUCTION–THE LAW
# OF SUPPLY AND DEMAND
## by W. Scott Morgan

There is, perhaps, no greater mistake made than the theory contended for by some of our cross-roads politicians and hair-brained
editors, that money has nothing to do with controlling prices;
that the law of supply and demand alone fixes the price of every
commodity. If these self-appointed political economists were to
allow the scales of prejudice to fall from their eyes long enough to
examine the true principles which underlie and govern commerce, they would learn that "price" is simply the expression of
the relation that exists between money and commodities or articles of commerce; and that they are as relative to each other as
one commodity is relative to another; and that both are governed

SOURCE: W. Scott Morgan, *History of the Wheel and Alliance and the
Impending Revolution* (Hardy, Arkansas: publ. by the author, 1889), ch. V,
pp. 511–518.

11

by this same law of supply and demand. Were it possible to remove the influence which this law exercises over money, and allow its actions to effect only the commodities of the country, their theory might be tenable, and we would have a true "standard of value." This school of political economists—and strange to say it includes many respectable and intelligent advocates—affirm that if wheat, corn, or any other product of labor is plentiful that prices will be correspondingly low; that if there is a large output of all the commodities there will be a general fall of prices. But they utterly fail to see that money is subject to the same law; that if it is plentiful it is cheap; that it does not take so much of the different commodities nor so much labor to procure it; and if money is scarce it is dear and requires more of the products of labor to obtain it. Money is said by some to be a measure of value. This is only true in part; for a dollar does not measure the value of a bushel of wheat any more than the bushel of wheat measures the value of the dollar. But their values are relative to each other and are both fixed by the law of supply and demand. Neither can it be established that gold or silver, or both, is a standard of value; for their price is fluctuating and quoted in the markets the same as other commodities; the price being governed by the law of supply and demand.

The dollar is only the unit of expression in fixing the relative value between money and commodities. If wheat is plenty and money scarce it takes more wheat to obtain a dollar than if wheat was scarce and money plenty. And this condition does not rest upon the fact that a bushel of wheat will make more flour or satisfy more hunger than when plenty, but simply because the relative conditions existing between wheat and money are changed; both being subject to the law of supply and demand. It is rather strange that those who are so ready to apply the law of supply and demand to the present condition of prices, and cry over-production, are so loth to apply the same law to the present supply of money.

As has been urged in the preceding chapters, and for reasons that will readily appear to the intelligent reader, the relation existing between money and commodities should be kept as near equal as possible, and this is only possible by keeping the volume of money uniformly apace with the increase of population and production. The result would be stable, and approximately uniform prices. The writers of both schools of this branch of political economy, that is, the advocates of the metallic and the paper system concur in the fact that plenty of money means cheap money as measured by the commodities of the country.

This is an open confession, that commodities measure the value of money, as well as that money measures the value of commodities. Hence, the importance of a fixed relation between the two.

Things are neither equal or equitable, when the holders of money, and evidences of debt which must be liquidated in money, have exclusive power to control and fix the relation between money, and commodities which must be parted with to secure money to pay those debts. And this condition does and will exist so long as the holders of this indebtedness have control over the issue of the money, or over any considerable portion of it. This condition is based upon the inequitable theory, that the creditor has the right to say to his debtor, "You must give me two bushels of wheat, corn, oats, or two pounds of cotton, beef or pork, where you only contracted to pay me one." It may be building up a nation of "grandeur and pomp," and "increasing our credit abroad," but, it is wrong to root the grandeur of the nation in the poverty of the people.

Over-production is impossible so long as the wants of the human family are unsupplied. Rather call it under-consumption. It is the proper term. The product of one thing creates a demand for another, inasmuch as the producer desires to exchange it for something else which he needs. This creates a demand for a medium of exchange and means of transportation. Medium of exchange and facilities for transportation are the two principal agents of distribution. These agents should exist in proportion to production. A proper system of distribution will overcome so-called "over-production."

It is to these two agents that the future statesman must address his attention if he would overcome and relieve the distress everywhere prevailing. With the proper means of distribution production will be stimulated, but instead of producing wide-spread distress and poverty, as is claimed by some, would add to the wealth, the happiness and comfort of the producing classes. To have over-production is as impossible as to become too wealthy. We may have under-consumption by cutting off the means of transportation or having an inadequate amount of currency or medium of exchange, and the product of certain commodities may become gorged on account of a deficiency in the means of distribution, and that distress exist, which is felt in times of excessive drouth, which is produced, not by a scarcity of water, but by improper distribution of it.

To remedy this we must have what nature has provided in her economic system, compensating laws, or laws that will properly distribute that which has been produced. It is rather strange that it has never occurred to the advocates of over-production, that it is those who produce so much who are the real sufferers, while a rich harvest is reaped by those who provide and control the means of distribution. The farmer who produces large quantities of the cereals may suffer for want of the clothing and shoes of which the men who make them have large quantities on hand. And the men who make the clothing and shoes may suffer for the breadstuffs of which the farmer has plenty. But it is not on account of an over-production of these necessaries of life and comfort, but owing to excessive rates of transportation and want of a sufficient medium of exchange. There are two things which the future patriotic statesman will take into consideration.

The first is, to stimulate production by encouraging labor. The second is, to provide the proper means of distribution. On these two points the greatest writer of the age, Victor Hugo, says: "For various reasons we can not discuss here, from the theoretical point of view, the questions raised by socialism, and we limit ourselves to an indication of them. All the questions which the socialists proposed—laying aside cosmogonic visions, reverie, and mysticism—may be carried back to two original problems, the first of which is, to produce wealth, and the second, to distribute it. The first problem contains the question of labor, the second, the question of wages; in the first, the point is the employment of strength, and in the second, the distribution of enjoyments. From a good employment of strength results public power, and from a good distribution of enjoyments, individual happiness. By good distribution we mean, not equal, but equitable, distribution, for the first quality is equity. From these two things, combined public power abroad and individual happiness at home, results social prosperity, that is to say, man happy, the citizen free, and the nation great.

"England solves the first of these two problems—she creates wealth admirably, but distributes it badly. This solution, which is completely on one side, fatally leads her to these two extremes, monstrous opulence and monstrous misery; all the enjoyments belong to the few, all the privations to the rest—that is to say, to the people, and privileges, exception, monopoly and feudalism spring up from labor itself. It is a false and dangerous situation to base public power on private want, and to root the grandeur of the state in the suffering of the individual; it is a badly composed grandeur, in which all the material elements are combined, in which no moral element enters. Communism and the agrarian law fancy that they solve the second question, but they are mistaken. Their distribution kills production, and equal division destroys emulation and consequently labor. It is a distribution made by the butcher who slaughters what he divides.

.    .    .    .    .

"Solve the two problems, encourage the rich and protect the poor, suppress misery, put an end to the unjust exhaustion of the weak by the strong; bridle the iniquitous jealousy which the man still on the road feels for him who has reached the journey's end. Adjust mathematically and paternally the wage of the laborer, blend gratuitous and enforced education with the growth of childhood, and render science the base of manhood; develop intelligence while occupying the arms, be at once a powerful people and a family of happy men; democratize properly, not by abolishing, but by universalizing it, so that every citizen without exception may be a land owner, an easier task than it may be supposed; in two words, know how to produce wealth and to distribute it, and you will possess at once material greatness, and moral greatness, and be worthy to call yourself France. Such was what socialism, above and beyond a few mistaken sects, said; this is what it sought in facts and stirred up in minds; they were admirable efforts and sacred attempts."—*Victor Hugo in Les Miserables, pp. 547, 548.*

In treating of the cause of the "present universal derangement of commerce and industry," the Silver Commission says:

"The real cause of the present universal derangement of commerce and industry must be ascertained before the proper remedy can be devised. The causes assigned are various and contradictory. Many of them never had any existence in fact. Others are inadequate or absurd in themselves, or by reason of being confined to narrow localities or special interests, cannot have proved a mischief which reaches all places and all poductive interests.

"Over-production is one of these alleged causes, although food, clothing, houses, and everything useful to mankind are, and probably always will be, in deficiency, as compared with the needs of them. The constant effort of the human race is, and ought to be, to multiply production.

"The aggregate effective demand for products, that is to say, the aggregate demand accompanied with the ability to purchase, always increases with production. Supply and demand mean substantially the same thing, and are nothing but two faces of the same fact. Every new supply of any product is the effective basis of a new demand for some other product. The capacity to buy is measured exactly by the extent of production, and there is practically no other limit to consumption than the limit of the means of payment. Over-production of particular things may occur, but that is soon corrected by the loss of profits in producing them. Over-production in the general and in the aggregate is impossible. The contrary opinion will be held only by those who will regret the discovery of the steam engine, the spinning-jenny, and the sewing and threshing machines, and who believe that while mankind have the skill to devise methods of increased production they have no capacity to provide for the distribution of the products of industry.

"Production is the sole and only source of wealth, and in fact is but another name for wealth. Over-production must therefore mean superabundant wealth, and the idea that either super-abundant wealth or the facilities for producing it can be the inciting cause of rapidly spreading poverty is repugnant to the common sense of mankind. All reputable authorities concur in treating the idea as the idlest of fancies, and wholly unworthy of serious notice."—*Report of Silver Commission, pages 117, 118.*[1]

It would seem useless to continue the discussion of this branch of our subject further. To say that over-production is the cause of "hard times," is to say that the people are too industrious; that they could make a better living if they did not work so hard; that they have raised so much they are starving to death, and manufacturing so many clothes that they are compelled to go naked. It is a little strange that those who claim that the law of supply and demand alone fix the price of products and attribute low prices to over-production, are frequently hard to make use of that other common expression, "there are none so far from market as those who have nothing to sell," and the author has himself heard a speaker attribute the "hard times" to both causes in the same speech.

[1 *Report and Accompanying Documents of the United States Monetary Commission Organized Under the Joint Resolution of August 15, 1876,* Senate Report No. 703, 44 Cong., 2 Sess., pp. 117–118. — Ed.]

**LAND MONOPOLY**
*The following selection illustrates the Populist myth of a golden age of American agriculture as well as the farmers' opposition to land monopoly and alien ownership.*

–3–

# LAND MONOPOLY
## by W. Scott Morgan

To the careful observer it is easy to see that the tendencies of the times is towards centralization. The natural consequence of class legislation is to concentrate the wealth of the country into the hands of a few, the inevitable result of which is to establish a land aristocracy on the one hand, and dependent tenants on the other.

. . . . . .

During the early existence of our government we had no extremes of wealth and poverty. We had neither millionaires or tramps. In 1842 Charles Dickens came from England to visit America. He wrote back from Boston to his friends in London:

"There is not a man in this town, nor this State, who has not a blazing fire, and meat for dinner every day in the year, nor would a flaming sword in the air attract so much attention as a beggar in the streets."

Then there were no castes or distinctions in society; no pomp

SOURCE: W. Scott Morgan, *History of the Wheel and Alliance and the Impending Revolution* (Hardy, Arkansas: publ. by the author, 1889), ch. XII, pp. 648–651, 671–677, 681–682.

and splendor to dazzle the eyes of the beholder. Democratic, socially, a republican form of government was natural, and rested equally and easily upon the shoulders of society. "Davy" Crockett, the bear hunter of Tennessee, was feted by the best society of Washington; and Henry Clay, the "mill boy of the slashes," was one of the first men of the nation. But a great change has taken place. A London journal recently declared that "there is not at this moment so wide a gulf between the rich and poor as in the United States," and adds, "there are as many beggars in each of the great American cities as there ever were of mendicants assembled about the steps of Roman churches." This journal then contrasts the collossal fortunes of the millionaires of our great cities, their gorgeous mansions, brilliant and dazzling balls and suppers, and elaborate display of costly diamonds and jewels, far surpassing royalty in brilliancy and costs. . . .

. . . When Dickens wrote from Boston, in 1842, we had but few millionaires and no money power. We had neither the financial machinery nor the legal privileges to make them. The United States bank had been swept out of existence; trusts were unknown; and railroads were built and operated upon legitimate business principles. Distinction depended upon honor and merit. There were no classes, no pomp or ostentatious display. Now we are cursed with all these evils. We adopted England's financial policy. We loaded the people with a burdensome debt as the basis of a plutocracy. We established the gold standard and contracted our currency volume, which squeezed billions of wealth out of the property of industry into the coffers of the creditor classes.

We created a law-favored aristocracy of wealth by the establishment of the national banking system.

We then bestowed upon it the vast credit of the nation, and gave it a patent right to monopolize it for its sole and exclusive benefit. To this aristocratic monopoly of public credit, Congress has delegated the sovereign power of the monetary prerogative. . . . The soul of American democracy and independence has been crushed out of our institutions, while the spirit of monarchial despotism is gestating in the organization of the national banking system. To-day, while our government bears the form of a republic, it exercises sovereign power as a despot, and the people are almost powerless in the grasp of this relentless and unyielding monster. . . .

The disposition of the public lands of the United States is a question of vital importance, but it now seems that the public attention is so thoroughly aroused to the evils attendant upon large and gratuitous land grants to corporations and individuals, that no political party could stem the tide of public indignation which would result from a repetition of the practice. It is to be regretted that other evils of equal importance have not met with the same universal disapproval. The history of land grants dates back to the year 1850. It is not known who first conceived the idea, but Stephen A. Douglas introduced the first bill in Congress granting land to aid in the construction of rialroads. This bill was hotly opposed, but supported by the persuasive eloquence of Mr. Douglas, it was passed and approved September 20th, 1850. It granted to the State of Illinois, for the use and benefit of the Illinois Central railroad company, 2,505,053 acres of land through the richest portion of the State. A provision stipulating, that in lieu of all other taxes, the company should pay into the State treasury an amount equal to seven per cent. of the gross earnings, was incorporated into the bill; but since the books of the company show that they still have 36 per cent. of their gross earnings left after paying all expenses, it would seem that the people are taxed to pay the seven per cent. The company have since realized about thirty million dollars from the sale of these lands. Within the next six years no less than forty-seven land grant bills passed Congress to aid in the construction of railroads in different States. These grants embraced about thirty million acres of land. It was not, however, until the close of the war that the most stupendous grants were made. During the few years immediately following the most reckless extravagance was indulged in, and the wildest schemes were aided by the chosen representatives of the people. The following table will show the number of acres granted to the different railroad companies from the time the system was first introduced. About 36,000,000 acres of these lands were first granted to the States, and by them to the railroads:

ACRES.

| | |
|---|---|
| Texas Pacific | 18,000,000 |
| Union Pacific | 12,000,000 |
| Kansas Pacific | 6,000,000 |
| Denver Pacific | 1,000,000 |
| Central Pacific | 11,000,000 |
| Oregon Central | 1,200,000 |
| Southern Pacific | 35,200,000 |
| Northern Pacific | 47,000,000 |
| Cairo & Fulton | 3,000,667 |
| Wisconsin Central | 1,800,000 |
| St. Paul & Pacific | 4,723,038 |
| Atlantic & Pacific | 42,000,000 |
| Oregon & California | 3,500,000 |
| Pensacola & Georgia | 1,568,229 |
| Mobile & Ohio River | 1,004,640 |
| St. Paul & Sioux City | 1,100,000 |
| Iowa Falls & Sioux City | 1,226,163 |
| St. Joe & Denver City | 1,700,000 |
| Missouri, Kansas & Texas | 1,520,000 |
| Pacific & Southwestern | 1,161,235 |
| Burlington & Missouri River | 2,441,600 |
| Jackson, Lansing & Saginaw | 1,052,169 |
| Chicago, Rock Island & Pacific | 1,261,181 |
| Cedar Rapids & Missouri | 1.298,739 |
| Missouri River, Fort Scott & Gulf | 2,350,000 |
| New Orleans, Baton Rouge & Vicksburg | 3,800,000 |
| Illinois Central and Mobile & Chicago | 2,596,053 |
| Atchison, Topeka & Santa Fe | 3,000,000 |

Of these 209,344,233 acres, estimated at $1,674,000,000, only a very small amount has been patented. This list has been carefully compiled from the records of the general land office, and is considered correct.

In addition to this the Pacific roads received six per cent. government bonds to the amount of $64,623,512. While the government was fighting to retain eleven States in the Union, spending millions of money and the best blood of the country, it permitted itself to become a party to robbing the pepole of a domain equal to more than the whole of the seceding States. This amount of land in one body would be almost equal to the thirteen original colonies. It is larger than the whole of England and France combined. In addition to the above there are millions of acres held by foreigners, and foreign and home syndicates. The following table comprises some of the European land owners with amount of land owned:

| | ACRES. |
|---|---|
| English syndicate, in Texas | 3,000,000 |
| Holland Land Company, in New Mexico | 4,500,000 |
| Sir Edward Reid, in Florida | 2,000,000 |
| English syndicate, in Mississippi | 1,800,000 |
| Marquis of Tweedsdale | 1,750,000 |
| Byron H. Evans | 700,000 |
| Anglo-American syndicate | 750,000 |
| Phillips, Marshall & Co | 1,300,000 |
| German syndicate | 1,000,000 |
| Duke of Sutherland | 425,000 |
| British Land Company, in Kansas | 320,000 |
| Wm. Whaley, M. P | 310,000 |
| Missouri Land Company, of Scotland | 465,000 |
| Robert Penant, of London | 260,000 |
| Dundee Land Company, of Scotland | 247,000 |
| Lord Dunmore | 120,000 |
| Benjamin Neugas | 100,000 |
| Lord Houghton | 60,000 |
| Lord Dunaven | 60,000 |
| English Land Company | 110,000 |
| Albert Peele, M. P | 10,000 |
| Sir J. L. Kay | 5,000 |
| Alex. Grant | 35,000 |
| English syndicate, in Missouri | 110,000 |
| M. Ellerhausen | 600,000 |
| Scotch syndicate, in Florida | 500,000 |
| A. Boysen, of Denmark | 50,000 |
| TOTAL | 20,557,500 |

The amount of land in the hands of these twenty-seven foreign speculators is equal to a territory as large as Ireland. Then we have our American syndicates and speculators. The late Col. Murphy left an estate of more than 4,000,000 acres. The Standard Oil Company owns 1,000,000 acres. Ex-Senator Dorsey has 500,-000 acres in New Mexico, and Diston has over 2,000,000 acres in Florida. Then, there is the Glenn, Vanderbilt and Dalrymple farms, and the great cattle ranches of Texas; and New York, even, has not escaped the Shylocks, such as Mr. Clark and Col. Church. The latter owns and collects rents from 180 farms, some of them containing more than 500 acres each, while his tenants, after paying the rents, can scarcely live.

An Indiana correspondent of the Chicago *Express* says the public lands of the United States, exclusive of the thirteen colonies and Texas, were as follows:

|  | ACRES. |
|---|---:|
| Thirteen colonies | 229,987,187 |
| Louisiana purchase | 756,961,280 |
| Florida | 37,931,520 |
| Texas | 65,130,880 |
| Gadsden | 29,142,400 |
| Alaska | 369,529,600 |
| Mexican treaty | 334,443,520 |
| TOTAL | 1,823,126,387 |

Land not available to be deducted:

|  | ACRES. |
|---|---:|
| Alaska | 369,529,600 |
| Indian and military reservations | 157,000,000 |
| Mountains and untillable land | 400,000,000 |
| TOTAL | 926,529,600 |

This leaves as available land nearly 900,000,000 acres. Of this 300,000,000 are owned by private parties and actual settlers. Congress has given to the States 160,000,000 acres, 79,000,000 to schools, as swamp lands 70,000,000 acres, as bounties for military and naval service 61,000,000, and 60,000,000 acres for canals, wagon roads, etc., a total of 528,000,000 acres. Now add 172,000,-000 acres already enumerated as granted to railroads and we find 700,000,000 acres out of the whole amount have been disposed of, and but 200,000,000 remain. Then the private and State claims that have not been considered in these figures amount to 85,000,-000 acres. Now what have we left? The small sum of 115,-000,000 acres, 22,000,000 acres less than has been given to the railroads alone. If we take the rate at which the public lands have been going for the last twenty-five years as a basis, there will not be, at the end of fifteen years more, one acre of government land to be had. Then these big land sharks will begin to reap their reward, unless compelled, through legislation, to put their lands in the market at once. By all means let us have a graduated land tax.

.    .    .    .    .

. . . Land monopoly is one of the worst forms of robbery. To encourage progress, induce invention and reward genius, it may be urged that inventors may for a time reap the benefits of their skill and industry. But such cannot be said of land, it is the gift of God. It is the source from whence the human family obtain their means of subsistence. From its fertile resources flows all wealth. Upon its proper and equitable distribution depends the happiness, comfort and prosperity of the people. "In the sweat of thy face shalt thou eat bread." This decree was uttered 6,000 years ago. It is as immutable as time itself. Labor is man's proper function. The word of God has made it honorable. Man smites the earth, and from its inexhaustible fountain of resources flow the means of comfort, happiness, and prosperity. Whoever works performs the natural functions of mankind. The idler is a drone; he shirks the immutable decree of Deity; he feeds upon the labor of others; he is a parasite upon society; he is a robber.

The earth is God's gift to man. To monopolize this is to enslave labor. To enslave labor is to strike at the very foundations of liberty; to violate the laws of justice and equity and rob the people of their God-given heritage. He who does it sins against God. The nation that permits it will be wiped from the face of the earth.

Usury and extortion lead to land monopoly. For this violation of the Divine law God has destroyed the nations.

.　　.　　.　　.　　.

Kind reader, history is repeating itself in our own fair land. Monopoly is eating out the very vitals of our existence. Usury and extortion have fastened their iron jaws upon every industry of the land. Labor is burdened beyond endurance. Trusts, syndicates and combinations demand extortion on everything we buy; and transportation companies, pools and middlemen levy tribute on everything we sell. We are traveling the same road to death that the nations gone before have traveled. We are told by the politicians that they will save us. So we have always been told. Our task becomes harder and life more burdensome. Reform never begins with the leaders. It comes from the people.

Will you follow in the same tracks that we have been treading for the past twenty years? Will you follow in the road to ruin, and let the history of other nations repeat itself in ours? Will you let this labor movement, this last effort, burn to ashes on our fallen altars? Then, indeed, will be actualized into history that which is written by the prophet: "Death on a white horse and hell following after him."

*Ashby was the Lecturer of the Northern Farmers Alliance. The selection here follows a discussion of land-grant and bond-aided railroads and the overcapitalization of railroads in general.*

–4–

# THE RAILROAD PROBLEM
## *by N. B. Ashby*

. . . In 1890 the 152,689 miles of railway in the United States were capitalized at $10,100,000,000 in round numbers, an average of about $65,000 per mile. We submit that no sane and competent, wholly disinterested, civil engineer would value this whole system of railways at more than $25,000 per mile, present worth, estimated at cost of reproducing road-beds, rolling-stock, and all equipments.

This leaves an average overvaluation of $40,000 per mile upon the railroads of the country, and this chiefly in the form of bonded indebtedness and "watered" stock. If it be granted that the railroads are worth on an average, the country over $25,000 per mile, the situation in 1890 stands thus: Actual value of aggregate roads, $3,817,225,000; water in form of bonds and over-issue of stocks, $6,107,560,000. Is not the normal condition of the railroads of the United States that of bankruptcy?

The railroad by nature is a monopoly. It controls the commerce of the country. This control gives it the power to levy taxes and collect tribute from every individual who buys or sells. Were the

SOURCE: N. B. Ashby, *The Riddle of the Sphinx* (Des Moines: Industrial Publishing Co., 1890), ch. V, pp. 128–142.

roads capitalized at the actual cost of economical construction and equipment, and were they managed with careful economy, and charges based upon yielding only fair dividends upon these lower valuations, it would still prove a heavy burden upon the people to pay the stockholders the semi-annual dividends of three or four per cent. But when the actual worth of the roads is increased three-fold, and the management is of that reckless kind which characterized the freebooter period, then the people mourn. To pay not more than four per cent. on the $6,000,000,000 of false railroad valuations, taxes the country annually $240,-000,000. The chairman of the committee of investigation[1] estimates that the Union Pacific Railroad takes $8,000,000 annually from the people living along its lines in overcharges. The overcharges upon Iowa commerce may be estimated conversatively at no less than $10,000,000 annually. Were all parts of the country and every individual treated as equals by the railways, the burden, although grievous, would be more endurable. But the railroads have ever assumed the prerogatives of sovereignty. They declare war upon each other or upon some competing waterway, and then boldly levy upon the interior for the thews and sinews of war. Disastrous losses from terminal and intersecting points, in the way of cuts, were recouped from the intermediate points. They assumed greater powers than those of Deity; they abrogated time and space; they changed the geography of the country. If rates were a guide. Omaha was situated between Chicago and Iowa, Denver was on the Mississippi, and San Francisco on the Missouri, while the interior towns of Iowa and Nebraska were located on Behring Strait. When the merchants of Columbus, Nebraska, complained that they were charged $3 per hundred on freight from San Francisco, that Omaha merchants, although ninety-one miles farther off on the same line, were getting at $1.40 per hundred, they were voicing the complaint of an abuse common in every town west of Chicago which was not the favorite of railroad managers. All the principal railroads in Iowa for years carried on just such a warfare against the towns of the

[1 Report of the Iowa Railroad Commissoners, 1888, cited in earlier portion of chapter, here omitted. — Ed.]

State, assuming the power to tax one place out of existence for the purpose of building up another. Nor were the towns east of Chicago exempt from the burdens imposed by railroad wars and favoritisms. Even New York City suffered for a long time from such brigandage.

The enormous revenues the railroads were drawing upon watered stock were burden enough when distributed equally upon all parts of the country. Favoritism was more than could be endured in peace. From 1871 to 1875 came the "Granger" revolt against discriminations. In Ohio, Michigan, Illinois, Minnesota, and Iowa it was the same battle-cry against extortion and favoritism. It was not a rebellion against excessive revenues on false valuations; excessive revenues were bearable as compared with the assumed right to ruin one section of the State or nation at pleasure to build up another. The granger rebelled against just such discrimination as later vexed the soul of the Columbus merchant; such a favoritism, for instance, as gave Council Bluffs a rate of from $25 to $45 per car to Chicago on hogs and cattle, while other Iowa towns on these same roads were forced to pay $70 per car for a less service; a favoritism in passenger service which carried the wealthy and the influential in politics on passes, and charged the citizen who could least afford it, five cents per mile. Granger legislation aimed to equalize freights and fares, and restrain the abnormal influences of railway mismanagement. Up to the time of the enactment of the "granger laws," the railway corporations had boldly asserted their right, as owners and managers of the railroads, to manage them arbitrarily. The grangers challenged the assumption that railways were private property, and subject only to the arbitrary control of the managers and officers. The government had favored the railway theory, and in the beginning of the contest there was arrayed against the farmer nearly the whole legal and newspaper talent of the country, as well as the hostility of political leaders, of whom the most had been seduced by the corruption of railway favors, in the way of passes and other favors and courtesies. By chance, the granger had the law in his favor. The power of corporations created by the State had been mooted early in our history, and most of the States had had the foresight to incorporate a provision in their constitutions retaining the power to modify the charters of corporations whenever the State should so choose. The success of the grangers established the principle of State and national control of railways, and this principle has been the foundation of all subsequent legislation respecting the control of railways.

After long agitation, public opinion came to the side of the granger, and it was hard to find the man who had not been an original "State-control" advocate. After long litigation in the courts, railway corporations were forced to accept the same view. They no longer object to the principle of State control; the whole fight now is against the exercise by the State of the principle. They are eager to profess their sincere belief in the principle, but ever ready to protest against any practical method of its enforcement. The granger was successful in establishing the principle for which he contended, but it was largely an abstract truth. He secured a permanent reduction in fares, and for a brief period was successful in securing equalization of freight rates.

But the question was complex, the corporations ever alert, and the granger was soon overreached. Instead of law, he accepted a compromise in the form of Railway Commissioners to act as a sort of board of arbitration. The salaries of his board were paid by the railway companies—their appointment, more often than otherwise, dictated by them. These commissioners practically became figure-heads, either through false sympathies, or because powerless to execute their own orders. This, at least, was the strait into which Iowa fell; and despite the principle of control, discrimination grew. But, however well State control might have been exercised in securing equal rates for the State, that control could not affect shipments going out of or coming into the State.

The railroads gave Minneapolis a milling in-transit rate. This discrimination crushed all local milling enterprises, and permitted the formation of a flour combine at Minneapolis which controlled both the price of wheat and the price of flour, and fixed the latter without reference to the cost of the former. The railroads combined to make the whole stock interests of the Northwest tributary to Chicago. We have traced, in a former chapter, how they built up the Union Stock-Yards and placed the stock market of the West in the hands of the unscrupulous "Big Four," who are still lords of kine and swine. By the power of discrimination, they placed the grain-farmer at the mercy of the Chicago elevators. They have set the Chicago Board of Trade over the grain markets, and given a den of gamblers "in options" the power to fix and keep the price of grain to the producer at the lowest cost of production.

Not satisfied with these achievements, the managers of railways went into all the cities and towns, villages and hamlets, along their lines, and attempted to dictate who should and who should not engage in business at such shipping-points. By the same methods which the Union Pacific Railroad employed to force the whole smelting business along their line to Omaha, and to give a few elevator firms and coal men the entire business of handling grain and coal, other roads endeavored to keep the shipping and retail trade solely in the hands of their favorites. These favors were in the nature of rebates. . . .

Here, then, is a prolific parent of the trust, the trade combine, and trade conspiracy. The Standard Oil trust was founded and grew into greatness upon railroad discriminations. In the case of Rice against the Standard Oil Company, it was testified that the railroads charged Rice higher rates for transporting oil than they charged the Standard Oil Company, and that the excess of rates collected from Rice was paid over to the Standard Oil people. With this powerful railroad leverage, the Standard Oil Company was enabled to crush all competition, and dictate the terms of a trust under which other companies might continue to do business. This same railroad power will be found, in a greater or less degree, behind every trust in the country, whether sugar trust, cotton-seed oil, whisky, or what not. In the same manner, a rebate to the local shipper enabled him to drive other men out of similar business, or compel them to combine with him on such terms as he should dictate. The local merchant favored with rebates enjoyed a similar power, and likewise used it. The result is that our country is honey-combed with trusts, forestallers, and trade combines, the latter of which is the controlling force in local trade.

This state of affairs aroused the people to an agitation of this question, which entered into congressional politics, and finally awoke Congress to a realization that the railroads could no longer be left to unrestrained individual management, and that there was need of government supervision. To correct these abuses, over which the whole country had become clamorous, Congress passed the Inter-State Commerce Law, which forbade pools, rebates, and discriminations; enacted the long-and-short-haul clause, and provided a board of five Railway Commissioners, with power to enforce the law. Iowa immediately followed up the act of Congress by a State law supplementary to the Inter-State Law, and made the board of Iowa Railroad Commissioners elective. Other States are rapidly supplementing the Inter-State Law, and there is a unison of movement toward strict State and national control of railway management.

.  .  .  .  .

The position of railroad corporations is opposition to all legal restraint. They claim to acknowledge and accept the principle of national and State control, but adherence is given only at the point of compulsion, and almost every act of the managers is to make all restrictions nugatory. The bond-aided roads are making a strong effort to lobby through Congress a bill extending the time of the payment of their indebtedness to the government from fifty to seventy years. Their intent is not to pay the debt, but to secure the government guarantee for continuing their robbery and outrages upon the public. The whole railroad power of the country is bringing to bear the full power of their influence to secure the repeal, or better, the emasculation, of the Inter-State Commerce Act. They want to be let alone, to do as they please with what they are pleased to term their own property. The law has struck at the pool and the combine, and as the government presses more vigorously, the railroad corporations are seeking to defy the law by the formation of a gigantic trust, which will consolidate the entire railway mileage of the country under the management of a single board of receivers, who will act as trustees. It is only a question of time when such a trust will be put into operation. The railroads hope to be able then to defy all restrictions of the nation or States, and so continue their *imperium in imperio* upon a much more arbitrary scale. The powers conferred upon railroad corporations have given into their hands the wealth of the nation, and have begotten the brood of millionaires enumerated by Mr. Shearman.[2] This brood will not lightly surrender the privileges which have made them the money kings of the world. The bankers' triangle will eventually secure the formation of a gigantic railroad trust, and against such a trust laws will be powerless. Since the above was written, the Chicago *Tribune* announces the probable formation of such a trust in the very near future, and says:

The object is not to unite all these railroad systems into one gigantic company, but the desired object is to be obtained by depositing a majority of the stocks and bonds of those roads with the bankers' triangle, thus giving it virtual control of all those properties, and placing it in a position to direct their financial and traffic affairs.

The present policy of national and State control has been powerless to remedy much of the evils of railroad abuse. Should a trust, as seems inevitable, be formed, the present laws would be inoperative of practical results. Present laws are even now powerless to squeeze the water from railroad values, as the stock quotations eloquently demonstrate. Under the present system the public must consent to continue paying freights and fares sufficient to furnish interest and dividends on threefold valuations, each man having the satisfaction simply of knowing he is faring no worse than his neighbor; for about all the present laws accomplish is to protect persons and places against "undue" favoritism. So long as all are treated alike, conflicting interests of managers are, under present laws, about the only obstacle in the way of making the burdens of transportation the limits of corporation greed. The

[2 Thomas G. Shearman, "The Owners of the United States," *The Forum*, VIII (November 1889), 262–273. — Ed.]

formation of a trust will remove that obstacle, but under present rules the country is paying annually not less than $300,000,000—interest and dividends—on the valuations of railway property which represent *"water."* This burden is weighing the life out of many industries, and yet government control, in evening rates, seems helpless to remedy it.

It was hoped that the Inter-State Commerce Law would squeeze the water out of railroad stocks; and the railroad managers have endeavored to create the impression that it was so doing. They put forward the claim that the Inter-State Law is bankrupting the roads, and hence insist upon its repeal. But, unfortunately, the stock markets show no tendency of railroad stock to unduly depreciate, and the tendencies of the roads to increase their capitalization goes on unchecked.

The normal condition of the railroad has been shown to be that of bankruptcy. Bankruptcy has always been a favorite method of railways whereby to increase the capitalization of the roads. When a road has failed, it has not paid out so much on the dollar, as in the case of failure on the part of an individual, but a new deal has been made, in which the whole indebtedness was refunded and issued as stock. Railroad bankruptcy is synonymous with increased capitalization. And such bankruptcy as the railroads claim to fear, under existing laws, would result in a new capitalization of these $10,000,000,000 of railway valuations at $12,000,000,000 instead, and the claim straightway for an increase of rates to meet dividends and interest on stock and debts. And a law of mere control is powerless to prevent. In fact, the cry that the capital invested in railways must be allowed to make a fair income, has ever been a most potent one. If it is demonstrated that much of this capital represents bogus issues of stock and bonds, it is met with the plea that it is now owned by the widow, the orphan, and the homeless, who purchased these bogus issues in good faith, and the innocent purchaser must be protected. In the present Congress are grave Senators and members who admit the fearful burdens entailed upon the country by the railroad system of over-valuations, and yet protest that the country must bear with it because "innocent purchasers" now hold the stocks and bonds of the over issue. Here, at the root of greatest evil, the axe of government control has proven itself powerless.

And yet, present methods have been wise, and have followed the only practical methods for which the people were ripe. The present Inter-State Law has effected much in remedying the evils which were most oppressive. It should be maintained and continually made more restrictive until such time as the government sees its way clear to assume the ownership of the entire railway system, or so much of it as will drive every road to a competitive basis, and thus eliminate false valuations and regulate charges by the cost of service based upon economcial management of roads capitalized at their actual worth. The Inter-State Commerce Law has, in a large measure, corrected the abuse practiced by the railroads in charging more for the short than for the long hauls. Upon all of the Chicago lines crossing Iowa and terminating at the Missouri River, the shippers from all points in Iowa, upon these lines, have been enabled to secure as low (or lower) rates as those given to the western terminals. The Iowa Railroad Commissioners, under the present laws, have kept the rates for the State in a fair degree of uniformity with the Inter-State rate, and are restoring a degree of confidence to the business interests of the State, by offering a certain measure of protection against the discriminations which formerly made business success a mere matter of favoritism. And we doubt not that many other States that profited by the national law and their State laws to a similar degree. . . .

But this is not all. Public functions should never be permitted to be controlled by private corporations. The very nature of railroad transportation is monopolistic. A railroad company cannot build a railroad with success until endued with the sovereign power of eminent domain. The public nature of railways is further shown by the fact that the roads were built almost totally by grants of the public domain, by municipal and township taxes, and by contributions of the people. Of the whole amount of public lands disposed of from June 30, 1880, to June 30, 1889, for all purposes, including homesteads, timber claims, etc., the railroads secured one-fifth. One-eighth of the whole territory of Iowa

—equal to one eighth out of every section—was granted to railways. The Illinois Central was granted 2,500,000 acres in Illinois. New York assisted the Erie to the extent of about $38,000,000. The whole people are placed under tribute to the railroad corporations to whom has been farmed out the public highways. The individual has no choice. He must pay toll to the railroad companies in freight charges upon what he buys and sells. Were the roads capitalized for no more than the actual cost of economical construction, and then managed with a view to give the lowest possible rates, the centralization of wealth which would necessarily follow would be dangerous to a republic. And vesting in the hands of private individuals the immense enginery of having absolute control of the commerce of a nation, whereby is enjoyed the power to tax and to grant immunities, is attended with dangers of so grave a character as to render the question of the perpetuity of republican institutions extremely uncertain. The conflicts growing out of this clash of private interests and power with the public welfare will eventually drive the government into such ownership as will eliminate the tribute power of the railways, or will drive the railroads into usurping the powers of government. And, in fact, they have already attempted this through the power of bribery in legislative hall and court, and the control of political conventions which nominate executives, lawmakers, and judges.

Hence there is a growing feeling that our government must own railways, or be owned by railway corporations. Such seems the inevitable, growing out of the public function to levy taxes having passed into the power of railway corporations, and having been used by them in a wholly irresponsible way. Nor is the government ownership of railroads a visionary or untried problem. Belgium owns the main lines of railways in its country. The government treats all private railways, like branch roads, as the wards of the State, and reserves the right to purchase any or all of them whenever it chooses. The State regulates the number of trains run upon private roads, prepares the train schedules, allows of no contracts between private companies without the approval of the State, and exacts low freight and passenger rates without favors or discriminations, and requires the rates to be certain and fixed, without flurries and fluctuations. The Belgium system is regarded as the best in the world. France reserved to herself the right to purchase her railways, which have been built in a large measure by State aid, and is now bending her energies toward the accomplishment of the purchase of her railways, despite the efforts of the Rothschild influence in France to persuade an abandonment of that policy. Prussia owns the main lines of her railways, and the State is rapidly becoming the chief owner of railway properties. The whole trend of the railway problem in Continental Europe is toward State ownership. The success of the govenments which have adopted this policy in securing cheap and uniform rates, without any of the disturbances and disgraceful proceedings which are characteristic of private ownership, is rapidly creating and hastening a policy of national ownership in all the governments of Europe. England has passed through a long fight with the railroads, and now has them under the severe and rigorous control of a board of commissioners, but leading English statesmen look upon government ownership as the ultimate solution of the problem.

## THE FARM MORTGAGE

*William Alfred "Whiskers" Peffer, born in Cumberland County, Pennsylvania, was a Kansas editor and Populist senator from that state, 1891–1897. His plain and unadorned disquisition on the farmers' woes was among the most widely read statements of Populist ideas.*

–5–

# THE DEBT BURDEN
## by *William Alfred Peffer*

The most pressing want of the farmer is to get rid of debts for which his home is mortgaged. It was not generally believed until recently that the clamor about individual indebtedness of our people had much foundation in truth. The most extravagant guesses upon the subject came short of the cold facts, which Mr. Porter, of the Census Bureau, is giving to us. The writer of this made an investigation of the subject, examining such sources of information as were within his reach, and came to the conclusion that $1,000,000,000 would about cover the entire indebtedness of the people in town and country for which their homes were mortgaged; but enough has already been shown by the Census Bureau to make it probable that the estimate is too short by at least 60 per cent. While the census figures have been given for only two States—Iowa and Alabama—yet such general statements are made in the bulletin reporting those two States as to show with reasonable certainty that the aggregate debts resting

SOURCE: William Alfred Peffer, *The Farmer's Side, His Troubles and Their Remedy* (New York: D. Appleton and Co., 1891), ch. III, pp. 179–184.

upon the people's homes will reach the enormous sum of $3,750,000,000. This seems incredible, yet how are we to avoid that conclusion in face of what really appears? There are 2,785 counties in the United States; every one of those counties was visited by one or more agents of the Government, who searched the records carefully, taking the entire period between 1880 and 1890, estimating as nearly as possible the amount of debt due on the 1st day of January, 1890; and those agents forwarded from their respective counties abstracts of mortgages—9,000,000 in number—covering ten years. At least 2,500,000 of them were in force on the 1st day of January, 1890. There are thousands of cases where a second mortgage was taken to secure the commissions and fees of the agents who negotiated the loans. The second mortgages, however, are not included in the list given in the census report; they are all taken as interest, and included in the interest account. For example, one county in Kansas—to wit, Linn County—reported about a year ago some 2,500 farm mortgages on record, of which 1,000 were of the class known as "second mortgages," given for commissions and other fees of the agents. In the census report all such second mortgages are included in the interest account, so that the report as given shows 9,000,000 original mortgages in sums which are unquestionably a lien upon the homes of the people.

Two thirds of the mortgages, or about that proportion, rest upon farms, one third upon city and town lots. That gives us now 1,666,666 on farms and 833,333 on lots.[1] Again the thought is

[1] The Census Bureau has not yet published a detailed report on this important matter. It appears, however, from what is already known that in some portions of the country the amount of mortgage debt due on the first day of January, 1890, was nearly, if not quite, one half as much as the aggregate amount recorded during the ten years. I had put the general average at two fifths, or 40 per cent. That gives us 3,600,000 mortgages due January 1, 1890, of which 2,400,000 may represent farm mortgages and 1,200,000 town mortgages. But it appears from Mr. Porter's recent statement, before referred to, that no mortgages are counted except only those on lands and lots occupied by *owners*, and that the total number of such mortgages in force January 1, 1890, does not exceed 2,500,000, or 28 per cent. Not more than two thirds of our 5,000,000 farms, or 3,333,333 farms, are occupied by their owners; and if, as appears, there are 1,666,666 mortgages on them, one half of them are mortgaged. If the Iowa average

repeated that this seems incredible, and yet here are the figures before us. But why should we be startled? Farmers are not reputed as accomplished financiers like men in other lines of business. It is generally conceded that railroad managers stand at the head of the best educated class of business men. For shrewdness, for foresight, for careful and close management, they are placed in the very forefront of commercial men; and yet it appears that the railroads of the country are indebted at least four times as much as they are worth. It is not usual among a certain class of economists to consider the stock account of a railroad company as indebtedness. It is regarded rather as a source of governmental power to be used in the political management of the road, not having reference to politics in the ordinary acceptation of that term, but the handling and manoeuvring of the business independently of persons who have a direct claim upon the assets of the company in the way of recorded indebtedness, or such indebtedness as is evidenced by paper that can be put upon the market, and paper that can be presented and payment upon it demanded; but there is no good reason for setting the stock account to one side and using only the bonded indebtedness when we are considering how much the railroad companies are involved. This thought may be made plainer by putting it in this way. Say that a certain railroad company is about to go out of business. The first thing it does is to pay its indebtedness. Every stockholder as well as every bondholder has a claim upon that road; say the bondholders' bond is $1,000, say the stockholders' stock is $1,000. The road—the property of the company of every sort and description making up what we call the "road"—is indebted to the stockholders $1,000 in the settlement, just as much,

---

($1,283 to the farm) holds good for the whole country, the total farm-mortgage debt of the people is $2,138,333,333. It is more than that, probably, because eastern loans are generally larger than western. Exact figures can not be given until complete census reports are published. I believe it is safe to put the aggregate farm-mortgage debt of the country at $2,500,000,000, which is 300 per cent more than my estimate before any census reports on the subject were published. And if town and city house mortgages equal one half those of the farms in amount, the sum total equals $3,750,000,000 on houses occupied only by persons who claim to own them.

just as honestly as it is indebted to the bondholders $1,000. It is for that reason, the reason that the stockholder has a claim on the road for every share of stock he owns, that in making up the estimate of total indebtedness stocks and bonds both are included. Taking that as a standard, the indebtedness of the railroads of the United States is at least four times what they would sell for if put upon the market to-day. And more than that, by taking a broader standard of measurement, they are in debt four times as much as their assessed valuation for taxes. In the Western States generally the roads are assessed at an average of $6,000 to $7,000 per mile; that is presumably what they are worth on the market; their capitalization amounts to from five to eight times that amount. In Kansas the capitalization of the railroads is $456,000,000 in round numbers, while their assessed valuation is put at $57,000,000; the books of the companies show the former amount, while the books of the tax gatherer show the latter amount; capitalization $8, value of the road $1. The farmers, while not being reputed as good managers, and while being rated as thriftless, wasteful, and extravagant, yet even at $2,500,000,000 for their aggregate mortgage indebtedness, they can show on the tax rolls of their respective counties an amount quite as large as that. In other words, the farmers' debts are not greater than the assessed valuation of their property, while their shrewder and more competent competitors in business—the railroad managers —have in some way fastened upon their roads debts in proportion vastly beyond that which rests upon the farmers.

And, as shown further by the census report, the interest on this indebtedness is exorbitant—three, four, five times, even twenty times the average increase of wealth produced by labor in the ordinary form, which is about 3 per cent. Farmers find that difficulties in the way of payment of their debts are increasing from year to year, that it is growing constantly harder to meet their obligations. If, then, enough money could be obtained by the farmers to pay off their indebtedness, other things being equal, they would be wholly relieved, because they are producing as much wheat and as much corn and as much cotton, and raising as many cattle and horses and swine as they ever did and more; they are producing as much hay and as many potatoes and as much of everything else which goes to make up the ordinary living of a family. Relieve them of their debt burden and they would be free indeed.

But there is a great deal more about it than the mere payment of a debt. To pay with borrowed money would leave them in no better condition than they are now, unless the money which they borrow can be obtained at a rate of interest that they can afford to pay. And there is where the difficulty appears. If money could be obtained at, say, 2 per cent, which business generally would afford and no more, it would be a comparatively easy matter for the farmers to pay interest on their debts out of the profits in their business, and at the same time have a small margin left every year to apply upon the principal. At a 2-per-cent rate the average farmer would pay out in the course of fifteen or twenty years at most; he would pay his debt and save his home. But how is he to obtain money at 2 per cent? How is he to obtain money at anything less than he is paying now? How is he to renew his loan except at the discretion of the owner of the money which he borrowed, or of the agent who negotiated the loan? He is at the mercy of his creditor, and that being true he is practically power-less, for the creditor is not a man to be trifled with. That brings us up to the question whether money can be obtained at lower rates of interest, and if so, how? For it may as well be admitted now as at any other time, the plain, naked truth is, that unless lower rates of interest can be obtained, one half of our farmers will be renters within the next ten years, and one half of the remainder in an-other ten years, and by the time the nineteenth century is ten years past the occupied lands of the country will be owned almost wholly by a comparatively few wealthy men. Let us, then, take up the subject of cheaper money.

**THE CROP-LIEN SYSTEM**

*The Reverend Charles H. Otken, Baptist minister and schoolmaster of Summit, Mississippi, published in 1894 his classic exposition,* The Ills of the South, *a circumspect critique lacking the populistic rhetoric but especially useful for its description of conditions in Southern agriculture.*

–6–

# THE CREDIT SYSTEM
## by *Charles H. Otken*

Credit is useful in an eminent degree. The business system prevailing with such hurtful and dangerous tendencies in the Southern States, is enslaving the people, and, by its insidious operations, concentrating productive wealth in the hands of the few. It reduces a large body of people to a state of beggary, fosters a discontented spirit, checks consumption, produces recklessness on the part of the consumer, places a discount on honesty, and converts commerce into a vast pawning shop where farmers pledge their lands for hominy and bacon upon ruinous terms in harmony with the pawning system.

. . . . . .

The features of the credit system in vogue in the Southern States during the last twenty-five years, differ widely from those of credit. It operates upon a different basis. The credit mode of

source: Charles H. Otken, *The Ills of the South or Related Causes Hostile to the General Prosperity of the Southern People* (New York: G. P. Putnam's Sons, 1894), Chapter II, pp. 12, 15–25, 27-29, 31–32.

doing business and the plan of the credit system are far apart. While credit is helpful, stimulating in the development of wealth, the credit system is depressing, discouraging—destroying hope. The one is rational, an aid to progress; the other is irrational, and clogs the forward movement of the people.

(1) This system is responsible for an indefiniteness as it respects the debtor, which amounts to tyranny. When A borrows a hundred dollars from B, he knows definitely the rate of interest he has agreed to pay B. The rate of interest is determined before the money is taken. By this method there is no such understanding. All the satisfaction the debtor can get is, he must pay certain prices. If the merchant has agreed to furnish him, it is sufficient for the farmer to know that he must pay these prices. Whether the prices are moderate, reasonable, unreasonable, exorbitant, or ruinous, does not concern the purchaser. It is a financial transaction which is as clear as the noonday sun to one party, the creditor, and as dark as a starless night to the other party, the debtor. Would that this statement were fiction instead of a hard, ugly fact! The purchaser is enveloped in mists. He travels in the dark twelve months in the year. He does not know whether he pays forty or a hundred per cent. profit. This is a secret not to be divulged. Human nature is weak. The power is all on one side, and the necessity for supplies, real or imaginary, on the other. The history of nineteen centuries has certainly taught the world one impressive lesson, that power, wherever found, has seldom been sparing in its exercise. It is not in the nature of power, generally speaking, to be merciful. It has not a tender heart. The milk of human charity comes not from this source. The power of this system is a subtle, expensive, crushing machinery.

.　　.　　.　　.　　.

(2) The debtor is bound to the creditor when once he has commenced to make a purchase. If he has incurred a debt with one merchant, he can not readily get credit from another merchant. The reason is obvious. The risk under the system is great. No merchant cares to take a customer who is already in debt to

another. If there is a mortgage the transfer is attended with difficulties. The purchaser, as a rule, has no option. He is tied up
under this peculiar plan. He may be dissatisfied with his merchant, whose prices may seem exorbitant; he may have found a
merchant whose terms are fairer, but if he is in debt, he is in no
condition to make the change. The debt chains the farmer to the
firm with whom he is trading. He can not buy where it suits him.
The price asked is the only chance to get what he wants, even if
that price amounts to confiscation. Blindly he must buy, if he
buys at all. "Competition" is a word not found in the debtor's
dictionary. "What power in civilized society," says Macaulay, "is
so great as that of the creditor over the debtor?"

(3) Those who buy supplies under this system can not tell how
much they have bought during the year until the cotton crop is
delivered. It is believed to be true of 75 per cent. The only check
to the making of purchases is upon the class of poor farmers
whose property is small, and whose crop consists in a half-dozen
bales of cotton. The limit is fixed at $50, $75, or $100. When
merchandise to the amount agreed upon has been bought, a halt
to further advances is called. The merchant may not be blamed
for refusing to extend the credit beyond the value of the expec-
tant crop. No such limit is fixed for the man whose real estate is
large, and whose personal property in the form of horses, mules,
and cattle is ample. If the purchaser has a family of somewhat
expensive tendencies, the account at the end of the year will
generally be larger than he expected. Upon what did the good,
easy, careless man base his expectation? He kept no account of
his purchases. In a vast number of cases, the bill, as it is com-
monly known, is called for in November and December of the
year. The wail of merchants in January is generally, "We have
large balances to carry over for next year." The size of the crop,
the price of cotton, and the purchases made, determine the size
and the number of balances. Few are the years that from 50 per
cent. to 75 per cent. of the farmers who thus bought supplies did
not come out in debt to their merchants at the close of the year.
These facts are gathered from conversations with many merchants and a large number of farmers. A slight improvement one

year is reversed by an unfavorable crop year the next. The indefinite plan of purchasing, and ignorance of the amount bought until the cotton has been sold, is a fruitful source of disaster to the country. "Fifty per cent. of the people," said a prominent merchant in 1891, "in my section are in debt, and from 25 to 35 per cent. are not in an easy condition." This incubus still tyrannizes the people. This method is ruinous to any people. It is called business in the sense of trade and transactions. It is all certainty and definiteness so far as the items bought, and the footing up of the merchant's ledger are concerned, and it is all uncertainty and indefiniteness so far as the farmer is concerned.

(4) The mode of doing business is the wicked foster-mother of much carelessness, and carelessness is not the basis of prosperity. It may be business to some people, but it has a greedy heart. "I haven't had a settlement," said a farmer of ordinary intelligence, "in six years." "Do you ask your merchant to make out your account at the end of the year?" "No! I sometimes ask him how we stand; and when he says, 'You are all right,' I'm satisfied. I have done business with him for twenty years, and have never asked him for a bill." Confidence is on the rack! "Are there many in your neighborhood who never call for an account?" "A right smart of them. The niggers never ask for a bill, and don't get it if they ask for it." Granting that all merchants are honest, the poor, ignorant negro, as well as the careless white farmer, in the absence of a written statement, has no opportunity to examine his year's transactions for himself. That honest merchant may be an infidel as respects the Bible, but his faith in keeping accounts is extraordinary; there is no flaw in this confidence. The amount of blind trusting he demands of these careless, ignorant people, is immense. Infidelity here would impose a good deal of labor. Such management bodes no good to the country. Not one merchant in ten thousand would be willing to do business with other merchants in this way. Dishonesty has the power to cheat and defraud in prices, in weights, and in measures, under such circumstances, with impunity. That the spirit of discontent should show itself, and the cry of "hard times" should be heard, ought not to surprise any one. "There is no money in farming," says the

planter. Certainly not, under such wild management. There is a big screw loose here, no matter how honest all parties may be. It is time to examine foundations. Silent and imperceptible are the causes that undermine the prosperity of a country. A magazine of explosives lies hid beneath this highly favored mode of business.

(5) When all the cotton made during the year has been delivered and sold, and the farmer comes out in debt on the 31st of December, that farmer has taken the first step toward bankruptcy. If he is a small farmer, $25, $50, or $75 is a heavy burden to carry. Take these cases: Hezekiah Drawbridge owes $25 at the close of the year; his credit limit was $75. Stephen Goff owes $50; his credit limit was $150. Buff Tafton owes $75; his credit limit was $250. The year during which these debts were made was fairly good, the purchases were moderate, there was no sickness in these families. The following year similar credit arrangements are made, and they purchase the full amount agreed upon between them and their merchants. From some unaccountable or accountable cause, the cotton crop is a little worse, or the price of cotton is a little less. The winding up of the second year's farm operations finds Drawbridge, Goff, and Tafton with the following debts confronting them, respectively: $65, $115, $155. The outlook is blue for these farmers, and they feel blue. Thus, or nearly thus, this system operates in thousands of cases. Each year the plunge into debt is deeper; each year the burden is heavier. The struggle is woe-begone. Cares are many, smiles are few, and the comforts of life are scantier. This is the bitter fruit of a method of doing business which comes to the farmer in the guise of friendship, but rules him with despotic power. To a large class of men, the inscription printed in large, bold characters over the door of the credit system is: "The man who enters here leaves hope behind," and it tells a sad and sorrowful history. Anxious days, sleepless nights, deep wrinkles, gray hairs, wan faces, cheerless old age, and perhaps abject poverty make up, in part, the melancholy story. The bitter reflection about the whole matter is, that, as a general rule, there was no substantial cause for this result.

(6) "A bad crop year, Mr. Tafton." "Mighty bad, mighty bad," replies Mr. Goff. "We are ruined. I reckon our merchants won't furnish us another year unless we give a mortgage on our land. I used to think that I would see any man in Halifax before I'd do that. It's come to that now, or starvation." The end of these men as freeholders is near at hand. Drawbridge, Goff, and Tafton, and their companions in misery, wear sad and long faces. On some dreary, cold day in December, when nothing can well be done on the farm, these men ride to town, each to execute that hard instrument called a mortgage, which in so many cases means ruin to themselves and their families. These ugly handcuffs are on, and they are hard to get off. This business method has peculiar attractions for these iron tools that chafe the flesh, but more the spirit. Independence! It is gone. Humiliation and dependence bow the head of the proud spirit. It is a rugged, thorny path these men must travel. A little earnest self-denial faithfully practiced for a few years, would have assured them ease, comfort, and competence.

(7) Thus it is that not a few farmers in the South who held a fee-simple title to their property, lost all in ten years. They worshipped Moloch. Their adoration destroyed their independence, their self-respect, their lands, and their chattels. There are men who made an average of fifteen to twenty-five bales of cotton a year, owned from five to ten head of mules, and from five hundred to one thousand acres of land, with comfortable residences and all necessary outhouses, who found themselves homeless and poor at the end of ten years. There is a cause. It sleeps within the womb of this business arrangement. There must be an enormous abuse lurking somewhere in these operations; it involves well-meaning and innocent men who keep no accounts, and, as a rule, apply no business principles to their farm work or their expenses, in hopeless poverty. Neither the merchants alone, as a class, nor the farmers alone, as a class, are to blame for this state of things; but the commercial contract, under whose articles they formed a joint copartnership to do business, deserves full and signal justice. It is a covenant to which the parties of the first part are thoroughly organized, thoroughly systematic in keeping accounts,

thoroughly acquainted with the cost and selling price of merchandise, and thoroughly informed as to their expenses. The parties of the second part are thoroughly unorganized, thoroughly unsystematic, thoroughly uninformed as to prices and as to their ability to pay them, thoroughly in the dark as to what their product will be or its price, and thoroughly in the dark as to their expense account. The parties to the covenant are unequally matched. System, exactness, power, and risks—risks, however, provided for by high prices, and often secured by liens—are on the one side; general inexactness, weakness, and heavy burdens in the form of prices are on the other side. The most certain thing about the covenant is, that the parties of the second part must pay the parties of the first part a definite sum. The price of cotton, sugar, molasses, rice, tobacco, and all other merchandise may fluctuate, but the debit side of the ledger maintains its figures with stubborn and relentless regularity. Hard times do not affect them. Storms and inundations do not change them. These figures remain unscathed amid social and political convulsions. Sickness and death can not discount them. Certainty and uncertainty have gone into copartnership as a basis for the country's prosperity.

(8) The many risks incident to this business involve many bad debts. The honest man must pay the debts of the dishonest man. Merchant Harlem does a $100,000 credit business per year. He has 600 customers, who make 3,000 bales of cotton. Twenty per cent. of the customers are first-class men; 150 men are in fair condition—they are somewhat in debt. A reverse in their farm work, a bad crop year, or serious sickness in their families, will bring them at once to the deadline where hope puts on its sickly hue. The remaining 250 obtain credit under a variety of conditions. That there should not be some rascals in this whole number, is as probable as that a cornfield should be without weeds. These bad debts, which ultimately may be charged up to profit and loss, will range from $1,000 to $5,000 per annum. This anticipated loss is considered when the selling price of the merchandise is marked. Were there no loss, the price would be less. Risk always raises the price of commodities. Every honest man

must help to pay his *pro rata* of the bad man's debts. There is not a merchant in the South, selling goods on credit, whose losses from this source have not amounted to thousands of dollars. This burden must be borne by the purchaser.

These are some of the ugly features of this business method. It has done much to debauch public sentiment. It has enslaved thousands of good people. It has brought about a state of dependence that reduces the great body of agricultural people to a condition of serfs, the name excepted. It deserves serious consideration. The situation is alarming to free men. It is no small matter that 3,000,000 farmers should be dependent upon 10,000 men. We blame not the merchant class. They have drifted into this channel, and have concluded there is no other way. Some like it, because, to them, it is a feast. This method of trading has lowered the tone of public morals. It is not a secret that perjury often walks the streets, unwhipped of justice. False swearing is common. Wealth obtained by dishonest means is respectable, and occupies a front seat on the dais—the seat of honor in the great temple of public sentiment; and that public sentiment, like a cracked bell, jangles out of tune. Robust honesty is still in the land, but it is timid and passive. It is shackled by environments. About 300 farmers are, on an average, at the mercy of one man. Year in and year out, for a quarter of a century, this submission has been endured. There is no money in the country, save during the winter months. All those who have dealings with the farming class, rendering to them valuable and necessary service, are involved in these impoverished circumstances. Enterprise is stunted. Progress is choked. Whatever is of the highest value to the country, relating to its material advancement, its intellectual and moral elevation, is depreciated and throttled by this ruinous method. . . .

.    .    .    .    .

The prosperity of the Southern people is very largely contingent on cash transactions and competition in business.

As late as 1893 we found these prices still ruling the market on a necessary article of consumption, flour. From February to September the average price of flour in the city of St. Louis was, for Patent, sold under three fancy names, $3.35; for Majestic, sold under five fancy names, $3.09; for Extra Fancy Grade, sold under three fancy names, $3.00; for Fancy Grade, sold under three fancy names, $2.65; for Choice Grade, sold under three fancy names, $2.40; for Plantation Grade, sold under three fancy names, $2.30. These fancy names, such as Challenge, Capitol, and Lillian, represent the same grade of flour. Each merchant adopts the brand that suits his taste. As will be noticed, for six grades of flour there are twenty different names or brands.

These quotations, a merchant assured us, were those of grocers. At the mills any grade of this flour can be bought at ten cents less, and perhaps fifteen cents less per barrel. Adding railroad freight, after deducting ten cents per barrel, to the last five grades, we have the following cost price at the point of delivery: Majestic, $3.91; Extra Fancy, $3.82; Fancy, $3.47; Choice, $3.22; Plantation, $3.12

This flour was sold *on credit* at $6.00 and $7.00 per barrel. We will suppose that one of the first three grades was sold at this price. In this case the profit on the Majestic was 53 per cent.; on the Extra Fancy, 57 per cent.; on the Fancy, 72 per cent. Others paid $7.50 as per bill seen, credit price. The average cost of Patent flour was $4.17. According to this price the profit on Patent flour was 79 per cent. If this was the price on any of the other grades, the profit on Majestic was 91 per cent.; on the Extra Fancy, 94 per cent.; and on the Fancy, 116.

A cash merchant informed us that he had sold a grade of flour equal to the Majestic, from January to October, for $4.50 cash on an average, at a net profit of 12½ per cent.; and that a farmer who bought his yearly supplies on a credit had paid for flour a grade below this at $6.00 per barrel. Had he bought for cash his flour would have cost him $4.29¾. He would have saved 44½ per cent. This is the difference between cash and credit prices. On 10,000 barrels of flour of this grade the farmers would save on a cash basis $17,025.

It is probable that the same difference between cash and credit

prices rules the market in regard to dry goods, domestics, sheet-
ing, prints, shoes, hats, hardware, agricultural implements, ready-
made clothing, and all the commodities usually bought by farmers at a general supply store. . . .

.    .    .    .    .

Five thousand dollars invested in trade, even if half is borrowed money, has a far better chance to make in a few years
twenty-five thousand, fifty thousand, and a hundred thousand
dollars, than has five thousand dollars in preparing for any of the
learned professions, or invested in a farm, to make a meagre
living. Survey the field of human industry in the Southern States,
and the fact is everywhere patent, emphasized in every vocation
and calling of life, that there is no general prosperity. In large
cities there are no doubt some prosperous physicians and lawyers,
and prosperous men in other callings of life. It is not so in the
country at large.

There should be no hostility between the merchant class, the
farming class, and all other classes. But this business method is
not only bringing bankruptcy to the farmers, but practically and
really it is damaging the just and reasonable interest of all other
classes, since, in a great agricultural community, the professions
and mechanics are largely the servants of the farming class.

An alarming state of affairs has impressed its die in recent
months upon the attention of the country. When people are prosperous, they have neither the time nor the disposition to engage
in lawlessness. Men who can not see afar off, moving in a narrow
circle, toiling hard, discouraged, despondent, in debt, the farm
under mortgage, ruin and poverty staring them in the face, are
easily led into desperate measures, and that to their own undoing.
But little sunshine streams into their lives. The situation of the
country, view it as we may, is serious.

**DEFLATION**

*A resident of Lansing, Michigan, and an active participant successively in the Greenback, Union Labor Party, and Populist causes, Mrs. Emery wrote one of the most widely circulated attacks on currency deflation. Her book is often cited as an outstanding expression of conspiracy theories harbored by the Populists.*

## –7–

# DEMONETIZATION OF SILVER
## by Sarah E. V. Emery

Having refunded and made payable in gold the bonds which had not cost their holders more than sixty cents on the dollar, the casual observer is satisfied that the last robbery has been perpetrated.[1] But the busy brain of avarice is ever reaching out—not after new truths—but for gain, *gain,* GAIN; and we next find these civilized brigands have consummated a scheme for the *demonetization of silver.* This act, passed in 1873, destroyed the money quality of silver, and thus produced a farther contraction of the currency. The object of this act was first to prevent the payment of the bonds, and second, to increase their value.

Never in this country had there been an investment so safe and yet so reliable. Shylock, with his hoarded millions, could rest on beds of down. Neither fire, flood, mildew nor blight brought anxiety to him. He seemed to rest in assurance of the Divine favor,

SOURCE: Mrs. Sarah E. V. Emery, *Seven Financial Conspiracies Which Have Enslaved the American People* (2d edition, Lansing, Michigan: Launt Thompson, 1888), Chapter VII, pp. 69–81.

[1 The Gold Act of March 18, 1869, and the Refunding Act of July 14, 1870. Ed.]

having obeyed the injunction to "lay up his treasure where moth and rust could not corrupt, nor thieves break through and steal." Indeed, the entire country had become sponsor for his wealth, for under the law every producer and millions of wage-workers had been instituted a vigilance committee to look after his welfare. Why should he not be opposed to having his bond investment disturbed? The government held that property in safe keeping, and did not charge a cent for the favor; it collected his interest and paid it over to him free of charge; it paid his gold interest in advance and exempted him from taxation; the insurance agent and tax gatherer were strangers to him, they did not molest or make him afraid, and being thus fortified, he was content to let the producers of wealth eke out a miserable existence while he fared sumptuously every day. But it was not the American capitalist alone who entered into this murderous scheme for demonetizing silver. In the *Banker's Magazine* of August, 1873, we find the following on this subject:

In 1872, silver being demonetized in France, England and Holland, a capital of $500,000 was raised, and Ernest Seyd of London was sent to this country with this fund, as agent of the foreign bond holders and capitalists, to effect the same object (demonetization of silver), which was accomplished.

There you have it, a paid agent of English capitalists sent to this country with $500,000 to buy the American Congress and rob the American people. In corroboration of this testimony we read from the *Congressional Record* of April 9, 1872, page 2,032, these words:[2]

Earnest Seyd of London, a distinguished writer and bullionist, who is now here, has given great attention to the subject of mint and coinage. After having examined the first draft of this bill (for the demonetization of silver) he made various sensible suggestions, which the committee adopted and embodied in the bill.

[2 "Mr. Ernest Seyd, of London, a distinguished writer, who has given great attention to the subject of mints and coinage, after examining the first draft of the bill, furnished many valuable suggestions which have been incorporated in this bill." *Congressional Globe*, 42 Cong., 2 Sess., pp. 2304–2305 (April 9, 1872). Ernest Seyd (1829 or 1830–1881) was a London banker and writer on finance and currency. — Ed.]

So says Mr. Hooper, who, at that time, was chairman of the committee on coinage, but I will farther add that I heard Hon. Gilbert DeLamartyr say that Judge Kelly told him that he (Kelly) saw the original draft of the bill for the demonetization of silver, and it was in Ernest Seyd's own handwriting.[3] God of our fathers! A British capitalist sent here to make laws for the American people. England failed to subjugate us by the bullet, but she stole into our Congressional halls and by the crafty use of gold, obtained possession of the ballot, and to-day American industry pays tribute to England, despite our blood-bought seal of independence.

Not only did the demonetization of silver prevent, or at least retard the payment of the bonds, but it added to the value of the gold in which these bonds were to be paid. Every dollar taken from circulation adds to the value of that which is left, hence the demonetization of silver increased the value of gold. After England had demonetized silver, our silver dollar, containing 412½ grains, was not worth as much in that country by at least ten cents on the dollar, as our gold dollar containing 25.8 grains of gold. By destroying the money quality of silver, bonds became payable in gold only, thus adding immensely to their value. A British capitalist, holding $100,000,000 of our four per cent. bonds, received an annual interest of $4,000,000, which paid in standard silver would be worth ten per cent., or $400,000 less than it would be if paid in gold. This would make a difference in his daily interest of $1,096. Is it not clear why English capitalists were anxious for the United States to demonetize silver? and why they could afford to send Ernest Seyd to this country with a capital of $500,000 to accomplish this object?

Just here will the reader stop for a moment and consider why the Rothschilds, who control the financial policy of England—as the brokers and security-holders of American control ours—why they could afford to pay, not only the paltry half million with

[3 Samuel Hooper (1808–1875), representative from Massachusetts, 1861–1875; Gilbert De La Matyr (1825–1892), Methodist minister and representative from Indiana, 1879–1881; William Darrah "Pig Iron" Kelley (1814–1890), representative from Pennsylvania, 1861–1890. — Ed.]

which they bought the demonetization of silver, but many millions more had it been necessary? Our civil war opened the eyes of England. She knew that her welfare, nay, almost her existence, depended upon America's supply of cotton, meat, and cereals; these were liable to fail, either in rebellion at home or in war with foreign nations. But she was the world's great creditor, for she held the bonds of all nations, and if she could make them payable in the dearest money in the world, it would enhance her securities many millions, and if she could insure herself an ample supply of wheat and cotton she would be independent of us under all circumstances. Now, since she owned and controlled all India—that great wheat and cotton country—she saw that, with India's cheap labor and the demonetization of American silver, she would have a double leverage over America and her productions. Silver money is used exclusively in India. England coins that money, and if, with eighty cents, she could buy silver, stamp and pass it for a dollar in payment for India's wheat and cotton, she not only gained the twenty per cent. from her own subjects, but in consequence of the demonetization of silver in America, her debtors here were compelled to pay her at least ten per cent. more than they would have paid had not silver been demonetized. Let it also be borne in mind that this discount, whether much or little, was so much new capital with which to open up the interior of India to compete with America and her productions.

The injury to the people of this country through the demonetization of silver can never, perhaps, be justly estimated. The panic of 1873, which ensued was one of the most disastrous that ever befell any people. Language fails in a description of the blighting misery that desolated the country, the ravages of war are scarcely comparable with it. From the demonetization of silver, in 1873, to its remonetization in 1878, may well be called the dark days of our Republic.[4] Bankruptcies and financial disaster brought in train their legitimate offspring, and the statistics of those and the ensuing years are voluminous with the most startling and loathsome crimes, murder, insanity, suicide, divorce,

[4 Coinage Act of 1873; Bland-Allison Act of 1878. — Ed.]

drunkenness, and all forms of immorality and crime have increased from that day to this in the most appalling ratio. Will any man say that legislation has had nothing to do with the startling increase of crime in our country? Every result is produced from certain causes, and it is no more certain that like begets like than that the increase of misery and crime in our country are the direct result of evil legislation. And it is impossible for a nation long to remain free whose laws are made granting special privileges to the few and ignoring the rights of the many. The contraction of the currency, commencing with the destruction of the greenbacks in 1866, and the stringency increased by the demonetization of silver in 1873, has been productive of more misery and crime to the people of this country than all the wars, pestilence, and famine with which they have ever been afflicted.

In regard to the policy of contraction, Prof. Walker, of Yale College,[5] who is not a politician, nor a statesman, but a cool, unbiased writer and teacher, says:

When the process of contraction commences, the first class on whom it falls is the merchants of the large cities, they find it difficult to get money to pay their notes, the next class is the manufacturer, the sale of his goods at once falls off; laborers and mechanics next feel the pressure, they are thrown out of employment; and, lastly, the farmer finds a dull sale for his produce; and all, unsuspicious of the real cause, have a vague idea that their difficulties are owing to the hard times. ° ° We have become so familiar with these periodical revolutions in trade, that we look upon them as the natural phenomenon of business, but it is not so.

Ricardo,[6] another eminent writer on political economy, says:

That commodities rise in price in proportion to the increase or diminution of money, I hold to be a fact that is incontrovertible.

John Stuart Mill[7] says:

[5 Francis Amesa Walker (1840–1897), professor of political economy and history at Yale University, 1873–1881; president of Massachusetts Institute of Technology, 1881–1897. — Ed.]

[6 David Ricardo (1772–1823), English economist. — Ed.]

[7 John Stuart Mill (1806–1873), English philosopher and economist. — Ed.]

If the whole volume of money in circulation were doubled, prices would double.

The monetary commission, created August 15, 1876, consisting of three United States senators, three members of the house, and three secretaries, made a report March 2, 1877, in which appear these words:[8]

The true and only cause of the stagnation in industry and commerce now everywhere felt, is the fact everywhere existing of falling prices, caused by a shrinkage in the volume of money.

Here we have the conclusion of nine prominent statesmen, who, after an exhaustive examination, emphatically declare that the "true and only cause" of the calamities that have befallen the people is "the shrinkage in the volume of money." To whom, then, shall we charge these calamities that have come upon us like a flood? Is it the extravagance of the people? Is it because too many of the necessaries of life have been produced? Because the farmer has been too industrious and prudent, or the manufacturers employed too many laborers in the production of his commodities? Is it because millions of children are employed in the mines and factories of the country, denied every blessing and privilege of childhood? Is it because the dram-shop is sucking away the sustenance of thousands of families, and bringing desolation into their homes? Is it because women are selling their souls to keep their bodies from starving, or because a band of train robbers are infesting the country and sending terror into the hearts of the people? No, it is none of these circumstances that have brought such disaster upon our country, but it is a selfish and criminal legislation that has overwhelmed us with these alarming conditions.

When the fiend of civil war was desolating the land, when the great heart of the nation throbbed in agony, and the people were bowed in mourning, then a band of men, with murderous pur-

[8 *Report and Accompanying Documents of the United States Monetary Commission Organized Under Joint Resolution of August 15, 1876*, Senate Report No. 703, 44 Cong., 2 Sess. (Washington, 1877), p. 121. — Ed.]

poses, went—not into the battlefield—but into the very sanctuary of our country, the holy place of government, and there, under the guise of patriot and benefactor, pillaged the soldier, and plotted the most diabolical scheme of robbery that ever blackened a historic page. Who were these men? Ah, history is writing their names in a most damning record, they are drenched with the blood of martyred children, and the agonizing cry of forty millions of enslaved people is ascending continually day and night. Do you ask for evidence that this people were deliberately robbed by a band of men at the head of our government, who were in league with the money power of Europe? If so, please read and ponder the "confidential" circular which was issued in 1862 by English capitalists, who commissioned one Hazard, a London banker, to propagate its principles among American bankers with a view of having the finance legislation of Congress pave the way for its final adoption as the settled policy of this nation. How well they succeeded is best told by millions of wrecked fortunes and ruined homes. Here is the infernal document:

Slavery is likely to be abolished by the war power, and chattel slavery destroyed. This, I and my European friends are in favor of, for slavery is but the owning of labor, and carries with it the care for the laborer; while the European plan, led on by England, is capital control of labor, by controlling wages. This can be done by controlling the money.

The great debt that capitalists will see to it is made out of the war, must be used as a measure to control the volume of money. To accomplish this, the bonds must be used as a banking basis. We are now waiting to get the secretary of the treasury to make his recommendation to congress. It will not do to allow the greenback, as it is called, to circulate as money any length of time, for we cannot control that.

About the middle of the present century Sir John Lubbock,[9] of England, declared:

There is likely to be an effort made by the capital class to fasten upon the world a rule through their wealth, *and by means of reduced*

[9] Sir John William Lubbock (1803–1865), English banker, mathematician, and astronomer. — Ed.]

*wages* place the masses upon a footing more degrading and dependant than has ever been known in history. The spirit of money worshippers seems to be rapidly developing in this direction.

A few years later Abraham Lincoln reiterated the same sentiment in his message to Congress in 1861. (See Barratt's Life of Lincoln, pages 309 and 310.) This important warning is omitted in the later histories.

Monarchy itself is sometimes hinted at as a possible refuge from the power of the people. In my present position I could scarcely be justified were I to omit raising a warning voice against the approach of returning despotism. There is one point to which I ask a brief attention. It is the effort to place *capital* on an equal footing with, if not above *labor*, in the structure of government. * * Let them beware of surrendering a political power which they already have, and which, if surrendered, will surely be used to close the door of advancement against such as they, and to fix new disabilities and burdens upon them, till all of liberty shall be lost.

These are the words of warning from our country's sainted martyr, but alas, how little heeded.

Again, near the close of the war, in reply to a letter from a friend in Illinois, President Lincoln said:

Yes, we may all congratulate ourselves that this cruel war is nearing to a close. It has cost a vast amount of treasure and blood. The best blood of the flower of American youth has been freely offered upon our country's altar that the nation might live. It has been indeed, a trying hour for the republic; but I see in the near future, a crisis approaching that unnerves me and causes me to tremble for the safety of my country.

As a result of the war, corporations have been enthroned, and an era of corruption in high places will follow, and the money power of the country will endeavor to prolong its reign by working upon the prejudices of the people until all wealth is aggregated in a few hands, and the Republic is destroyed. I feel at this moment more anxiety for the safety of my country than ever before, even in the midst of the war. God grant that my suspicion may prove groundless.

## PLUTOCRACY AND THE TRUSTS

*James Baird Weaver, Populist candidate for president in 1892 and Greenback candidate in 1880, was a resident of Iowa. He had a varied career in gold mining, storekeeping, mail carrying, the law, and politics, after reaching the rank of brigadier general in the Civil War. His book,* A Call to Action, *served as a campaign document in the presidential canvass of 1892.*

## –8–

# A CALL TO ACTION
## by James Baird Weaver

### DIVES AND LAZARUS

#### CONTRASTS

If the master builders of our civilization one hundred years ago had been told that at the end of a single century, American society would present such melancholy contrasts of wealth and poverty, of individual happiness and widespread infelicity as are to be found to-day throughout the Republic, the person making the unwelcome prediction would have been looked upon as a misanthropist, and his loyalty to Democratic institutions would have been seriously called in question. Our federal machine, with its delicate inter-lace work of National, State and municipal supervision, each intended to secure perfect individual equality,

SOURCE: James Baird Weaver, *A Call to Action: An Interpretation of the Great Uprising, Its Source and Causes* (Des Moines: Iowa Printing Co., 1892), ch. XII, pp. 362–364, 368–369, 374–375; ch. XIV, pp. 387–394; ch. XX, pp. 441–445.

was expected to captivate the world by its operation and insure domestic contentment and personal security to a degree never before realized by mankind.

But there is a vast difference between the generation which made the heroic struggle for Self-government in colonial days, and the third generation which is now engaged in a mad rush for wealth. The first took its stand upon the inalienable rights of man and made a fight which shook the world. But the leading spirits of the latter are entrenched behind class laws and revel in special privileges. It will require another revolution to overthrow them. That revolution is upon us even now.

Two representative characters—Dives and Lazarus—always make their appearance side by side in disturbing contrast just before the tragic stage of revolution is reached. They were present at the overthrow of ancient civilizations; the hungry multitude stood outside the gates when Belshazzar's impious feast was spread; they were both at the cave of Adullam when the scepter was about to depart from the tyrant Saul to the hands of the youthful David; they stood side by side when Alaric thundered at the gates of Rome; they confronted one another in the fiery tempest of the French revolution and they are sullenly face to face in our own country to-day. We will devote a few pages to the delineation of these forces as they appear in our civilization at the present period.

### SOCIAL EXTRAVAGANCE

In the year 1884, as we are told by Ward McAllister, in his book entitled "Society as I Found It," a wealthy gentleman gave a banquet at Delmonico's at which the moderate number of seventy-two guests, ladies and gentlemen, were entertained. The gentlemen giving the banquet had unexpectedly received from the Treasury of the United States a rebate of $10,000 for duties which had been exacted from him through some alleged misconception of the law. He resolved to spend the entire sum in giving a single dinner which should excel any private entertainment ever given in New York. He consulted Charles Delmonico, who engaged to carry out his wishes. The table was constructed with a miniature lake in the center thirty feet in length, enclosed by a network of golden wire which reached to the ceiling, forming a great cage. Four immense swans were secured from one of the parks and placed in this lake. High banks of flowers of every hue surrounded the lake and covered the entire table, leaving barely enough room for the plates and wine glasses. The room was festooned with flowers in every direction. Miniature mountains and valleys with carpets of flowers made vocal with sparkling rivulets, met the eye on every hand. Golden cages filled with sweet singing birds hung from the ceiling and added their enchantment to the gorgeous spectacle. Soft, sweet music swept in from adjoining rooms, and all that art, wealth and imagination could do was done to make the scene one of unexampled beauty. And then the feast! All the dishes which ingenuity could invent or the history of past extravagance suggest, were spread before the guests. The oldest and costliest wines known to the trade flowed like the water that leaped down the cascades in the banqueting hall. The guests were wild with exultation and delight and tarried far into the night. But in a few brief hours the romanticism had passed, the carousal was broken, and the revelers were face to face with the responsibilities which none of us can evade. The fool and his money had parted.

### SILVER, GOLD AND DIAMOND DINNERS

Some time after the "swan dinner" was given, three of the swell leaders of New York society planned to give each a handsome entertainment which should set all New York talking. Each instructed the head of the celebrated *cafe* to spare no expense and to make his dinner the best of the three. So magnificent were these entertainments that Lorenzo Delmonico designated them as the silver, gold and diamond dinners. Each had peculiarities which distinguished it from the others. At one of them each lady found snugly concealed in her napkin a gold bracelet with the monogram of Jerome Park in the center in chased gold.

. . . . .

## AT THE RICH MAN'S GATE

About the time these princely entertainments were given, and in the same year with some of them, one of the metropolitan journals caused a careful canvass to be made of the unemployed of that city. The number was found to be *one hundred and fifty thousand persons who were daily unsuccessfully seeking work within the city limits of New York*. Another one hundred and fifty thousand earn less than sixty cents per day. Thousands of these are poor girls who work from eleven to sixteen hours per day.

In the year 1890, over twenty-three thousand families, numbering about one hundred thousand people, were forcibly evicted in New York City owing to their inability to pay rent, and one-tenth of all who died in that city during the year were buried in the Potters Field.

## AT CHICAGO

In the latter part of the year 1891, a committee from a Chicago Trade and Labor Assembly, at the request of a body of striking cloakmakers, made an investigation of the condition of that class of workers in the city. They were accompanied by an officer of the City Health Department, the City Attorney and artists and reporters of the local press. They found that thirteen thousand persons were engaged in the manufacture of clothing in Chicago, over one-half of whom were females. In order to reduce the cost of production the firms engaged in the manufacture of clothing have adopted the European Sweating System, which is in brief, as follows: The material for garments is cut to size and shape and delivered by the large firms to individual contractors known as sweaters, who relieve the firm of all other care or expense, taking the goods to what are known as sweating dens, usually located in the poorest neighborhoods of the great city. These sweaters are employed by the most opulent firms. The committee visited a large number of these dens, nearly all of which were dwelling houses which served as living and sleeping rooms for the sweater's family and the employes. In one room ten feet by forty, they found thirty-nine young girls, twelve children between ten and twelve years of age, eleven men and the sweater and his wife. The room and all the surroundings were filthy in the extreme. The rates of wages were of course very low, and yet the fear of discharge rendered it almost impossible to obtain satisfactory information. The committee found two thousand one hundred children at work in these dismal places who were under age and employed in violation of existing laws against child labor. Sanitary laws were also overridden in all of these miserable abodes. . . .

### AND HAS IT COME TO US SO SOON?

We trust the brief pages of this chapter may suffice to call the attention of the reader to the ghastly condition of American society and to remind him of the imperative call which is made upon him as an individual to do all in his power to arrest the alarming tendencies of our times. In the opinion of the writer, unless the people of America shall immediately take political matters into their own hands, the contrasts suggested in this chapter portend a tragic future. The millionaire and the pauper cannot, in this country, long dwell together in peace, and it is idle to attempt to patch up a truce between them. Enlightened self respect and a quickened sense of justice are impelling the multitude to demand an interpretation of the anomalous spectacle, constantly presented before their eyes, of a world filled with plenty and yet multitudes of people suffering for all that goes to make life desirable. They are calling to know why idleness should dwell in luxury and those who toil in want; and they are inquiring why one-half of God's children should be deprived of homes upon a planet which is large enough for all. The world will find a solution for these insufferable afflictions in the glorious era but just ahead. Even now the twilight discloses the outlines of a generous inheritance for all and we hear the chirping of sweet birds making ready to welcome with melody and gladness the advent of the full orbed day.

*TRUSTS*

A Trust is defined to be a combination of many competing concerns under one management. The object is to increase profits through reduction of cost, limitation of product and increase of the price to the consumer. The term is now applied, and very properly, to all kinds of combinations in trade which relate to prices, and without regard to whether all or only part of the objects named are had in view.

Combinations which we now call trusts have existed in this country for a considerable period, but they have only attracted general attention for about ten years. We have in our possession copies of the agreements of the Standard Oil and Sugar Trusts. The former is dated January 2, 1882, and the latter August 6, 1887.

Trusts vary somewhat in their forms of organization. This is caused by the character of the property involved and the variety of objects to be attained. The great trusts of the country consist of an association or consolidation of a number of associations engaged in the same line of business—each company in the trust being first separately incorporated. The stock of these companies is then turned over to a board of trustees who issue back trust certificates in payment for the stock transferred. The trust selects its own board of directors and henceforth has complete control of the entire business and can regulate prices, limit or stimulate production as they may deem best for the parties concerned in the venture. The trust is not necessarily incorporated. Many of the strongest, such as the "Standard Oil Trust," the "Sugar Trust," and "The American Cotton Seed Oil Trust" and others are not. They are the invisible agents of associated artificial intangible beings. They are difficult to find, still harder to restrain and so far as present experience has gone they are practically a law unto themselves.

The power of these institutions has grown to be almost incalculable. Trustees of the Standard Oil Trust have issued certificates to the amount of $90,000,000, and each certificate is worth to-day $165 in the market, which makes their real capital at least

$148,500,000, to say nothing of the added strength of their recent European associations. They have paid quarterly dividends since their organization in 1882. The profits amount to $20,000,000 per year. The Trust is managed by a Board of Trustees all of whom reside in New York. The combine really began in 1869, but the present agreement dates no further back than January, 1882. The only record kept of the meetings of these Trustees is a note stating that the minutes of the previous meeting were read and approved. The minutes themselves are then destroyed. These facts were brought to light by an investigation before the New York Senate February, 1888. Col. George Bliss and Gen. Roger A. Pryor acted as council for the people and a great many things were brought out concerning the Standard, and a multitude of other combines, which had not before been well understood. John D. Rockefeller, Charles Pratt, Henry M. Rogers, H. M. Flagler, Benjamin Brewster, J. N. Archibald, William Rockefeller and W. H. Tilford are the trustees and they personally own a majority of the stock. Seven hundred other persons own the remainder. This trust holds the stock of forty-two corporations, extending into thirteen States. The Cotton Seed Oil Trust holds the stock of eighty-five corporations extending into fifteen States.

Trust combinations now dominate the following products and divisions of trade: Kerosene Oil, Cotton Seed Oil, Sugar, Oat meal, Starch, White Corn Meal, Straw Paper, Pearled Barley, Coal, Straw Board, Lumber, Castor Oil, Cement, Linseed Oil Lard, School Slate, Oil Cloth, Salt, Cattle, Meat Products, Gas, Street Railways, Whisky, Paints, Rubber, Steel, Steel Rails, Steel and Iron Beams, Cars, Nails, Wrought Iron Pipes, Iron Nuts, Stoves, Lead, Copper, Envelopes, Wall Paper, Paper Bags, Paving Pitch, Cordage, Coke, Reaping, Binding and Mowing Machines, Threshing Machines, Plows, Glass, Water Works, Warehouses, Sand Stone, Granite, Upholsterers' Felt, Lead Pencils, Watches and Watch Cases, Clothes Wringers, Carpets, Undertakers' Goods and Coffins, Planes, Breweries, Milling, Flour, Silver Plate, Plated Ware and a vast variety of other lines of trade.

.    .    .    .    .

ARE TRUSTS LEGAL?

It is clear that trusts are contrary to public policy and hence in conflict with the Common law. They are monopolies organized to destroy competition and restrain trade. Enlightened public policy favors competition in the present condition of organized society. It was held in 1880, Central Ohio Salt Company *vs.* Guthrie, 35 Ohio St., 666, that a trust was illegal and void. The Pennsylvania courts held the same way against the Coal Trust of that State. Morris Coal Company *vs.* Vorday, 68 Pa. St., 173.

In 1869 a coal company in New York had contracted to buy coal from several firms upon condition that they would not sell coal to other persons in that locality. The party buying the coal did not pay for it, whereupon suit was brought to collect. The court refused to enforce the bargain, holding that the contract was illegal. Arnot *vs.* Pittison Coal Company, 68 N. Y., 588. The same rule was upheld by the courts at Louisiana in 1859. In Illinois a Grain Dealer's Combine was held to be illegal. The question arose in a suit brought to compel a proper division of the profits. The court refused to enforce the agreement. See Croft *vs.* McConoughy, 79 Ill., 346. The same character of decisions will be found in perhaps a majority of the States. Indeed, since the days when Coke was Lord Chief Justice of England, more than a century and a half ago, the courts in both England and America have held such combinations to be illegal and void. See "Case of the Monopolies," 11 Coke, 84.

It is contended by those interested in Trusts that they tend to cheapen production and diminish the price of the article to the consumer. It is conceded that these results may follow temporarily and even permanently in some instances. But it is not the rule. When such effects ensue they are merely incidental to the controlling object of the association. Trusts are speculative in their purposes and formed to make money. Once they secure control of a given line of business they are masters of the situation and can dictate to the two great classes with which they deal—the producer of the raw material and the consumer of the finished product. They limit the price of the raw material so as to impoverish the producer, drive him to a single market, reduce the price of every class of labor connected with the trade, throw out of employment large numbers of persons who had before been engaged in a meritorious calling and finally, prompted by insatiable avarice, they increase the price to the consumer and thus complete the circle of their depredations. Diminished prices is the bribe which they throw into the market to propitiate the public. They will take it back when it suits them to do so.

The Trust is organized commerce with the Golden Rule excluded and the trustees exempted from the restraints of conscience.

They argue that competition means war and is therefore destructive. The Trust is eminently docile and hence seeks to destroy competition in order that we may have peace. But the peace which they give us is like that which exists after the leopard has devoured the kid. This professed desire for peace is a false pretense. They dread the war of competition because the people share in the spoils. When rid of that they always turn their guns upon the masses and depredate without limit or mercy. The main weapons of the trust are threats, intimidation, bribery, fraud, wreck and pillage. Take one well authenticated instance in the history of the Oat Meal Trust as an example. In 1887 this Trust decided that part of their mills should stand idle. They were accordingly closed. This resulted in the discharge of a large number of laborers who had to suffer in consequence. The mills which were continued in operation would produce seven million barrels of meal during the year. Shortly after shutting down the Trust advanced the price of meal one dollar per barrel and the public was forced to stand the assessment. The mills were more profitable when idle than when in operation.

The Sugar Trust has it within its power to levy a tribute of $30,000,000 upon the people of the United States by simply advancing the price of sugar one cent per pound for one year.

If popular tumult breaks out and legislation in restraint of these depredations is threatened, they can advance prices, extort campaign expenses and corruption funds from the people and force the disgruntled multitude to furnish the sinews of war for their own destruction. They not only have the power to do these things, but it is their known mode of warfare and they actually practice it from year to year.

The most distressing feature of this war of the Trusts is the fact that they control the articles which the plain people consume in their daily life. It cuts off their accumulations and deprives them of the staff upon which they fain would lean in their old age.

### THE REMEDY

For nearly three hundred years the Anglo-Saxon race has been trying to arrest the encroachments of monopoly and yet the evil has flourished and gained in strength from age to age. The courts have come to the aid of enlightened sentiment, pronounced all such combinations contrary to public policy, illegal and their contracts void; and still they have continued to thrive. Thus far repressive and prohibitory legislation have proved unavailing. Experience has shown that when men, for the sake of gain, will openly violate the moral law and infringe upon the plain rights of their neighbors, they will not be restrained by ordinary prohibitory measures. It is the application of force to the situation and force must be met with force. The States should pass stringent penal statutes which will visit personal responsibility upon all agents and representatives of the trust who aid or assist in the transaction of its business within the State. The General Government, through its power to lay and collect taxes, should place an excise or internal revenue tax of from 25 to 40 per cent on all manufacturing plants, goods, wares or merchandise of whatever kind and wherever found when owned by or controlled in the interest of such combines or associations, and this tax should be a first lien upon such property until the tax is paid. The details of such a bill would not be difficult to frame. Such a law would destroy the Trust root and branch. Whenever the American people really try to overthrow these institutions they will be able to do so and to further postpone action is a crime.

### WHAT OF THE FUTURE?

One of the main charges against Charles the First, was that he had fostered and created monopolies. His head went to the block.

Nearly every great struggle of the English race has been caused by the unjust exactions of tribute—against the extortions of greed. Our own war for Independence was a war against taxes. Our late internal struggle was for the freedom of labor and the right of the laborer to possess and enjoy his own. That struggle is still on and it is now thundering at our gates with renewed energy. It will not down, though the Trust heap Ossa upon Pelion. The people will rise and overturn the despoilers though they shake the earth by the displacement.

These vast struggles are great teachers and the world is learning rapidly. We are coming to know that great combinations reduce the cost of production and soon the world will grasp the idea that the people can combine and protect themselves. In this combine, in this co-operation of all, there will be no discrimination and the bounties of Heaven will be open alike to the weak and the powerful. We welcome the conflict. There is no time to lose nor can the battle begin too soon.

## DANGER AND DUTY

The American people have entered upon the mightiest civic struggle known to their history. Many of the giant wrongs which they are seeking to overthrow are as old as the race of man and are rock-rooted in the ignorant prejudices and controlling customs of every nation in christendom. We must expect to be confronted by a vast and splendidly equipped army of extortionists, usurers and oppressors marshalled from every nation under heaven. Every instrumentality known to man,—the state with its civic authority, learning with its lighted torch, armies with their commissions to take life, instruments of commerce essential to commercial intercourse, and the very soil upon which we live, move and have our being—all these things and more, are being perverted and used to enslave and impoverish the people. The Golden Rule is rejected by the heads of all the great departments of trade, and the law of Cain, which repudiates the obligations that we are mutually under to one another, is fostered and made the rule of action throughout the world. Corporate feudality has taken the place of chattle slavery and vaunts its power in every state.

The light of past civilization is shining full upon us all, and knowing that cause and effect follow closely upon each other, we believe that we fairly discern the outlines of the main events which the near future has in store for the American people. We do not claim to see clearly all the concomitant phenomena destined to follow the social earthquake just at hand. Such prevision is not accorded to man. But of this much we are certain: In their flight from their task masters the people have about reached the Red Sea. We can not retreat. Either the floods will be parted for us and close, as of old, upon our pursurers, or a life and death struggle will ensue between oppressors and oppressed—between those who would destroy and enslave and those who are seeking to enter into the inheritance prepared for them by a beneficent Father. Our danger lurks in the alternative stated. It behooves every man who desires a peaceful solution of our ever increasing complications to do all in his power to make the deliverance peaceful and humane. To further postpone the controversy is to invite chaos and challenge the arbitrament of the sword. Our past experience should be sufficient to warn us to steer clear of this abyss of peril and the hell of war.

All the Nations of antiquity were scourged exactly as our people are now being scourged. They were afflicted, they complained, rebelled and perished—oppressors and oppressed together. Their innate sense of justice enabled them to discern clearly between right and wrong, but their passion for revenge and thirst for blood made it impossible for the people to retain power even when the fortunes of war had placed it in their hands.

But thanks to the all-conquering strength of Christian enlightenment we are at the dawn of the golden age of popular power. We have unshaken faith in the integrity and final triumph of the people. But their march to power will not be unobstructed. The universal uprising of the industrial forces will result in unifying the monopolistic and plutocratic elements also, and through the business and social influences of these potential and awakened forces, thousands of well-meaning professional and business men of all classes will be induced, for a time, to make common cause against us. This makes it necessary for the friends of reform to put forth herculean efforts to disabuse the minds of well-meaning people concerning the underlying objects of the movement, and this calls for systematic, energetic, and constant educational work, covering the whole range of the reforms proposed. It is also the surest method of overcoming the obstacle of indifference among the people.

We must also be prepared to see the two well-organized and equipped political parties march to the assistance of each other at critical points along the line. The leaders will spare no effort to accomplish this end. Two influences, now at work, are ample to at least partially precipitate this result—the use of money and the community of danger inspired by the appearance of the new political force. The great mass of voters should be faithfully warned of this danger before designing leaders have made the attempt to mislead them. In this manner the evil consequences of their efforts can be largely averted.

### THE GREAT DANGER

If the economic revolution now in progress in the United States is not speedily successful, the industrial people will have no one to blame but themselves. Through suffering and research they have learned the causes of their distress. They have organized, decided upon remedies and made known their demands. They have the numbers to make their wishes effective. The Constitution and laws of the country place the whole matter within their hands. The great initial battles have been fought in the Courts and this constitutes their Gibraltar and impregnable vantage ground. Nothing is now needed but a proper use of the ballot.

If the friends of reform will make one united and fearless effort the victory will be won. Fidelity to truth, to home, to family and to the brotherhood of purpose is all that is required. Capital possesses one thing which labor does not—ready cash. They will not hesitate to make the best possible use of it. But labor possesses that which capital does not—numbers. They should be made effective. Will they longer refuse to make use of the peaceful weapon which their fathers placed in their hands? If we will not with courage and conscience choose the methods of peace, the sword is inevitable. Persistent oppression on the one hand and neglect to make proper use of the ballot on the other, in the very nature of things, call for the application of force as the only solution. Avenging armies always follow close upon the heels of legalized injustice. If we would escape the sword we must at once conquer through the power of truth and through knowledge incarnated and set in motion.

Let us all remember that the various organizations, now so powerful, cannot always be maintained. They will decay with time and fall to pieces from lack of purpose or the discouragements of defeat. Our enemies well understand this and are urging procrastination and pleading for time. As well might the general of an army send a bearer of dispatches, under a flag of truce, to ask the commander of the opposing forces when he would like to have the engagement brought on. If the general consulted were weak in numbers he would decide to postpone the battle until such time as the forces of his adversary could be wasted by death, disease and desertion.

### STRIKE NOW!

We have challenged the adversary to battle and our bugles have sounded the march. If we now seek to evade or shrink from the conflict it will amount to a confession of cowardice and a renunciation of the faith. Let us make the year 1892 memorable for all time to come as the period when the great battle for industrial emancipation was fought and won in the United States. It is glorious to live in this age, and to be permitted to take part in this heroic combat is the greatest honor that can be conferred upon mortals. It is an opportunity for every man, however humble, to strike a blow that will permanently benefit his race and make the world better for his having lived. Throughout all history we have had ample evidence that the new world is the theater upon which the great struggle for the rights of man is to be made, and the righteous movement now in progress should again forcibly remind us of our enviable mission, under Providence, among the nations of the earth.

# III
# ALLIANCE AND
# POPULIST PLATFORMS

---

## THE ST. LOUIS DEMANDS,
## DECEMBER 1889

*The Northern and Southern Alliances met simultaneously at St. Louis in December 1889 to explore the possibility of uniting the two orders. The negotiations broke down on several points, especially on the name of the order and the racial segregation and secret ritual practiced by the Southern Alliance. Both, however, adopted platforms that were remarkably similar and advanced most of the demands later endorsed by the People's party. Delegates from the Knights of Labor also endorsed the Southern Alliance's platform.*

## –9–

## SOUTHERN ALLIANCE AND
## KNIGHTS OF LABOR

Sᴛ. Lᴏᴜɪs, Mᴏ., *December 6, 1889*

Agreement made this day by and between the undersigned committee representing the National Farmers Alliance and Industrial Union on the one part, and the undersigned committee representing the Knights of Labor on the other part, Witnesseth: The undersigned committee representing the Knights of Labor having read the demands of the National Farmers Alliance and Industrial Union which are embodied in this agreement, hereby endorse the same on behalf of the Knights of Labor, and for the purpose of giving practical effect to the demands herein set forth, the legislative committees of both organizations will act in con-

sᴏᴜʀᴄᴇ: *The National Economist,* III (December 21, 1889), 214–215.

cert before Congress for the purpose of securing the enactment of laws in harmony with the demands mutually agreed.

And it is further agreed, in order to carry out these objects, we will support for office only such men as can be depended upon to enact these principles in statute law uninfluenced by party caucus.

The demands hereinbefore referred to are as follows:

1. That we demand the abolition of national banks and the substitution of legal tender treasury notes in lieu of national bank notes, issued in sufficient volume to do the business of the country on a cash system; regulating the amount needed on a per capita basis as the business interests of the country expands; and that all money issued by the Government shall be legal tender in payment of all debts, both public and private.

2. That we demand that Congress shall pass such laws as shall effectually prevent the dealing in futures of all agricultural and mechanical productions; preserving a stringent system of procedure in trials as shall secure the prompt conviction, and imposing such penalties as shall secure the most perfect compliance with the law.

3. That we demand the free and unlimited coinage of silver.

4. That we demand the passage of laws prohibiting the alien ownership of land, and that Congress take early steps to devise some plan to obtain all lands now owned by aliens and foreign syndicates; and that all lands now held by railroad and other corporations in excess of such as is actually used and needed by them, be reclaimed by the Government and held for actual settlers only.

5. Believing in the doctrine of "equal rights to all and special privileges to none," we demand that taxation, National or State, shall not be used to build up one interest or class at the expense of another.

We believe that the money of the country should be kept as much as possible in the hands of the people, and hence we demand that all revenues, National, State or county, shall be limited to the necessary expenses of the Government economically and honestly administered.

6. That Congress issue a sufficient amount of fractional paper currency to facilitate exchange through the medium of the United States mail.

7. We demand that the means of communication and transportation shall be owned by and operated in the interest of the people as is the United States postal system.

For the better protection of the interests of the two organizations, it is mutually agreed that such seals or emblems as the National Farmers Alliance and Industrial Union of America may adopt, will be recognized and protected in transit or otherwise by the Knights of Labor, and that all seals and labels of the Knights of Labor will in like manner be recognized by the members of the National Farmers Alliance and Industrial Union of America.

# –10–

# NORTHERN ALLIANCE

*Whereas*, the farmers of the United States are most in number of any order of citizens, and with the other productive classes have freely given of their blood to found and maintain the nation; therefore be it

*Resolved*, that the public land, the heritage of the people, be reserved for actual settlers only, and that measures be taken to prevent aliens from acquiring titles to lands in the United States and Territories, and that the law be rigidly enforced against all railroad corporations which have not complied with the terms of their contract, by which they have received large grants of land.

2. We demand the abolition of the national banking system and that the government issue full legal tender money direct to the people in sufficient volume for the requirements of business.

3. We favor the payment of the public debt as rapidly as possi-

SOURCE: *Political Science Quarterly*, VI (June 1891), pp. 293–294.

ble, and we earnestly protest against maintaining any bonds in existence as the basis for the issue of money.

4. We favor a graded income tax, and we also favor a tax on real-estate mortgages.

5. We demand economy and retrenchment as far as is consistent with the interests of the people in every department of the government, and we will look with special disfavor upon any increase of the official salaries of our representatives or government employees.

6. We favor such a revision and reduction of the tariff that the taxes may rest as lightly as possible upon productive labor and that its burdens may be upon the luxuries and in a manner that will prevent the accumulation of a United States Treasury surplus.

7. The stability of our government depends upon the moral, manual and intellectual training of the young, and we believe in so amending our public school system that the education of our children may inculcate the essential dignity necessary to be a practical help to them in after life.

8. Our railroads should be owned and managed by the government, and be run in the interest of the people upon an actual cash basis.

9. That the government take steps to secure the payment of the debt of the Union and Central Pacific railroads and their branches by foreclosure and sale, and any attempt to extend the time again for the payment of the same beyond its present limit will meet with our most emphatic condemnation.

10. We are in favor of the early completion of a ship canal connecting the great lakes with the Gulf of Mexico, and a deep water harbor on the southern coast in view of opening trade relations with the Central and South American states, and we are in favor of national aid to a judicious system of experiments to determine the practicability of irrigation.

11. We sympathize with the just demands of labor of every grade and recognize that many of the evils from which the farming community suffers oppress universal labor, and that therefore producers should unite in a demand for the reform of unjust

systems and the repeal of laws that bear unequally upon the people.

12. We favor the Australian system, or some similar system of voting, and ask the enactment of laws regulating the nomination of candidates for public office.

13. We are in favor of the diversification of our productive resources.

14. We [will] favor and assist to office such candidates only as are thoroughly identified with our principles and who will insist on such legislation as shall make them effective.

THE SUBTREASURY PLAN, DECEMBER 1889

*The report of the "Committee on the Monetary System" was approved by the St. Louis convention of the Southern Alliance in 1889. C. W. Macune, past president of the Southern Alliance and editor of The National Economist, its official journal, presented the report and was probably its author. The source of the plan, however, may have been an article, "The Hope of the South," by Harry Skinner, a North Carolina Allianceman and later a Populist congressman, in Frank Leslie's Illustrated Newspaper, LXIX (November 30, 1889), 290. Efforts to get a subtreasury bill through Congress met with repeated failure, but the plan does have some resemblance to programs established under the Warehouse Act of 1916 for federal licensing of private warehouses and the New Deal's crop loan program under the Commodity Credit Corporation of 1933.*

–11–

# REPORT OF THE COMMITTEE ON THE MONETARY SYSTEM

The financial policy of the general government seems to-day to be peculiarly adapted to further the interests of the speculative class at the expense and to the manifest detriment of the productive class, and while there are many forms of relief offered, there has up to the present time been no true remedy presented which has secured a support universal enough to render its adoption probable. Neither of the political parties offers a remedy adequate to our necessities, and the two parties that have been in power since the war have pursued practically the same financial policy. The

SOURCE: *The Sub-Treasury System as Proposed by the Farmers Alliance,* Library of National Economist Extras, I (Washington, June 1891), pp. 9–14.

situation is this: The most desirable and necessary reform is one that will adjust the financial system of the general government so that its provisions cannot be utilized by a class, which thereby becomes privileged, and is in consequence contrary to the genius of our government, and which is to-day the principal cause of the depressed condition of agriculture. Regardless of all this, the political parties utterly ignore these great evils and refuse to remove their cause, and the importunities of the privileged class have, no doubt, often led the executive and legislative branches of the government to believe that the masses were passive and reconciled to the existence of this system whereby a privileged class can, by means of the power of money to oppress, exact from labor all that it produces except a bare subsistence. Since, then, it is the most necessary of all reforms, and receives no attention from any of the prominent political parties, it is highly appropriate and important that our efforts be concentrated to secure the needed reform in this direction, provided all can agree upon such measures. Such action will in no wise connect this movement to any partisan effort, as it can be applied to the party to which each member belongs.

In seeking a true and practical remedy for the evils that now flow from the imperfections in our financial system let us first consider what is the greatest evil, and on what it depends. The greatest evil, the one that outstrips all others so far that it is instantly recognized as the chief, and known with certainty to be more oppressive to the productive interests of the country than any other influence, is that which delegates to a certain class the power to fix the price of all kinds of produce and of all commodities. This power is not delegated directly, but it is delegated indirectly by allowing such class to issue a large per cent of the money used as the circulating medium of the country, and having the balance of such circulating medium, which is issued by the government, a fixed quantity that is not augmented to correspond with the necessities of the times. In consequence of this the money issued by the privileged class, which they are at liberty to withdraw at pleasure, can be, and is, so manipulated as to control the volume of circulating medium in the country sufficiently to produce fluctuations in general prices at their pleasure. It may be likened unto a simple illustration in philosophy: The inflexible volume of the government issue is the fulcrum, the volume of the bank issue is the lever power, and price is the point at which power is applied, and it is either raised or lowered with great certainty to correspond with the volume of bank issue. Any mechanic will instantly recognize the fact that the quickest and surest way of destroying the power of the lever to raise or lower price is to remove the resistance offered by the fulcrum—the inflexible volume of government issue. The power to regulate the volume of money so as to control price is so manipulated as to develop and apply a potent force, for which we have in the English language no name; but it is the power of money to oppress, and is demonstrated as follows: In the last four months of the year the agricultural products of the whole year having been harvested, they are placed on the market to buy money. The amount of money necessary to supply this demand is equal to many times the actual amount in circulation. Nevertheless the class that controls the volume of the circulating medium desire to purchase these agricultural products for speculative purposes, so they reduce the volume of money by hoarding, in the face of the augmented demand, and thereby advance the exchangeable value of the then inadequate volume of money, which is equivalent to reducing the price of the agricultural products. True, agriculturists should hold their products and not sell them at these ruinously low prices. And no doubt they would if they could, but to prevent that, practically all debts, taxes and interests are made to mature at that time, and they being forced to have money at a certain season when they have the product of their labor to sell, the power of money to oppress by its scarcity is applied until it makes them turn loose their products so low that their labor expended does not average them fifty cents per day. This illustrates the power of money to oppress; the remedy, as before, lies in removing the power of the fulcrum—the inflexible government issue—and supplying a government issue, the volume of which shall be increased to correspond with the actual addition to the wealth of the nation presented by agriculture at harvest time, and diminished as such agricultural products are consumed. Such a flexibility of volume would guarantee a stability of price based on cost of production which would be compelled to reckon the pay for agricultural labor at the same rates as other employments. Such flexibility would rob money of its most potent power—the power to oppress—and place a premium on productive effort. But how may so desirable a result be secured? Let us see. By applying the same principles now in force in the monetary system of the United States with only slight modifications in the detail of their execution. The government and the people of this country realize that the amount of gold and silver, and the certificates based on these metals, do not comprise a volume of money sufficient to supply the wants of the country, and in order to increase the volume, the government allows individuals to associate themselves into a body corporate, and deposit with the government bonds which represent national indebtedness, which the government holds in trust and issues to such corporation paper money equal to 90 per cent of the value of the bonds, and charges said corporation interest at the rate of 1 per cent per annum for the use of said paper money. This allows the issue of paper money to increase the volume of the circulating medium on a perfectly safe basis, because the margin is a guarantee that the banks will redeem the bonds before they mature. But now we find that the circulation secured by this method is still not adequate; or to take a very conservative position, if we admit that it is adequate on the average, we know that the fact of its being entirely inadequate for half the year makes its inflexibility an engine of oppression, because a season in which it is inadequate must be followed by one of superabundance in order to bring about the average, and such a range in volume means great fluctuations in prices which cut against the producer, both in buying and selling, because he must sell at a season when produce is low, and buy when commodities are high. The system, now in vogue by the United States government of supplementing its circulating medium by a safe and redeemable paper money, should be pushed a little further and conducted in such a manner as to secure a certain augmentation of supply at the season of the year in which the agricultural additions to the wealth of the nation demand money, and a diminution in such supply of money as said agricultural products are consumed. It is not an average adequate amount that is needed, because under it the greatest abuses may prevail, but a certain adequate amount that adjusts itself to the wants of the country at all seasons. For this purpose let us demand that the United States government modify its present financial system:

1. So as to allow the free and unlimited coinage or the issue of the silver certificates against an unlimited deposit of bullion.

2. That the system of using certain banks as United States depositories be abolished, and in place of said system establish in every county in each of the States that offers for sale during the year five hundred thousand dollars worth of farm products, including wheat, corn, oats, barley, rye, rice, tobacco, cotton, wool and sugar, all together, a sub-treasury office, which shall have in connection with it such warehouses or elevators as are necessary for carefully storing and preserving such agricultural products as are offered it for storage; and it should be the duty of such sub-treasury department to receive such agricultural products as are offered for storage and make a careful examination of such products and class same as to quality and give a certificate of the deposit showing the amount and quality, and that United States legal tender paper money equal to 80 per cent of the local current value of the products deposited has been advanced on same on interest at the rate of 1 per cent per annum, on the condition that the owner or such other person as he may authorize will redeem the agricultural product within twelve months from the date of the certificate, or the trustees will sell same at public auction to the highest bidder for the purpose of satisfying the debt. Besides the 1 per cent interest the sub-treasurer should be allowed to charge a trifle for handling and storage, and a reasonable amount for insurance, but the premises necessary for conducting this business should be secured by the various counties donating to the general Government the land, the Government building the very best modern buildings, fire-proof and substantial. With this method in vogue the farmer, when his product was harvested,

would place it in storage where it would be perfectly safe, and he would secure four-fifths of its value to supply his pressing necessity for money at 1 per cent per annum. He would negotiate and sell his warehouse or elevator receipt whenever the current price suited him, receiving from the person to whom he sold only the difference between the price agreed upon and the amount already paid by the sub-treasurer. When, however, these storage certificates reached the hand of the miller or factory, or other consumer; he to get the product would have to return to the sub-treasurer the sum of money advanced, together with the interest on same and the storage and insurance charges on the product. This is no new or untried scheme; it is safe and conservative; it harmonizes and carries out the system already in vogue on a really safer plan, because the products of the country that must be consumed every year are really the very best security in the world, and with more justice to society at large. For a precedent, attention is called to the following: In December, 1848, the London Times announced the inevitable failure of the French republic and disintegration of French society in the near future, but so wise was the administration of the statesmen of that nation that two months later it was forced to eat its own words—saying in its columns February 16, 1849:

As a mere commercial speculation with the assets which the bank held in hand it might then have stopped payment and liquidated its affairs, with every probability that a very few weeks would enable it to clear off its liabilities. But this idea was not for a moment entertained by M. D'Argout, and he resolved to make every effort to keep alive what may be termed the circulation of the life-blood of the community. The task was overwhelming. Money was to be found to not only meet the demands on the bank, but the necessities, both public and private, of every rank in society. It was essential to enable the manufacturers to work, lest their workmen, driven to desperation, should fling themselves among the most violent enemies of public order. It was essential to provide money for the food of Paris, for the pay of troops, and for the daily support of the industrial establishments of the nation. A failure on any one point would have led to a fresh convulsion, but the panic had been followed by so great a scarcity of the metallic currency, that a few days later, out of a payment of 26,000-000 fallen due, only 47,000 francs could be recovered in silver.

In this extremity, when the bank alone retained any available sums of money, the government came to the rescue, and on the night of the 15th of March, the notes of the bank were, by a decree, made a legal tender, the issue of these notes being limited in all to 350,000,000, but the amount of the lowest of them reduced for the public convenience to 100 francs. One of the great difficulties mentioned in the report was to print these 100-franc notes fast enough for the public consumption. In ten days the amount issued in this form had reached 80,000,000 francs.

To enable the manufacturing interests to weather the storm at a moment when all the sales were interrupted, a decree of the national assembly had directed warehouses to be opened for the reception of all kinds of goods, and provided that the registered invoice of the goods so deposited should be made negotiable by indorsement. The Bank of France discounted these receipts. In Havre alone eighteen millions were thus advanced on colonial produce, and in Paris fourteen millions on merchandise; in all, sixty millions were made available for the purposes of trade. Thus the great institution had placed itself as it were in direct contact with every interest of the community, from the minister of the treasury down to the trader in a distant outport. Like a huge hydraulic machine, it employed its colossal powers to pump a fresh stream into the exhausted arteries of trade to sustain credit, and preserve the circulation from complete collapse.—From the Bank Charter Act, and the Rate of Interest, London, 1873.

This is proof positive, and a clear demonstration, in 1848, what this system could accomplish when a necessity existed for resorting to it. But since that time every conceivable change has tended toward rendering such a system easier managed and more necessary. The various means of rapid transportation and the facilities for the instantaneous transmission of intelligence, make it no disadvantage for the produce of a country to be stored at home until demanded for consumption, and the great savings that will follow the abolition of local shipments shows what great economy such a system is. In this day and time, no one will for a moment deny that all the conditions for purchasing and sale will attach to the Government certificates showing amount, quality, and running charges that attach to the product.

The arguments sustaining this system will present themselves to your minds as you ponder over the subject. The one fact stands out in bold relief, prominent, grand, and worthy the best efforts of our hearts and hands, and that is "this system will emancipate productive labor from the power of money to oppress" with speed and certainty. Could any object be more worthy? Surely not, and none could be devised that would more enlist your sympathies.

Our forefathers fought in the revolutionary war, making sacrifices that will forever perpetuate their names in history, to emancipate productive labor from the power of a monarch to oppress. Their battle cry was "liberty." Our monarch is a false, unjust, and statutory power given to money, which calls for a conflict on our part to emancipate productive labor from the power of money to oppress. Let the watch word again be, "Liberty!"

## THE OCALA PLATFORM, DECEMBER 1890

*At its annual meeting in Ocala, Florida, December 1890, the Southern Alliance faced demands that it endorse a third-party movement. Delegates from Kansas, which with North and South Dakota had switched to the Southern Alliance, were especially vigorous in advocating the idea, but Southern members, having won many successes within the Democratic party in the recent elections, were reluctant to follow. Agreement was reached, however, on a statement of demands and goals, which closely resembled the St. Louis platform of the previous year.*

–12–

# REPORT OF THE COMMITTEE ON DEMANDS

1 a. We demand the abolition of national banks.

b. We demand that the government shall establish sub-treasuries or depositories in the several States, which shall loan money direct to the people at a low rate of interest, not to exceed two per cent per annum, on non-perishable farm products, and also upon real estate, with proper limitations upon the quantity of land and amount of money.

c. We demand that the amount of the circulating medium be speedily increased to not less than $50 per capita.

2. That we demand that Congress shall pass such laws as shall effectually prevent the dealing in futures of all agricultural and mechanical productions; preserving a stringent system of procedure in trials as shall secure the prompt conviction, and imposing

SOURCE: *The National Economist,* IV (December 20, 1890), p. 216.

such penalties as shall secure the most perfect compliance with the law.

3. We condemn the silver bill recently passed by Congress, and demand in lieu thereof the free and unlimited coinage of silver.

4. We demand the passage of laws prohibiting alien ownership of land, and that Congress take prompt action to devise some plan to obtain all lands now owned by aliens and foreign syndicates; and that all lands now held by railroads and other corporations in excess of such as is actually used and needed by them be reclaimed by the government, and held for actual settlers only.

5. Believing in the doctrine of equal rights to all and special privileges to none, we demand that our national legislation shall be so framed in the future as not to build up one industry at the expense of another; and we further demand a removal of the existing heavy tariff tax from the necessities of life that the poor of our land must have; we further demand a just and equitable system of graduated tax on incomes; we believe that the money of the country should be kept as much as possible in the hands of the people, and hence we demand that all national and State revenues shall be limited to the necessary expenses of the government economically and honestly administered.

6. We demand the most rigid, honest, and just State and national governmental control and supervision of the means of public communication and transportation, and if this control and supervision does not remove the abuse now existing, we demand the government ownership of such means of communication and transportation.

7. We demand that Congress of the United States submit an amendment to the constitution providing for the election of United States Senators by direct vote of the people of each State.

**THE OMAHA PLATFORM, JULY 1892**

*This, the first national platform of the People's party, may be taken to represent the essential demands of the Populists. The preamble and much of the platform were written by Ignatius Donnelly, of Minnesota.*

# –13–
# NATIONAL PEOPLE'S PARTY PLATFORM

Assembled upon the 116th anniversary of the Declaration of Independence, the People's Party of America, in their first national convention, invoking upon their action the blessing of Almighty God, put forth in the name and on behalf of the people of this country, the following preamble and declaration of principles:

## PREAMBLE

The conditions which surround us best justify our co-operation; we meet in the midst of a nation brought to the verge of moral, political, and material ruin. Corruption dominates the ballot-box, the Legislatures, the Congress, and touches even the ermine of the bench. The people are demoralized; most of the States have been compelled to isolate the voters at the polling places to prevent universal intimidation and bribery. The newspapers are largely subsidized or muzzled, public opinion silenced, business prostrated, homes covered with mortgages, labor impoverished, and the land concentrating in the hands of capitalists. The urban

SOURCE: *The World Almanac, 1893* (New York, 1893), pp. 83–85.

workmen are denied the right to organize for self-protection, imported pauperized labor beats down their wages, a hireling standing army, unrecognized by our laws, is established to shoot them down, and they are rapidly degenerating into European conditions. The fruits of the toil of millions are boldly stolen to build up colossal fortunes for a few, unprecedented in the history of mankind; and the possessors of those, in turn, despite the Republic and endanger liberty. From the same prolific womb of governmental injustice we breed the two great classes—tramps and millionaires.

The national power to create money is appropriated to enrich bondholders; a vast public debt payable in legal tender currency has been funded into gold-bearing bonds, thereby adding millions to the burdens of the people.

Silver, which has been accepted as coin since the dawn of history, has been demonetized to add to the purchasing power of gold by decreasing the value of all forms of property as well as human labor, and the supply of currency is purposely abridged to fatten usurers, bankrupt enterprise, and enslave industry. A vast conspiracy against mankind has been organized on two continents, and it is rapidly taking possession of the world. If not met and overthrown at once it forebodes terrible social convulsions, the destruction of civilization, or the establishment of an absolute despotism.

We have witnessed for more than a quarter of a century the struggles of the two great political parties for power and plunder, while grievous wrongs have been inflicted upon the suffering people. We charge that the controlling influences dominating both these parties have permitted the existing dreadful conditions to develop without serious effort to prevent or restrain them. Neither do they now promise us any substantial reform. They have agreed together to ignore, in the coming campaign, every issue but one. They propose to drown the outcries of a plundered people with the uproar of a sham battle over the tariff, so that capitalists, corporations, national banks, rings, trusts, watered stock, the demonetization of silver and the oppressions of the usurers may all be lost sight of. They propose to sacrifice our homes, lives, and children on the altar of mammon; to destroy the multitude in order to secure corruption funds from the millionaires.

Assembled on the anniversary of the birthday of the nation, and filled with the spirit of the grand general and chief who established our independence, we seek to restore the government of the Republic to the hands of "the plain people," with which class it originated. We assert our purposes to be identical with the purposes of the National Constitution; to form a more perfect union and establish justice, insure domestic tranquillity, provide for the common defence, promote the general welfare, and secure the blessings of liberty for ourselves and our posterity.

We declare that this Republic can only endure as a free government while built upon the love of the whole people for each other and for the nation; that it cannot be pinned together by bayonets; that the civil war is over, and that every passion and resentment which grew out of it must die with it, and that we must be in fact, as we are in name, one united brotherhood of free men.

Our country finds itself confronted by conditions for which there is no precedent in the history of the world; our annual agricultural productions amount to billions of dollars in value, which must, within a few weeks or months, be exchanged for billions of dollars' worth of commodities consumed in their production; the existing currency supply is wholly inadequate to make this exchange; the results are falling prices, the formation of combines and rings, the impoverishment of the producing class. We pledge ourselves that if given power we will labor to correct these evils by wise and reasonable legislation, in accordance with the terms of our platform.

We believe that the power of government—in other words, of the people—should be expanded (as in the case of the postal service) as rapidly and as far as the good sense of an intelligent people and the teachings of experience shall justify, to the end that oppression, injustice, and poverty shall eventually cease in the land.

While our sympathies as a party of reform are naturally upon the side of every proposition which will tend to make men intelligent, virtuous, and temperate, we nevertheless regard these questions, important as they are, as secondary to the great issues now pressing for solution, and upon which not only our individual prosperity but the very existence of free institutions depend; and we ask all men to first help us to determine whether we are to have a republic to administer before we differ as to the conditions upon which it is to be administered, believing that the forces of reform this day organized will never cease to move forward until every wrong is remedied and equal rights and equal privileges securely established for all the men and women of this country.

## PLATFORM

We declare, therefore—

*First.*—That the union of the labor forces of the United States this day consummated shall be permanent and perpetual; may its spirit enter into all hearts for the salvation of the Republic and the uplifting of mankind.

*Second.*—Wealth belongs to him who creates it, and every dollar taken from industry without an equivalent is robbery. "If any will not work, neither shall he eat." The interests of rural and civic labor are the same; their enemies are identical.

*Third.*—We believe that the time has come when the railroad corporations will either own the people or the people must own the railroads, and should the government enter upon the work of owning and managing all railroads, we should favor an amendment to the Constitution by which all persons engaged in the government service shall be placed under a civil-service regulation of the most rigid character, so as to prevent the increase of the power of the national administration by the use of such additional government employés.

FINANCE.—We demand a national currency, safe, sound, and flexible, issued by the general government only, a full legal tender for all debts, public and private, and that without the use of banking corporations, a just, equitable, and efficient means of distribution direct to the people, at a tax not to exceed 2 per cent. per annum, to be provided as set forth in the sub-treasury plan of the Farmers' Alliance, or a better system; also by payments in discharge of its obligations for public improvements.

1. We demand free and unlimited coinage of silver and gold at the present legal ratio of 16 to 1.

2. We demand that the amount of circulating medium be speedily increased to not less than $50 per capita.

3. We demand a graduated income tax.

4. We believe that the money of the country should be kept as much as possible in the hands of the people, and hence we demand that all State and national revenues shall be limited to the necessary expenses of the government, economically and honestly administered.

5. We demand that postal savings banks be established by the government for the safe deposit of the earnings of the people and to facilitate exchange.

TRANSPORTATION.—Transportation being a means of exchange and a public necessity, the government should own and operate the railroads in the interest of the people. The telegraph, telephone, like the post-office system, being a necessity for the transmission of news, should be owned and operated by the government in the interest of the people.

LAND.—The land, including all the natural sources of wealth, is the heritage of the people, and should not be monopolized for speculative purposes, and alien ownership of land should be prohibited. All land now held by railroads and other corporations in excess of their actual needs, and all lands now owned by aliens should be reclaimed by the government and held for actual settlers only.

## EXPRESSION OF SENTIMENTS

Your Committee on Platform and Resolutions beg leave unanimously to report the following:

*Whereas,* Other questions have been presented for our consideration, we hereby submit the following, not as a part of the

Platform of the People's Party, but as resolutions expressive of the sentiment of this Convention:

1. *Resolved,* That we demand a free ballot and a fair count in all elections, and pledge ourselves to secure it to every legal voter without Federal intervention, through the adoption by the States of the unperverted Australian or secret ballot system.

2. *Resolved,* That the revenue derived from a graduated income tax should be applied to the reduction of the burden of taxation now levied upon the domestic industries of this country.

3. *Resolved,* That we pledge our support to fair and liberal pensions to ex-Union soldiers and sailors.

4. *Resolved,* That we condemn the fallacy of protecting American labor under the present system, which opens our ports to the pauper and criminal classes of the world and crowds out our wage-earners; and we denounce the present ineffective laws against contract labor, and demand the further restriction of undesirable emigration.

5. *Resolved,* That we cordially sympathize with the efforts of organized workingmen to shorten the hours of labor, and demand a rigid enforcement of the existing eight-hour law on Government work, and ask that a penalty clause be added to the said law.

6. *Resolved,* That we regard the maintenance of a large standing army of mercenaries, known as the Pinkerton system, as a menace to our liberties, and we demand its abolition; and we condemn the recent invasion of the Territory of Wyoming by the hired assassins of plutocracy, assisted by Federal officers.

7. *Resolved,* That we commend to the favorable consideration of the people and the reform press the legislative system known as the initiative and referendum.

8. *Resolved,* That we favor a constitutional provision limiting the office of President and Vice-President to one term, and providing for the election of Senators of the United States by a direct vote of the people.

9. *Resolved,* That we oppose any subsidy or national aid to any private corporation for any purpose.

10. *Resolved,* That this convention sympathizes with the

Knights of Labor and their righteous contest with the tyrannical combine of clothing manufacturers of Rochester, and declare it to be the duty of all who hate tyranny and oppression to refuse to purchase the goods made by the said manufacturers, or to patronize any merchants who sell such goods.

# IV
# THE POPULIST SPIRIT

---

## THE PRODUCER RHETORIC

*Dunning, associate editor of* The National Economist, *the weekly organ of the Southern Alliance, published a compendium of Alliance doctrine in 1891. This statement from his history of agricultural organizations is characteristic of the Populist dualism in viewing the social struggle as one of producers versus predators, the people versus the money power. The theory assumed a natural harmony of interests among the producing classes.*

## –14–
## INTRODUCTORY HISTORY
### by Nelson A. Dunning

Aristocratic ideas, backed up by intelligence and refinement, may serve a good purpose in toning down the untamed spirit, and broadening the nature of a native American; but when this station in society is reached through the medium of a bank account, human nature revolts, and the average person becomes disgusted. This spirit of avarice, or desire to make money, has become the bane of our social relations, and threatens the perpetuity of the government itself. The desire for wealth is increased as the power and privileges which it brings become more clearly understood. When the brains of a Webster or a Calhoun must wait unnoticed in the anteroom, while the plethoric pocket-book of some conscienceless speculator, monopolist, or trickster, brings to its owner the privileges of the parlor, and the softest seat at the feast,

SOURCE: Nelson A. Dunning, *The Farmers' Alliance History and Agricultural Digest* (Washington: The Alliance Publishing Co., 1891), ch. I, pp. 3–9.

intelligence and moral rectitude will always be at a discount, while fraud and corruption will bring a premium. In order that such conditions may exist, some portions of the people must suffer. This becomes a self-evident truth to all who will give the matter even the least consideration. The possession of wealth may be assumed, as a rule, to bring about the differences that are seen in society, and, because of this, becomes the essential object for which a large portion of our people are contending.

It is evident that all cannot be rich, and it is also true that none should be poor because of economic conditions. All economists agree that labor is the sole producer of wealth. If this proposition be true, it might be proper to ask: Why does not the producer of this wealth possess it, after production? What intervening cause steps in between the producer and this wealth, and prevents his owning and enjoying what his brain and brawn have created? No one seems to question the right or justice of each individual enjoying the fruits of his own labor. But the recognition of this right does not prevent the separation of production and possession, nor does it indicate a remedy for the evil. The idea of labor in production, at the present time, is associated with only a portion of our people. It represents, under the prevailing ideas of society, an undesirable condition, from which all, or nearly all, seek to be freed. The man or woman does not live who desires to labor every day in every year of their whole sojourn upon earth. Such a desire would be unnatural, a sin against the future, and a libel upon the past. Nine-tenths of the labor performed at the present time is done with the belief that this hard labor will bring about future ease and comfort. But when these efforts are honestly and earnestly continued for a series of years, and the anticipated reward does not come, and the plain fact is demonstrated that labor brings no reward, some give up in despair, while others determine to ascertain the cause, if possible.

It was to satisfy the American farmer that his calling had either become obsolete, or his environment unnatural, that agricultural organizations, for political or economic purposes, were brought into existence. Up to 1860 the economic privileges of the farmer were somewhat near a parity with other branches of productive industry. The systematic spoliation of the present was, to a large extent, practically unknown. Special laws and privileges, which operated directly against the national interests of agriculture, existed only in a mild degree. At that period immense fortunes were almost unknown, and aristocracy was confined to the better educated and more refined. Neither poverty nor crime existed in the same proportion as now, and the general trend of events was toward conservatism in all economic conditions. Moderate fortunes, moderate sized farms, and moderate business enterprises, were not only the rule of the times, but were maintained under the protecting care of society's consent. Of course there were exceptions, but not in the offensive and disturbing sense in which they now exist. All must admit that the parasitic age had not begun at this date, and that labor in production paid less tribute than at the present time. Emerson says: "The glory of the farmer is that, in the division of labors, it is his part to create. All trade rests at last on his primitive activity. He stands close to Nature; he obtains from the earth the bread and the meat. The food which was not he causes to be." It is because of the truth contained in this statement that the farmer complains. It is because he simply creates for others, with but a feeble voice, if any, in determining the measure of his remuneration, that he has at last been compelled to enter an earnest protest. Willing as he is to create, and anxious to serve all other classes with the fruits of his industry and skill, yet the farmer has learned, by sad experience, that his toil has gone unrequited, and his anxiety has been construed into servility. The American farmer, in his present condition, is a living example of the folly and disaster which inevitably follow, where one class of citizens permits another class to formulate and administer all economic legislation. In other words, he is the victim of misplaced confidence, and has at last undertaken to regain his lost advantages and rights. The late Civil War gave an impetus to all productive labor. All efforts in that direction were profitable for a time, and the business of agriculture was looked upon with much favor. Vast sums of money were expended in the purchase and improvement of farming lands, and the success of that branch of industry seemed assured. The war ended in the spring of 1865, and that year closed amid universal prosperity in the North, East, and West. The people were out of debt, all labor was employed, and all the conditions which wait upon a prosperous and industrious people were seen on every hand.

The people of the South had begun the task of repairing the ravages of war and rebuilding their shattered fortunes with a determination which admitted of no failure, and the whole country echoed with the busy hum of industry. During the year which followed, these conditions continued, but in the latter part of 1867 a change was observed. It had been brought about quietly. No one seemed to know how, but the effects were none the less positive. Agriculture was the first to feel this changed condition, and undertook to counteract it by a closer economy and increased production. The first compelled the manufacturer to curtail his production or lessen its value. Either course reduced the remuneration of the laborer, and compelled him to purchase less or buy cheaper. This reacted upon the farmer. The second overstocked the market, and reduced the price of the whole product, and enabled those who could to dictate their own terms. This condition has obtained among the farmers to the present time. In the vain endeavor to extricate themselves from their surroundings, having faith in the prospect of better times, the farmers borrowed money on note or mortgage to tide them over, only to find that the future brought no relief. This dark cloud of debt and disappointment hung lower and lower each succeeding year, until the storm of 1873 swept over the country, leaving in its course the wrecks of many thousand financial disasters.

In 1867 the first agricultural organization of promise appeared in the Grange, or Patrons of Husbandry. This organization sought to better the condition of the farmer by eliminating the so-called middleman,—the merchant or dealer. It assumed that the profit, which lodged somewhere between the producer and consumer, was the cause of nearly all the disaster that waited upon agricultural effort. This idea took hold of the people, and the result was an immense organization, with every promise of success. The experiment, aside from its educational results, was almost an entire failure.

Since this time the causes which have depressed agriculture have been discovered, throughout the length and breadth of the land, by those who were interested, those who sympathized, to be the politician and the demagogue; but the discovery produced little or no effect. It remained for the farmer himself, after several ineffectual attempts, to solve the problem, and in so doing challenge the respect and admiration of the thinking world. The solution of this question, and the demand for its enactment into law, have no parallel in all history. It is an uprising of the conservative element of the people, the brain and brawn of the nation. It is a protest against present conditions; a protest against the unequal distribution of the profits arising from labor in production; a protest against those economic methods which give to labor a bare living, and make capital the beneficiary of all life's pleasures and comforts. It is a protest against continual toil on the one hand, and continual ease and comfort on the other. It is a protest against forced economy, debt, and privation to the producer, and peace, plenty, happiness, and prosperity to the non-producer.

The farmers have learned the secret, that organization, unity of action, and continuity of purpose, on their part, will in the end unite all sections, enrich all communities, and make every citizen equal before just laws. Intelligence to organize, fellow-feeling enough to unite, and manhood sufficient to stand firm, are the necessary requirements to bring this about. Organization is now the order of the day. It is the motive power that rules and guides the world. Without it the best of causes will not succeed, while with it the worse cause may prosper for a time. In the great struggle of life, as society is now constituted, organized evil must be met with organized good; organized greed with organized equity. In the combination of kindred forces lie the astonishing results of modern undertakings.

Individual enterprises are at a discount in the commercial world for many reasons. The individual may die and the whole business pass necessarily into the hands of those less competent to direct; or the individual may make a false move and thereby jeopardize the entire venture through an error in his single judgment; or, again, he may fall under the influence of bad habits and wreck the business through neglect or fast living. All these con-

tingencies are impossible with an organization properly constituted. Members of the organization may die, but the organization
continues. The aggregate business intelligence of the whole
membership is used, and not the single ideas of one. Organizations go on, live on; gathering experience which is stored up;
gathering special information which is safely put away; increasing in wealth of which the outside world has no knowledge; using
their power when least expected, and for objects that require
years of patient waiting and calculation to perfect and mature.
These considerations not only recommend a system of organization to all progressive minds, but make them absolutely necessary
for success in modern business. One thing is certain,—organization as a factor of our modern civilization has come to stay. It
cannot be eliminated, but may be, to a greater or less extent,
confined in its operation within legitimate bounds. Its benefits
will be sought under all conditions and by all classes of people,
and those who ignore its power or underestimate its strength are
sure to have cause for regret in the end.

The difficulty of organization among farmers is not wholly confined to a want of information, but shows itself in neighborhood
factions of numerous kinds, individual or local jealousies, family
or political differences, and a multitude of other insignificant but
annoying obstructions that have to be avoided, smoothed over, or
settled. These are never met with among men who organize from
a business standpoint. The farmers, as a class, have been betrayed
in almost everything, with a regularity truly astonishing. They
have struggled against all odds, and have submitted to the result
with a fortitude absolutely wonderful, but the time has come
when something must be done. Some united action is demanded
in defence of their own rights, and the maintenance of agriculture. This fact is too plain and too imperative to be longer ignored. It is a question now between liberty and serfdom, and
must be decided without delay. Some will ask: What shall we
organize for? For the same reasons that our enemies do; for
individual benefits through combined effort. Organize to watch
them, to consider their motives, and, if possible, checkmate their
designs, when aimed at you or your business. This is a selfish

world, and they who fail to realize this fact are quite sure to find it out when too late. Organize for better laws; for through legislation comes prosperity or adversity.

During the past quarter of a century, the farmers of this country have labored, and others have made the laws. What has been the result? The non-producer has thrived while the producer has grown poor. Not only have the non-producers organized against the farmers, but almost all other producers. There is hardly a manufactured product, or ever a raw material, that is not subject to the guidance of an organization or combination of the whole, excepting the products of the farm. This means the spoliation of all who cannot meet this force with similar power. That being true, the farmer becomes the easy prey of all, and receives the treatment his own neglect brings upon him. All non-producers are the avowed enemies of producers, and should be so considered in all propositions of economics. When they organize, it is for the purpose of increasing their strength, which in turn makes them a correspondingly more dangerous enemy, and increases the necessity of stronger defence. In the vast amount of national legislation of the past twenty-five years, there is not one single act which was passed in the interest of the farmer. Search through the whole mass, and not one will be found that was introduced, passed, and put upon the statute books, for the sole benefit of agriculture. Until this is changed, and labor in production is made to bring a reward, industry is useless and economy is folly.

.    .    .    .    .

**A POPULIST UTOPIA**

*The eccentric genius of Populism, Ignatius Donnelly, of Nininger, Minnesota, followed a varied career as lawyer, farmer, editor, lecturer, author, reformer, and politician. He was successively a Republican, Liberal Republican, Granger, Greenbacker, Allianceman, and Populist. His futuristic novel,* Caesar's Column, *set in 1988, projected into the future the consequences of what Donnelly saw as the destructive trends of his times. His protagonist, who lives in Africa, visits New York and finds the city a center of technological miracles and plutocratic luxury based upon mass misery. A "Brotherhood of Destruction" finally overthrows the system in a cataclysmic uprising that destroys civilization in America and Europe. At the end a few people escape to Uganda to establish a kind of Christian socialist utopia. The apocalyptic vision of Donnelly's novel is also reflected in the preamble to the Populist platform of 1892, which he wrote. In the following selection the African visitor, Gabriel Weltstein, engages in a dialogue with Maximilian Petion, an agent of the Brotherhood of Destruction.*

## –15–

# GABRIEL'S UTOPIA

## by *Ignatius Donnelly*

"But what would you do, my good Gabriel," said Maximilian, smiling, "if the reformation of the world were placed in your hands? Every man has an Utopia in his head. Give me some idea of yours."

"First," I said, "I should do away with all interest on money. Interest on money is the root and ground of the world's troubles. It puts one man in a position of safety, while another is in a

SOURCE: Ignatius Donnelly, *Caesar's Column: A Story of the Twentieth Century* (Chicago: F.J. Schulte and Co., 1891), Ch. XII, pp. 116–133.

condition of insecurity, and thereby it at once creates a radical distinction in human society."

"How do you make that out?" he asked.

"The lender takes a mortgage on the borrower's land or house, or goods, for, we will say, one-half or one-third their value; the borrower then assumes all the chances of life in his efforts to repay the loan. If he is a farmer, he has to run the risk of the fickle elements. Rains may drown, droughts may burn up his crops. If a merchant, he encounters all the hazards of trade; the bankruptcy of other tradesmen; the hostility of the elements sweeping away agriculture, and so affecting commerce; the tempests that smite his ships, etc. If a mechanic, he is still more dependent upon the success of all above him, and the mutations of commerical prosperity. He may lose employment; he may sicken; he may die. But behind all these risks stands the money-lender, in perfect security. The failure of his customer only en-riches him; for he takes for his loan property worth twice or thrice the sum he has advanced upon it. Given a million of men and a hundred years of time, and the slightest advantage pos-sessed by any one class among the million must result, in the long run, in the most startling discrepancies of condition. A little evil grows like a ferment—it never ceases to operate; it is always at work. Suppose I bring before you a handsome, rosy-cheeked young man, full of life and hope and health. I touch his lip with a single *bacillus* of *phthisis pulmonalis*—consumption. It is invisible to the eye; it is too small to be weighed. Judged by all the tests of the senses, it is too insignificant to be thought of; but it has the capacity to multiply itself indefinitely. The youth goes off singing. Months, perhaps years, pass before the deadly disorder begins to manifest itself; but in time the step loses its elasticity; the eyes become dull; the roses fade from the cheeks; the strength departs, and eventually the joyous youth is but a shell—a cadaverous, shrunken form, inclosing a shocking mass of putridity; and death ends the dreadful scene. Give one set of men in a community a financial advantage over the rest, however slight—it may be al-most invisible—and at the end of centuries that class so favored will own everything and wreck the country. A penny, they say, put out at interest the day Columbus sailed from Spain, and compounded ever since, would amount now to more than all the assessed value of all the property, real, personal and mixed, on the two continents of North and South America."

"But," said Maximilian, "how would the men get along who wanted to borrow?"

"The necessity to borrow is one of the results of borrowing. The disease produces the symptoms. The men who are enriched by borrowing are infinitely less in number than those who are ruined by it; and every disaster to the middle class swells the number and decreases the opportunities of the helplessly poor. Money in itself is valueless. It becomes valuable only by use—by exchange for things needful for life or comfort. If money could not be loaned, it would have to be put out by the owner of it in business enterprises, which would employ labor; and as the enterprise would not then have to support a double burden—to wit, the man engaged in it and the usurer who sits securely upon his back—but would have to maintain only the former usurer—that is, the present employer—its success would be more certain; the general prosperity of the community would be increased thereby, and there would be therefore more enterprises, more demand for labor, and consequently higher wages. Usury kills off the enterprising members of a community by bankrupting them, and leaves only the very rich and the very poor; for every dollar the employers of labor pay to the lenders of money has to come eventually out of the pockets of the laborers. Usury is therefore the cause of the first aristocracy, and out of this grow all the other aristocracies. Inquire where the money came from that now oppresses mankind, in the shape of great corporations, combinations, etc., and in nine cases out of ten you will trace it back to the fountain of interest on money loaned. The coral island is built out of the bodies of dead coral insects; large fortunes are usually the accumulations of wreckage, and every dollar represents disaster."

"Well," said Maximilian, "having abolished usury, in your Utopia, what would you do next?"

"I would set to work to make a list of all the laws, or parts of laws, or customs, or conditions which, either by commission or omission, gave any man an advantage over any other man; or which tended to concentrate the wealth of the community in the hands of a few. And having found out just what these wrongs or advantages were, I would abolish them *instanter*."

"Well, let us suppose," said Maximilian, "that you were not immediately murdered by the men whose privileges you had destroyed—even as the Gracchi were of old—what would you do next? Men differ in every detail. Some have more industry, or more strength, or more cunning, or more foresight, or more acquisitiveness than others. How are you to prevent these men from becoming richer than the rest?"

"I should not try to," I said. "These differences in men are fundamental, and not to be abolished by legislation; neither are the instincts you speak of in themselves injurious. Civilization, in fact, rests upon them. It is only in their excess that they become destructive. It is right and wise and proper for men to accumulate sufficient wealth to maintain their age in peace, dignity and plenty, and to be able to start their children into the arena of life sufficiently equipped. A thousand men in a community worth $10,000 or $50,000, or even $100,000 each, may be a benefit, perhaps a blessing; but one man worth fifty or one hundred millions, or, as we have them now-a-days, one thousand millions, is a threat against the safety and happiness of every man in the world. I should establish a maximum beyond which no man could own property. I should not stop his accumulations when he had reached that point, for with many men accumulation is an instinct; but I should require him to invest the surplus, under the direction of a governmental board of management, in great works for the benefit of the laboring classes. He should establish schools, colleges, orphan asylums, hospitals, model residences, gardens, parks, libraries, baths, places of amusement, music-halls, sea-side excursions in hot weather, fuel societies in cold weather, etc., etc. I should permit him to secure immortality by affixing his name to his benevolent works; and I should honor him still further by placing his statue in a great national gallery set apart to perpetuate forever the memory of the benefactors of the race."

"But," said Maximilian, with a smile, "it would not take long for your rich men, with their surplus wealth, to establish all those works you speak of. What would you do with the accumulations of the rest?"

"Well," said I, "we should find plenty to do. We would put their money, for instance, into a great fund and build national railroads, that would bring the productions of the farmers to the workmen, and those of the workmen to the farmers, at the least cost of transportation, and free from the exactions of speculators and middlemen. Thus both farmers and workmen would live better, at less expense and with less toil."

"All very pretty," said he; "but your middlemen would starve."

"Not at all," I replied; "the cunning never starve. There would be such a splendid era of universal prosperity that they would simply turn their skill and shrewdness into some new channels, in which, however, they would have to give something of benefit, as an equivalent for the benefits they received. Now they take the cream, and butter, and beef, while some one else has to raise, feed and milk the cow."

"But," said he, "all this would not help our farmers in their present condition—they are blotted off the land."

"True," I replied; "but just as I limited a man's possible wealth, so should I limit the amount of land he could own. I would fix a maximum of, say, 100 or 500 acres, or whatever amount might be deemed just and reasonable. I should abolish all corporations, or turn them back into individual partnerships. Abraham Lincoln, in the great civil war of the last century, gave the Southern insurgents so many days in which to lay down their arms or lose their slaves. In the same way I should grant one or two years' time, in which the great owners of land should sell their estates, in small tracts, to actual occupants, to be paid for in installments, on long time, without interest. And if they did not do so, then, at the end of the period prescribed, I should confiscate the lands and sell them, as the government in the old time sold the public lands, for so much per acre, to actual settlers, and turn the proceeds over to the former owners."

"But, as you had abolished interest on money, there could be no mortgages, and the poor men would starve to death before they could raise a crop."

"Then," I replied, "I should invoke the power of the nation, as was done in that great civil war of 1861, and issue paper money, receivable for all taxes, and secured by the guarantee of the faith and power of five hundred million people; and make advances to carry these ruined peasants beyond the first years of distress— that money to be a loan to them, without interest, and to be re- paid as a tax on their land. Government is only a machine to insure justice and help the people, and we have not yet devel- oped half its powers. And we are under no more necessity to limit ourselves to the governmental precedents of our ancestors than we are to confine ourselves to the narrow boundaries of their knowledge, or their inventive skill, or their theo- logical beliefs. The trouble is that so many seem to regard government as a divine something which has fallen down upon us out of heaven, and therefore not to be improved upon or even criticised; while the truth is, it is simply a human device to secure human happiness, and in itself has no more sacredness than a wheelbarrow or a cooking-pot. The end of everything earthly is the good of man; and there is nothing sacred on earth but man, because he alone shares the Divine conscience."

"But," said he, "would not your paper money have to be re- deemed in gold or silver?"

"Not necessarily," I replied. "The adoration of gold and silver is a superstition of which the bankers are the high priests and man- kind the victims. Those metals are of themselves of little value. What should make them so?"

"Are they not the rarest and most valuable productions of the world?" said Maximilian.

"By no means," I replied; "there are many metals that exceed them in rarity and value. While a kilogram of gold is worth about $730 and one of silver about $43.50, the same weight of iridium (the heaviest body known) costs $2,400; one of palladium, $3,075; one of calcium nearly $10,000; one of stibidium, $20,000; while vanadium, the true 'king of metals,' is worth $25,000 per kilogram, as against $730 for gold or $43.50 for silver."

"Why, then, are they used as money?" he asked.

"Who can tell? The practice dates back to prehistoric ages. Man always accepts as right anything that is in existence when he is born."

"But are they not more beautiful than other metals? And are they not used as money because acids will not corrode them?"

"No," I replied; "some of the other metals exceed them in beauty. The diamond far surpasses them in both beauty and value, and glass resists the action of acids better than either of them."

"What do you propose?" he asked.

"Gold and silver," I said, "are the bases of the world's currency. If they are abundant, all forms of paper money are abundant. If they are scarce, the paper money must shrink in proportion to the shrinkage of its foundation; if not, there come panics and convulsions, in the effort to make one dollar of gold pay three, six or ten of paper. For one hundred and fifty years *the production of gold and silver has been steadily shrinking, while the population and business of the world have been rapidly increasing*.

"Take a child a few years old; let a blacksmith weld around his waist an iron band. At first it causes him little inconvenience. He plays. As he grows older it becomes tighter; it causes him pain; he scarcely knows what ails him. He still grows. All his internal organs are cramped and displaced. He grows still larger; he has the head, shoulders and limbs of a man and the waist of a child. He is a monstrosity. He dies. This is a picture of the world of to-day, bound in the silly superstition of some prehistoric nation. But this is not all. Every decrease in the quantity, actual or relative, of gold and silver increases the purchasing power of the dollars made out of them; and the dollar becomes the equivalent for a larger amount of the labor of man and his productions. This makes the rich man richer and the poor man poorer. The iron band is displacing the organs of life. As the dollar rises in value, man sinks. Hence the decrease in wages; the increase in the power of wealth; the luxury of the few; the misery of the many."

"How would you help it?" he asked.

"I would call the civilized nations together in council, and devise an international paper money, to be issued by the different nations, but to be receivable as legal tender for all debts in all countries. It should hold a fixed ratio to population, never to be exceeded; and it should be secured on all the property of the civilized world, and acceptable in payment of all taxes, national, state and municipal, everywhere. I should declare gold and silver legal tenders only for debts of five dollars or less. An international greenback that was good in New York, London, Berlin, Melbourne, Paris and Amsterdam, would be good anywhere. The world, released from its iron band, would leap forward to marvelous prosperity; there would be no financial panics, for there could be no contraction; there would be no more torpid 'middle ages,' dead for lack of currency, for the money of a nation would expand, *pari passu*, side by side with the growth of its population. There would be no limit to the development of mankind, save the capacities of the planet; and even these, through the skill of man, could be increased a thousand-fold beyond what our ancestors dreamed of. The very seas and lakes, judiciously farmed, would support more people than the earth now maintains. A million fish ova now go to waste where one grows to maturity.

"The time may come when the slow processes of agriculture will be largely discarded, and the food of man be created out of the chemical elements of which it is composed, transfused by electricity and magnetism. We have already done something in that direction in the way of synthetic chemistry. Our mountain ranges may, in after ages, be leveled down and turned into bread for the support of the most enlightened, cultured, and, in its highest sense, religious people that ever dwelt on the globe. All this is possible if civilization is preserved from the destructive power of the ignorant and brutal Plutocracy, who now threaten the safety of mankind. They are like the slave-owners of 1860; they blindly and imperiously insist on their own destruction; they strike at the very hands that would save them."

"But," said Maximilian, "is it not right and necessary that the intellect of the world should rule the world?"

"Certainly," I replied; "but what is intellect? It is breadth of comprehension; and this implies gentleness and love. The man whose scope of thought takes in the created world, and apprehends man's place in nature, cannot be cruel to his fellows. Intellect, if it is selfish, is wisely selfish. It perceives clearly that such a shocking abomination as our present condition cannot endure. It knows that a few men cannot safely batten down the hatches over the starving crew and passengers, and then riot in drunken debauchery on the deck. When the imprisoned wretches in the hold become desperate enough—and it is simply a question of time—they will fire the ship or scuttle it, and the fools and their victims will all perish together. True intellect is broad, foresighted, wide-ranging, merciful, just. Some one said of old that 'the gods showed what they thought of riches by the kind of people they gave them to.' It is not the poets, the philosophers, the philanthropists, the historians, the sages, the scholars, the really intellectual of any generation who own the great fortunes. No; but there is a subsection of the brain called *cunning;* it has nothing to do with elevation of mind, or purity of soul, or knowledge, or breadth of view; it is the lowest, basest part of the intellect. It is the trait of foxes, monkeys, crows, rats and other vermin. It delights in holes and subterranean shelters; it will not disdain filth; it is capable of lying, stealing, trickery, knavery. Let me give you an example:

"It is recorded that when the great war broke out in this country against slavery, in 1861, there was a rich merchant in this city, named A. T. Stewart. Hundreds of thousands of men saw in the war only the great questions of the Union and the abolition of human bondage—the freeing of four millions of human beings, and the preservation of the honor of the flag; and they rushed forward eager for the fray. They were ready to die that the Nation and Liberty might live. But while their souls were thus inflamed with great and splendid emotions, and they forgot home, family, wealth, life, everything, Stewart, the rich merchant, saw simply the fact that the war would cut off communication between the North and the cotton-producing States, and that this would result in a rise in the price of cotton goods; and so, amid the wild agitations of patriotism, the beating of drums and the blaring of trumpets, he sent out his agents and bought up all the cotton goods he could lay his hands on. He made a million dollars, it is said, by this little piece of cunning. But if all men had thought and acted as Stewart did, we should have had no Union, no country, and there would be left to-day neither honor nor manhood in all the world. The nation was saved by those poor fellows who did not consider the price of cotton goods in the hour of America's crucial agony. Their dust now billows the earth of a hundred battle-fields; but their memory will be kept sweet in the hearts of men forever! On the other hand, the fortune of the great merchant, as it did no good during his life, so, after his death, it descended upon an alien to his blood; while even his wretched carcass was denied, by the irony of fate, rest under his splendid mausoleum, and may have found its final sepulchre in the stomachs of dogs!

"This little incident illustrates the whole matter. It is not *Intellect* that rules the world of wealth, it is *Cunning. Muscle* once dominated mankind—the muscle of the baron's right arm; and *Intellect* had to fly to the priesthood, the monastery, the friar's gown, for safety. Now *Muscle* is the world's slave, and *Cunning* is the baron—the world's master.

"Let me give you another illustration: Ten thousand men are working at a trade. One of them conceives the scheme of an invention, whereby their productive power is increased tenfold. Each of them, we will say, had been producing, by his toil, property worth four dollars and a half per day, and his wages were, we will say, one dollar and a half per day. Now, he is able with the new invention to produce property worth forty-five dollars per day. Are his wages increased in due proportion, to fifteen dollars per day, or even to five dollars per day? Not at all. *Cunning* has stepped in and examined the poor workman's invention; it has bought it from him for a pittance; it secures a patent—a monopoly under the shelter of unwise laws. The workmen still get their $1.50 per day, and *Cunning* pockets the remainder. But this is not all: If one man can now do the work of ten, then there are nine men thrown out of employment. But the nine men must live; they want the one man's place; they are hungry; they will work for less; and down go wages, until they reach the lowest limit at which the workmen can possibly live. Society has produced one millionaire and thousands of paupers. The millionaire cannot eat any more or wear any more than one prosperous yeoman and therefore is of no more value to trade and commerce; but the thousands of paupers have to be supported by the taxpayers, and they have no money to spend, and they cannot buy the goods of the merchants, or the manufacturers, and all business languishes. In short, the most utterly useless, destructive and damnable crop a country can grow is—millionaires. If a community were to send to India and import a lot of man-eating tigers, and turn them loose on the streets, to prey on men, women and children, they would not inflict a tithe of the misery that is caused by a like number of millionaires. And there would be this further disadvantage: the inhabitants of the city could turn out and kill the tigers, but the human destroyers are protected by the benevolent laws of the very people they are immolating on the altars of wretchedness and vice."

"But what is your remedy?" asked Max.

"Government," I replied; "government—national, state and municipal—is the key to the future of the human race.

"There was a time when the town simply represented cowering peasants, clustered under the shadow of the baron's castle for protection. It advanced slowly and reluctantly along the road of civic development, scourged forward by the whip of necessity. We have but to expand the powers of government to solve the enigma of the world. Man separated is man savage; man gregarious is man civilized. A higher development in society requires that this instrumentality of co-operation shall be heightened in its powers. There was a time when every man provided, at great cost, for the carriage of his own letters. Now the government, for an infinitely small charge, takes the business off his hands. There was a time when each house had to provide itself with water. Now the municipality furnishes water to all. The same is true of light. At one time each family had to educate its own children; now the state educates them. Once every man went armed to protect himself. Now the city protects him by its armed police. These hints must be followed out. The city of the future must furnish doctors for all; lawyers for all; entertainments for all; business guidance for all. It will see to it that no man is plundered, and no man starved, who is willing to work."

"But," said Max, "if you do away with interest on money and thus scatter coagulated capital into innumerable small enterprises, how are you going to get along without the keen-brained masters of business, who labor gigantically for gigantic personal profits; but who, by their toil and their capital, bring the great body of producers into relation with the great body of consumers? Are these men not necessary to society? Do they not create occasion and opportunity for labor? Are not their active and powerful brains at the back of all progress? There may be a thousand men idling, and poorly fed and clothed, in a neighborhood: along comes one of these shrewd adventurers; he sees an opportunity to utilize the bark of the trees and the ox-hides of the farmers' cattle, and he starts a tannery. He may accumulate more money than the thousand men he sets to work; but has he not done more? Is not his intellect immeasurably more valuable than all those unthinking muscles?"

"There is much force in your argument," I replied, "and I do not think that society should discourage such adventurers. But the muscles of the many are as necessary to the man you describe as his intellect is to the muscles; and as they are all men together there should be some equity in the distribution of the profits. And remember, we have gotten into a way of thinking as if numbers and wealth were everything. It is better for a nation to contain thirty million people, prosperous, happy and patriotic, than one hundred millions, ignorant, wretched and longing for an opportunity to overthrow all government. The over-population of the globe will come soon enough. We have no interest in hurrying it. The silly ancestors of the Americans called it 'national development' when they imported millions of foreigners to take up the public lands, and left nothing for their own children.

"And here is another point: Men work at first for a competence —for enough to lift them above the reach of want in those days which they know to be rapidly approaching, when they can no longer toil. But, having reached that point, they go on laboring for vanity—one of the shallowest of the human passions. The man who is worth $100,000 says to himself, 'There is Jones; he is worth $500,000; he lives with a display and extravagance I cannot equal. I must increase my fortune to half a million.' Jones, on the other hand, is measuring himself against Brown, who has a million. He knows that men cringe lower to Brown than they do to him. He must have a million—half a million is nothing. And Brown feels that he is overshadowed by Smith, with his ten millions; and so the childish emulation continues. Men are valued, not for themselves, but for their bank account. In the meantime these vast concentrations of capital are made at the expense of mankind. If, in a community of a thousand persons, there are one hundred millions of wealth, and it is equally divided between them, all are comfortable and happy. If, now, ten men, by cunning devices, grasp three-fourths of all this wealth, and put it in their pockets, there is but one-fourth left to divide among the nine hundred and ninety, and they are therefore poor and miserable. Within certain limits accumulation in one place represents denudation elsewhere.

"And thus, under the stimulus of shallow vanity," I continued, "a rivalry of barouches and bonnets—an emulation of waste and extravagance—all the powers of the minds of men are turned—not to lift up the world, but to degrade it. A crowd of little creatures—men and women—are displayed upon a high platform, in the face of mankind, parading and strutting about, with their noses in the air, as tickled as a monkey with a string of beads, and covered with a glory which is not their own, but which they have been able to purchase; crying aloud: 'Behold what I *have got!*' not, 'Behold what I *am!*'

"And then the inexpressible servility of those below them! The fools would not recognize Socrates if they fell over him in the street; but they can perceive Crœsus a mile off; they can smell him a block away; and they will dislocate their vertebræ abasing themselves before him. It reminds one of the time of Louis XIV. in France, when millions of people were in the extremest misery even unto starvation; while great grandees thought it the acme of earthly bliss and honor to help put the king to bed, or take off his dirty socks. And if a common man, by any chance, caught a glimpse of royalty changing its shirt, he felt as if he had looked into heaven and beheld Divinity creating worlds. Oh, it is enough to make a man loathe his species."

"Come, come," said Maximilian, "you grow bitter. Let us go to dinner before you abolish all the evils of the world, or I shall be disposed to quit New York and buy a corner lot in Utopia."

## POPULISM AND RACE

*Watson, agrarian rebel of Georgia, served one term in the House of Representatives, 1891–1893, and ran as Populist candidate for vice-president in 1896. In this piece he justifies the Populist effort to effect a political alliance of white and Negro farmers. In his later career Watson reversed his position, led the movement for the disfranchisement of Negroes in Georgia, and through his periodical,* Tom Watson's Magazine, *and its successors conducted scurrilous campaigns of hate and slander against Catholics and Jews.*

–16–

# THE NEGRO QUESTION
# IN THE SOUTH
## by *Thomas E. Watson*

The Negro Question in the South has been for nearly thirty years a source of danger, discord, and bloodshed. It is an ever-present irritant and menace.

Several millions of slaves were told that they were the prime cause of the civil war; that their emancipation was the result of the triumph of the North over the South; that the ballot was placed in their hands as a weapon of defence against their former masters; that the war-won political equality of the black man with the white, must be asserted promptly and aggressively, under the leadership of adventurers who had swooped down upon the conquered section in the wake of the Union armies.

No one, who wishes to be fair, can fail to see that, in such a

SOURCE: Thomas E. Watson, "The Negro Question in the South," *The Arena*, VI (October 1892), 540–550.

condition of things, strife between the freedman and his former owner was inevitable. In the clashing of interests and of feelings, bitterness was born. The black man was kept in a continual fever of suspicion that we meant to put him back into slavery. In the assertion of his recently acquired privileges, he was led to believe that the best proof of his being on the right side of any issue was that his old master was on the other. When this was the case, he felt easy in his mind. But if, by any chance, he found that he was voting the same ticket with his former owner, he at once became reflective and suspicious. In the irritable temper of the times, a whispered warning from a Northern "carpet-bagger," having no justification in rhyme or reason, outweighed with him a carload of sound argument and earnest expostulation from the man whom he had known all his life; who had hunted with him through every swamp and wooded upland for miles around; who had wrestled and run foot-races with him in the "Negro quarters" on many a Saturday afternoon; who had fished with him at every "hole" in the creek; and who had played a thousand games of "marble" with him under the cool shade of the giant oaks which, in those days, sheltered a home they had both loved.

In brief, the end of the war brought changed relations and changed feelings. Heated antagonisms produced mutual distrust and dislike—ready, at any accident of unusual provocation on either side, to break out into passionate and bloody conflict.

Quick to take advantage of this deplorable situation, the politicians have based the fortunes of the old parties upon it. Northern leaders have felt that at the cry of "Southern outrage" they could not only "fire the Northern heart," but also win a unanimous vote from the colored people. Southern politicians have felt that at the cry of "Negro domination" they could drive into solid phalanx every white man in all the Southern states.

Both the old parties have done this thing until they have constructed as perfect a "slot machine" as the world ever saw. Drop the old, worn nickel of the "party slogan" into the slot, and the machine does the rest. You might beseech a Southern white tenant to listen to you upon questions of finance, taxation, and transportation; you might demonstrate with mathematical precision that herein lay his way out of poverty into comfort; you might have him "almost persuaded" to the truth, but if the merchant who furnished his farm supplied (at tremendous usury) or the town politician (who never spoke to him excepting at election times) came along and cried "Negro rule!" the entire fabric of reason and common sense which you had patiently constructed would fall, and the poor tenant would joyously hug the chains of an actual wretchedness rather than do any experimenting on a question of mere sentiment.

Thus the Northern Democrats have ruled the South with a rod of iron for twenty years. We have had to acquiesce when the time-honored principles we loved were sent to the rear and new doctrines and polices we despised were engrafted on our platform. All this we have had to do to obtain the assistance of Northern Democrats to prevent what was called "Negro supremacy." In other words, the Negro has been as valuable a portion of the stock in trade of a Democrat as he was of a Republican. Let the South ask relief from Wall Street; let it plead for equal and just laws on finance; let it beg for mercy against crushing taxation, and Northern Democracy, with all the coldness, cruelty, and subtlety of Mephistopheles, would hint "Negro rule!" and the white farmer and laborer of the South had to choke down his grievance and march under Tammany's orders.

Reverse the statement, and we have the method by which the black man was managed by the Republicans.

Reminded constantly that the North had emancipated him; that the North had given him the ballot; that the North had upheld him in his citizenship; that the South was his enemy, and meant to deprive him of his suffrage and put him "back into slavery," it is no wonder he has played as nicely into the hands of the Republicans as his former owner has played into the hands of the Northern Democrats.

Now consider: here were two distinct races dwelling together, with political equality established between them by law. They lived in the same section; won their livelihood by the same pursuits; cultivated adjoining fields on the same terms; enjoyed together the bounties of a generous climate; suffered together the rigors of cruelly unjust laws; spoke the same language; bought and sold in the same markets; classified themselves into churches under the same denominational teachings; neither race antagonizing the other in any branch of industry; each absolutely dependent on the other in all the avenues of labor and employment; and yet, instead of being allies, as every dictate of reason and prudence and self-interest and justice said they should be, they were kept apart, in dangerous hostility, that the sordid aims of partisan politics might be served!

So completely has this scheme succeeded that the Southern black man almost instinctively supports any measure the Southern white man condemns, while the latter almost universally antagonizes any proposition suggested by a Northern Republican. We have, then, a solid South as opposed to a solid North; and in the South itself, a solid black vote against the solid white.

That such a condition is most ominous to both sections and both races, is apparent to all.

If we were dealing with a few tribes of red men or a few sporadic Chinese, the question would be easily disposed of. The Anglo-Saxon would probably do just as he pleased, whether right or wrong, and the weaker man would go under.

But the Negroes number 8,000,000. They are interwoven with our business, political, and labor systems. They assimilate with our customs, our religion, our civilization. They meet us at every turn,—in the fields, the shops, the mines. They are a part of our system, and they are here to stay.

Those writers who tediously wade through census reports to prove that the Negro is disappearing, are the most absurd mortals extant. The Negro is not disappearing. A Southern man who looks about him and who sees how rapidly the colored people increase, how cheaply they can live, and how readily they learn, has no patience whatever with those statistical lunatics who figure out the final disappearance of the Negro one hundred years hence. The truth is, that the "black belts" in the South are getting blacker. The race is mixing less than it ever did. Mulattoes are less common (in proportion) than during the times of slavery. Miscegenation is further off (thank God) than ever. Neither the blacks nor the whites have any relish for it. Both have a pride of race which is commendable, and which, properly directed, will lead to the best results for both. The home of the colored man is chiefly with us in the South, and there he will remain. It is there he is founding churches, opening schools, maintaining newspapers, entering the professions, serving on juries, deciding doubtful elections, drilling as a volunteer soldier, and piling up a cotton crop which amazes the world.

II

This preliminary statement is made at length that the gravity of the situation may be seen. Such a problem never confronted any people before.

Never before did two distinct races dwell together under such conditions.

And the problem is, can these two races, distinct in color, distinct in social life, and distinct as political powers, dwell together in peace and prosperity?

Upon a question so difficult and delicate no man should dogmatize—nor dodge. The issue is here; grows more urgent every day, and must be met.

It is safe to say that the present status of hostility between the races can only be sustained at the most imminent risk to both. It is leading by logical necessity to results which the imagination shrinks from contemplating. And the horrors of such a future can only be averted by honest attempts at a solution of the question which will be just to both races and beneficial to both.

Having given this subject much anxious thought, my opinion is that the future happiness of the two races will never be assured until the political motives which drive them asunder, into two distinct and hostile factions, can be removed. There must be a new policy inaugurated, whose purpose is to allay the passions and prejudices of race conflict, and which makes its appeal to the sober sense and honest judgment of the citizen regardless of his color.

To the success of this policy two things are indispensable—a common necessity acting upon both races, and a common benefit assured to both—without injury or humiliation to either.

Then, again, outsiders must let us alone. We must work out our own salvation. In no other way can it be done. Suggestions of Federal interference with our elections postpone the settlement and render our task the more difficult. Like all free people, we love home rule, and resent foreign compulsion of any sort. The Northern leader who really desires to see a better state of things in the South, puts his finger on the hands of the clock and forces them backward every time he intermeddles with the question. This is the literal truth; and the sooner it is well understood, the sooner we can accomplish our purpose.

What is that purpose? To outline a policy which compels the support of a great body of both races, from those motives which imperiously control human action, and which will thus obliterate forever the sharp and unreasoning political divisions of to-day.

The white people of the South will never support the Republican Party. This much is certain. The black people of the South will never support the Democratic Party. This is equally certain.

Hence, at the very beginning, we are met by the necessity of new political alliances. As long as the whites remain solidly Democratic, the blacks will remain solidly Republican.

As long as there was no choice, except as between the Democrats and the Republicans, the situation of the two races was bound to be one of antagonism. The Republican Party represented everything which was hateful to the whites; the Democratic Party, everything which was hateful to the blacks.

Therefore a new party was absolutely necessary. It has come, and it is doing its work with marvellous rapidity.

Why does a Southern Democrat leave his party and come to ours?

Because his industrial condition is pitiably bad; because he struggles against a system of laws which have almost filled him with despair; because he is told that he is without clothing because he produces too much cotton, and without food because corn is too plentiful; because he sees everybody growing rich off the products of labor except the laborer; because the millionnaires who manage the Democratic Party have contemptuously ignored his plea for a redress of grievances and have nothing to say to him beyond the cheerful advice to "work harder and live closer."

Why has this man joined the PEOPLE'S PARTY? Because the same grievances have been presented to the Republicans by the farmer of the West, and the millionnaires who control that party have replied to the petition with the soothing counsel that the Republican farmer of the West should "work more and talk less."

Therefore, if he were confined to a choice between the two old parties, the question would merely be (on these issues) whether the pot were larger than the kettle—the color of both being precisely the same.

### III

The key to the new political movement called the People's Party has been that the Democratic farmer was as ready to leave the Democratic ranks as the Republican farmer was to leave the Republican ranks. In exact proportion as the West received the assurance that the South was ready for a new party, it has moved. In exact proportion to the proof we could bring that the West had broken Republican ties, the South has moved. *Without* a decided break in both sections, neither would move. *With* that decided break, both moved.

The very same principle governs the race question in the South. The two races can never act together permanently, harmoniously, beneficially, till each race demonstrates to the other a readiness to leave old party affiliations and to form new ones, based upon the profound conviction that, in acting together, both races are seeking new laws which will benefit both. On no other basis under heaven can the "Negro Question" be solved.

.    .    .    .    .

### V

The People's Party will settle the race question. First, by enacting the Australian ballot system. Second, by offering to white and black a rallying point which is free from the odium of former discords and strifes. Third, by presenting a platform immensely beneficial to both races and injurious to neither. Fourth, by making it to the *interest* of both races to act together for the success of the platform. Fifth, by making it to the *interest* of the colored man to have the same patriotic zeal for the welfare of the South that the whites possess.

Now to illustrate. Take two planks of the People's Party platform: that pledging a free ballot under the Australian system and that which demands a distribution of currency to the people upon pledges of land, cotton, etc.

The guaranty as to the vote will suit the black man better than the Republican platform, because the latter contemplates Federal interference, which will lead to collisions and bloodshed. The Democratic platform contains no comfort to the Negro, because, while it denounces the Republican programme, as usual, it promises nothing which can be specified. It is a generality which does not even possess the virtue of being "glittering."

The People's Party, however, not only condemns Federal interference with elections, but also distinctly commits itself to the method by which every citizen shall have his constitutional right to the free exercise of his electoral choice. We pledge ourselves to isolate the voter from all coercive influences and give him the free and fair exercise of his franchise under state laws.

Now couple this with the financial plank which promises equality in the distribution of the national currency, at low rates of interest.

The white tenant lives adjoining the colored tenant. Their houses are almost equally destitute of comforts. Their living is confined to bare necessities. They are equally burdened with heavy taxes. They pay the same high rent for gullied and impoverished land.

They pay the same enormous prices for farm supplies. Christmas finds them both without any satisfactory return for a year's toil. Dull and heavy and unhappy, they both start the plows again when "New Year's" passes.

Now the People's Party says to these two men, "You are kept apart that you may be separately fleeced of your earnings. You are made to hate each other because upon that hatred is rested the keystone of the arch of financial despotism which enslaves you both. You are deceived and blinded that you may not see how this race antagonism perpetuates a monetary system which beggars both."

This is so obviously true it is no wonder both these unhappy laborers stop to listen. No wonder they begin to realize that no change of law can benefit the white tenant which does not benefit the black one likewise; that no system which now does injustice to one of them can fail to injure both. Their every material interest is identical. The moment this becomes a conviction, mere selfishness, the mere desire to better their conditions, escape onerous taxes, avoid usurious charges, lighten their rents, or change their precarious tenements into smiling, happy homes, will drive these two men together, just as their mutually inflamed prejudices now drive them apart.

Suppose these two men now to have become fully imbued with the idea that their material welfare depends upon the reforms we demand. Then they act together to secure them. Every white reformer finds it to the vital interest of his home, his family, his fortune, to see to it that the vote of the colored reformer is freely cast and fairly counted.

Then what? Every colored voter will be thereafter a subject of industrial education and political teaching.

Concede that in the final event, a colored man will vote where his material interests dictate that he should vote; concede that in the South the accident of color can make no possible difference in the interests of farmers, croppers, and laborers; concede that under full and fair discussion the people can be depended upon to ascertain where their interests lie—and we reach the conclusion that the Southern race question can be solved by the People's Party on the simple proposition that each race will be led by self-interest to support that which benefits it, when so presented that neither is hindered by the bitter party antagonisms of the past.

Let the colored laborer realize that our platform gives him a better guaranty for political independence; for a fair return for his work; a better chance to buy a home and keep it; a better chance to educate his children and see them profitably employed; a better chance to have public life freed from race collisions; a better chance for every citizen to be considered as a *citizen* regardless of color in the making and enforcing of laws,—let all this be fully realized, and the race question at the South will have settled itself through the evolution of a political movement in which both whites and blacks recognize their surest way out of wretchedness into comfort and independence.

The illustration could be made quite as clearly from other planks in the People's Party platform. On questions of land, transportation and finance, especially, the welfare of the two races so clearly depends upon that which benefits either, that intelligent discussion would necessarily lead to just conclusions.

Why should the colored man always be taught that the white man of his neighborhood hates him, while a Northern man, who taxes every rag on his back, loves him? Why should not my tenant come to regard me as his friend rather than the manufacturer who plunders us both? Why should we perpetuate a policy which drives the black man into the arms of the Northern politician?

Why should we always allow Northern and Eastern Democrats to enslave us forever by threats of the Force Bill?

Let us draw the supposed teeth of this fabled dragon by founding our new policy upon justice—upon the simple but profound truth that, if the voice of passion can be hushed, the self-interest of both races will drive them to act in concert. There never was a day during the last twenty years when the South could not have flung the money power into the dust by patiently teaching the Negro that we could not be wretched under any system which would not afflict him likewise; that we could not prosper under any law which would not also bring its blessings to him.

To the emasculated individual who cries "Negro supremacy!" there is little to be said. His cowardice shows him to be a degeneration from the race which has never yet feared any other race. Existing under such conditions as they now do in this country, there is no earthly chance for Negro domination, unless we are ready to admit that the colored man is our superior in will power, courage, and intellect.

Not being prepared to make any such admission in favor of any race the sun ever shone on, I have no words which can portray my contempt for the white men, Anglo-Saxons, who can knock their knees together, and through their chattering teeth and pale lips admit that they are afraid the Negroes will "dominate us."

The question of social equality does not enter into the calculation at all. That is a thing each citizen decides for himself. No statute ever yet drew the latch of the humblest home—or ever will. Each citizen regulates his own visiting list—and always will.

The conclusion, then, seems to me to be this: the crushing burdens which now oppress both races in the South will cause each to make an effort to cast them off. They will see a similarity of cause and a similarity of remedy. They will recognize that each should help the other in the work of repealing bad laws and enacting good ones. They will become political allies, and neither can injure the other without weakening both. It will be to the interest of both that each should have justice. And on these broad lines of mutual interest, mutual forbearance, and mutual support the present will be made the stepping-stone to future peace and prosperity.

## FREE SILVER

*"Coin" Harvey, of Chicago, a native of West Virginia who had tried the law, ranching, silver prospecting, and editing, finally achieved success with the slender classic* Coin's Financial School. *It became the bible of the silverites. In his book the youthful "Professor Coin" repeatedly confounded the goldbugs with his unanswerable logic. Harvey followed his success with a novel elaborating the conspiracy theory of deflation,* A Tale of Two Nations, *and other works that used the figure of Professor Coin. All of the first chapter of* Coin's Financial School *and most of the last are included here.*

<br>

# –17–
# COIN'S FINANCIAL SCHOOL
## by *William H. Harvey*

So much uncertainty prevailing about the many facts connected with the monetary question, very few are able to intelligently understand the subject.

Hard times are with us; the country is distracted; very few things are marketable at a price above the cost of production; tens of thousands are out of employment; the jails, penitentiaries, workhouses and insane asylums are full; the gold reserve at Washington is sinking; the government is running at a loss with a deficit in every department; a huge debt hangs like an appalling cloud over the country; taxes have assumed the importance of a mortgage, and 50 per cent of the public revenues are likely to go delinquent; hungered and half-starved men are banding into

SOURCE: William H. Harvey, *Coin's Financial School* (Chicago: Coin Publishing Co., 1894), ch. I, pp. 3–20; ch. VI, pp. 12–128, 130–133, 135, 143–147.

armies and marching toward Washington; the cry of distress is heard on every hand; business is paralyzed; commerce is at a standstill; riots and strikes prevail throughout the land; schemes to remedy our ills when put into execution are smashed like box-cars in a railroad wreck, and Wall street looks in vain for an excuse to account for the failure of prosperity to return since the repeal of the silver purchase act.

It is a time for wisdom and sound sense to take the helm, and Coin, a young financier living in Chicago, acting upon such a suggestion, established a school of finance to instruct the youths of the nation, with a view to their having a clear understanding of what has been considered an abstruse subject; to lead them out of the labyrinth of falsehoods, heresies and isms that distract the country.

## THE FIRST DAY

The school opened on the 7th day of May, 1894.

There was a good attendance, and the large hall selected in the Art Institute was comfortably filled. Sons of merchants and bankers, in fact all classes of business, were well represented. Journalists, however, predominated. Coin stepped on to the platform, looking the smooth little financier that he is, and said:

"I am pleased to see such a large attendance. It indicates a desire to learn and master a subject that has baffled your fathers. The reins of the government will soon be placed in your hands, and its future will be molded by your honesty and intelligence.

"I ask you to accept nothing from me that does not stand the analysis of reason; that you will freely ask questions and pass criticisms, and if there is any one present who believes that all who differ from *him* are lunatics and fools, he is requested to vacate his seat and leave the room."

The son of Editor Scott, of the *Chicago Herald*, here arose and walked out. Coin paused a moment, and then continued: "My object will be to teach you the A, B, C of the questions about money that are now a matter of every-day conversation.

THE MONEY UNIT

"In money there must be a unit. In arithmetic, as you are aware, you are taught what a unit is. Thus, I make here on the blackboard the figure 1. That, in arithmetic, is a unit. All countings are sums or multiples of that unit. A unit, therefore, in mathematics, was a necessity as a basis to start from. In making money it was equally as necessary to establish a unit. The constitution gave the power to Congress to 'coin money and regulate the value thereof.' Congress adopted silver and gold as money. It then proceeded to fix the unit.

"That is, it then fixed what should constitute one dollar, the same thing that the mathematician did when he fixed one figure from which all others should be counted. Congress fixed the monetary unit to consist of 37¼ grains of pure silver, and provided for a certain amount of alloy (baser metals) to be mixed with it to give it greater hardness and durability. This was in 1792, in the days of Washington and Jefferson and our revolutionary forefathers, who had a hatred of England, and an intimate knowledge of her designs on this country.

"They had fought eight long years for their independence from British domination in this country, and when they had seen the last red-coat leave our shores, they settled down to establish a permanent government, and among the first things they did was to make 371¼ grains of silver the unit of values. That much silver was to constitute a dollar. And each dollar was a unit. They then provided for all other money to be counted from this unit of a silver dollar. Hence, dimes, quarters and half-dollars were exact fractional parts of the dollar so fixed.

"Gold was made money, but its value was counted from these silver units or dollars. The ratio between silver and gold was fixed at 15 to 1, and afterward at 16 to 1. So that in making gold coins their relative weight was regulated by this ratio.

"This continued to be the law up to 1873. During that long period, the unit of values was never changed and always contained 371¼ grains of pure silver. While that was the law it was impossible for any one to say that the silver in a silver dollar was only worth 47 cents, or any other number of cents less than 100 cents, or a dollar. For it was itself the unit of values. While that was the law it would have been as absurd to say that the silver in a silver dollar was only worth 47 cents, as it would be to say that this figure 1 which I have on the blackboard is only forty-seven one-hundredths of one.

"When the ratio was changed from 15 to 1 to 16 to 1 the silver dollar or unit was left the same size and the gold dollar was made smaller. The latter was changed from 24.7 grains to 23.2 grains pure gold, thus making it smaller. This occurred in 1834. The silver dollar still remained the unit and continued so until 1873.

"Both were legal tender in the payment of all debts, and the mints were open to the coinage of all that came. So that up to 1873, we were on what was known as a bimetallic basis, but what was in fact a silver basis, with gold as a companion metal enjoying the same privileges as silver, except that silver fixed the unit, and the value of gold was regulated by it. This was bimetallism.

"Our forefathers showed much wisdom in selecting silver, of the two metals, out of which to make the unit. Much depended on this decision. For the one selected to represent the unit would thereafter be unchangeable in value. That is, the metal in it could never be worth less than a dollar, for it would be the unit of value itself. The demand for silver in the arts or for money by other nations might make the quantity of silver in a silver dollar sell for more than a dollar, but it could never be worth less than a dollar. Less than itself.

"In considering which of these two metals they would thus favor by making it the unit, they were led to adopt silver because it was the most reliable. It was the most favored as money by the people. It was scattered among all the people. Men having a design to injure business by making money scarce, could not so easily get hold of all the silver and hide it away, as they could gold. This was the principal reason that led them to the conclusion to select silver, the more stable of the two metals, upon which to fix the unit. It was so much handled by the people and preferred by them, that it was called the people's money.

"Gold was considered the money of the rich. It was owned

principally by that class of people, and the poor people seldom handled it, and the very poor people seldom ever saw any of it."

Here young Medill, of the *Chicago Tribune*, held up his hand, which indicated that he had something to say or wished to ask a question. Coin paused and asked him what he wanted.

He arose in his seat and said that his father claimed that we had been on a gold basis ever since 1837, that prior to 1873 there never had been but eight million dollars of silver coined. Here young Wilson, of the *Farm, Field, and Fireside*, said he wanted to ask, who owns the *Chicago Tribune*?

Coin tapped the little bell on the table to restore order, and ruled the last question out, as there was one already before the house by Mr. Medill.

"Prior to 1873," said Coin, "there were one hundred and five millions of silver coined by the United States and eight million of this was in silver dollars. When your father said that 'only eight million dollars in silver' had been coined, he meant to say that 'only eight million silver dollars had been coined.' He also neglected to say—that is—he forgot to state, that ninety-seven millions had been coined into dimes, quarters and halves.

"About one hundred millions of foreign silver had found its way into this country prior to 1860. It was principally Spanish, Mexican and Canadian coin. It had all been made legal tender in the United States by act of Congress. We needed more silver than we had, and Congress passed laws making all foreign silver coins legal tender in this country. I will read you one of these laws—they are scattered all through the statutes prior to 1873." Here Coin picked up a copy of the laws of the United States relating to loans and the currency, coinage and banking, published at Washington. He said: "A copy could be obtained by any one on writing to the Treasury Department."

He then read from page 240, as follows:

*And be it further enacted,* That from and after the passage of this act, the following foreign silver coins shall pass current as money within the United States, and be receivable by tale, for the payment of all debts and demands, at the rates following, that is to say: the Spanish pillar dollars, and the dollars of Mexico, Peru and Bolivia, etc.

"On account of the scarcity of silver, both Jefferson and Jackson recommended that dimes, quarters and halves would serve the people better than dollars, until more silver bullion could be obtained. This was the reason why only about eight million of the one hundred and five million of silver were coined into dollars.

"During this struggle to get more silver," continued Coin, "France made a bid for it by establishing a ratio of 15½ to 1, and as our ratio was 16 to 1, this made silver in France worth $1.03⅛ when exchanged for gold, and as gold would answer the same purpose as silver for money, it was found that our silver was leaving us. So Congress in 1853, had our fractional silver coins made of light weight to prevent their being exported.

"So that we had prior to 1873 one hundred and five millions of silver coined by us, and about one hundred million of foreign silver coin, or about two hundred and five million dollars in silver in the United States, and were doing all we could to get more and to hold on to what we had. Thus silver and gold were the measure of values. It should be remembered that no silver or gold was in circulation between 1860 and 1873. Two hundred and five millions were in circulation before 1861."

Then looking at young Medill, Coin asked him if he had answered his question. The young journalist turned red in the face and hung his head, while young Wilson muttered something about Englishmen owning the *Tribune*.

### YOUNG SCOTT RETURNS

Young Scott was seen entering the room; he was carrying in his hand a book. He stopped and addressed Coin, saying that he wished to apologize for his conduct, and was now here to stay if permitted to do so.

Coin told him that so long as he accorded to others the right to entertain views different from his, his name would be kept on the roll as a student at the "Financial School."

Thereupon Mr. Scott said: "I am informed that you have stated that silver was the unit of value prior to 1873; that this unit was composed of 371¼ grains of pure silver or 412 grains of standard silver. Now I want to know if it is not a fact that both gold and silver at that time were each the unit in its own measurement? And that we had a double measurement of values, which was liable to separate and part company at any time? And when the metals did separate, was not the effect like having two yard-sticks of different lengths? I wish to call your attention to the statute on page 213 of the book you read from where it says an eagle or ten-dollar gold piece is ten *units*. Does not this indicate positively that a gold unit was also provided for?"

And with this he sat down looking as proud as a cannoneer who has just fired a shot that has had deadly effect in the enemy's ranks.

Coin had nodded when the proposition of the *unit* was stated; looked amused at the double unit proposition advanced, and now replied: "The law I referred to this morning was passed April 2, 1792, and remained the law till 1873. You will find it in my valuable Handbook. I now read it from the United States Statutes:

*Dollars or units,* each to be of the value of a Spanish milled dollar as the same is now current, and to contain three hundred and seventy-one grains and four-sixteenth parts of a grain of pure, or four hundred and sixteen grains of standard silver.

"If you omit the words referring to the Spanish milled dollar, it will then read: *'Dollars or units, each to contain 371 grains and 4 parts of a grain of pure silver.'*

"This is the statute that fixed the *unit* and is the only statute on the subject till we come to 1873.

"Now, what you referred to is this. It is in section 9, and reads as follows:

*Eagles*—each to be of the *value of* ten dollars or units.

"And on the ratio of 15 to 1, fixed in the same act, this made an eagle contain 247 grains of pure gold, or 270 grains of standard gold. You will observe that the law does not say, as you stated, that an 'Eagle or ten-dollar gold piece *is* ten units.' It says: *'Of the value of ten dollars or units.'* In other words, a ten-dollar gold piece shall *be of the value of ten silver dollars.*

"Or to state it in another way: As the law fixed 371¼ grains of pure silver as a unit, the quantity of gold in a gold dollar would be regulated by the ratio fixed from time to time.

"Now," addressing Mr. Scott, "if I have not read your law right, I want you to say so. This is the place to settle all questions of fact. Your law does not say a gold piece has so many *units* in it, but instead of that, it does say, the gold pieces are *to be of the value* of so many *units.*"

The young journalist from Washington street had not seen the distinction, and had jumped at conclusions. When he did see the hole he was in, he leaned over to Evans of the *Economist,* who sat next to him, and asked him to help him out. Evans thought he had mastered the subject of political economy several years ago, and had named his paper *"The Economist."* He found now, that he had not gone very deep into the subject. His text-books had been the *Tribune, Herald, Record* and *Journal.* He did not know that they, too, were getting their information in about the same way.

So now when his friend Scott was in trouble, he greatly sympathized with him. But he could not help him, and was seen to shake his head. Scott sat silently in his seat.

"You will observe," continued Coin, "that the law in fixing a *dollar* or *unit* does not say, as in the case of gold, that it shall be of the value of 371¼ grains of silver, but that the *dollar* or *unit* was *silver* and its quantity should be 371¼ grains. The amount of alloy added to this quantity of pure silver was afterward changed, but this amount of pure silver, 371¼ grains, has always remained the same and was the unit of values until 1873."

A bright looking kid was now seen standing on a chair in the back part of the room holding up his hand and cracking his finger and thumb. He was asked what he wanted and said:

"I want to know what is meant by *standard* silver?" Coin then explained that this meant with the government a standard rule for mixing alloy with silver and gold. And when so mixed is called standard silver or standard gold. Before it is mixed with the alloy it is called pure silver or pure gold. The standard of both gold and silver is such that by 1,000 parts by weight, 900 shall be of pure metal, and 100 of alloy. The alloy of silver coins is copper. In gold coins it is copper and silver, but the silver shall in no case exceed one-tenth of the whole alloy. Standard silver and standard gold is the metal when mixed with its alloy.

"I now think we understand," said Coin, "what the unit of value was prior to 1873. We had the silver dollar as the unit. And we had both gold and silver as money walking arm in arm into the United States mints.

## THE CRIME OF 1873

"We now come to the act of 1873," continued Coin. "On February 12, 1873, Congress passed an act purporting to be a revision of the coinage laws. This law covers 15 pages of our statutes. It repealed the *unit* clause in the law of 1792, and in its place substituted a law in the following language:

> That the gold coins of the United States shall be a one-dollar piece which at the standard weight of twenty-five and eight-tenths grains *shall be the unit of value.*

"It then deprived silver of its right to unrestricted free coinage, and destroyed it as legal tender money in the payment of debts, except to the amount of five dollars.

"At that time we were all using paper money. No one was handling silver and gold coins. It was when specie payments were about to be resumed that the country appeared to realize what had been done. The newspapers on the morning of February 13, 1873, and at no time in the vicinity of that period, had any account of the change. General Grant, who was President of the United States at that time, said afterwards, that he had no idea of it, and would not have signed the bill if he had known that it demonetized silver.

"In the language of Senator Daniel of Virginia, it seems to have gone through Congress 'like the silent tread of a cat.'

"An army of a half million of men invading our shores, the warships of the world bombarding our coasts, could not have made us surrender the money of the people and substitute in its place the money of the rich. A few words embraced in fifteen pages of statutes put through Congress in the rush of bills did it. The pen was mightier than the sword.

"But we are not here to deal with sentiment. We are here to learn facts. Plain, blunt facts.

"The law of 1873 made gold the *unit* of values. And that is the law to-day. When silver was the unit of value, gold enjoyed *free coinage,* and was legal tender in the payment of all debts. Now things have changed. Gold is the unit and silver does not enjoy free coinage. It is refused at the mints. We might get along with gold as the *unit,* if silver enjoyed the same right gold did prior to 1873. But that right is now denied to silver. When silver was the unit, the unlimited demand for gold to coin into money, made the demand as great as the supply, and this held up the value of gold bullion."

Here Victor F. Lawson, Jr., of the Chicago *Evening News,* interrupted the little financier with the statement that his paper, the *News,* had stated time and again that silver had become so plentiful it had ceased to be a precious metal. And that this statement believed by him to be a fact had more to do with his prejudice to silver than anything else. And he would like to know if that was not a fact?

"There is no truth in the statement," replied Coin. "On page 21 of my Handbook you will find a table on this subject, compiled by Mulhall, the London statistician. It gives the quantity of gold and silver in the world both coined and uncoined at six periods—at the years 1600, 1700, 1800, 1848, 1880, and 1890. It shows that in 1600 there were 27 tons of silver to one ton of gold. In 1700, 34 tons of silver to one ton of gold. In 1800, 32 tons of silver to one ton of gold. In 1848, 31 tons of silver to one ton of gold. In 1880, 18 tons of silver to one ton of gold. In 1890, 18 tons of silver to one ton of gold.

"The United States is producing more silver than it ever did, or was until recently. But the balance of the world is producing much less. They are fixing the price on our silver and taking it away from us, at their price. The report of the Director of the

Mint shows that since 1850 the world has produced less silver than gold, while during the first fifty years of the century the world produced 78 per cent more silver than gold. Instead of becoming more plentiful, it is less plentiful. So it is less, instead of more.

"Any one can get the official statistics by writing to the treasurer at Washington, and asking for his official book of statistics. Also write to the Director of the Mint and ask him for his report. If you get no answer write to your Congressman. These books are furnished free and you will get them.

"At the time the United States demonetized silver in February, 1873, silver as measured in gold was worth $1.02. The argument of depreciated silver could not then be made. Not one of the arguments that are now made against silver was then possible. They are all the bastard children of the crime of 1873.

"It was demonetized secretly, and since then a powerful money trust has used deception and misrepresentations that have led tens of thousands of honest minds astray."

William Henry Smith, Jr., of the Associated Press, wanted to know if the size of the gold dollar was ever changed more than the one time mentioned by Coin, viz., in 1834.

"Yes," said Coin. "In 1837 it was changed from 23.2 to 23.22. This change of 2/100ths was for convenience in calculation, but the change was made in the gold coin—never in the silver dollar (the *unit*) till 1873.

Adjourned.

.    .    .    .    .

## THE SIXTH DAY

The manner in which the little lecturer had handled his subject on the fifth day had greatly enhanced his popularity. What he had said, had been in the nature of a revelation to nearly all that heard it, and his grouping of facts had made a profound impression.

What created the most comment, was his statement as to the

space in which all the gold and silver of the world could be placed. In all the hotel lobbies it was the subject of conversation. The bare statement that all the gold in the world could be put in a cube of 22 feet appeared ridiculous—absurd.

Few that had entertained the single gold standard view of the monetary question were willing to believe it. They argued that it was impossible; that the business of the world could not be transacted on such an insignificant amount of property for primary money. They said, "Wait till the morning papers come out; the *Tribune* would puncture it, the *Inter Ocean, Herald,* in fact all of the papers would either admit it by their silence, contradict it or give the facts."

At the Grand Pacific Hotel the cashier was kept busy answering requests to see a twenty-dollar gold piece. They wanted to measure it—to get its diameter and thickness. As none was to be had, they had to content themselves with measuring up silver dollars and figuring out how much space all the silver in the world would occupy. This resulted in confirming Coin's statement.

Mr. George Sengel, a prominent citizen of Fort Smith, Arkansas, while discussing the subject with a large party in the rotunda of the Palmer House, stood up in a chair and addressed the crowd, saying:

"Gentlemen, I have just been up in Coin's room and examined the government reports as to the amount of gold and silver in the world, and have made the calculation myself as to the quantity of it, and I find that the statements made are true. All the gold and silver in the world obtainable for money can be put in the office of this hotel, and all the gold can be put in this office and not materially interfere with the comfort of the guests of the house.

"I have been until to-day in favor of a single gold standard, but hard times, and this fact that all the gold in the world available for money can be put in a space of twenty-two feet each way, has knocked it out of me. Count on me and old Arkansas for bimetallism."

Mr. Sengel's speech was greeted with applause, and he was followed by others expressing similar views.

The morning papers gave full reports of the previous day's lecture. All editorially confirmed Coin's statement as to the quantity of gold and silver in the world, and the space it would occupy, except the *Herald* and *Tribune;* they were silent on the subject.

It was generally known that Coin would discuss independent action of the United States on the last day, and from the number that tried to gain admission, a hall many times as large could have been easily filled.

At the hour for opening the hall large crowds surrounded the entrance to the Art Institute, and the corridors were filled with people. In the large hall where the lectures were delivered the walls had been decorated with the American colors. This had been seen to by a committee of bimetallists; they had given special attention to the decorations around the platform, and though assuming many forms, each piece had been made from United States' flags. The scene presented was striking and patriotic.

When the doors were opened the hall was soon filled and thousands were turned away.

Coin was escorted by a committee of bimetallists in carriages from his hotel to the Art Institute, each carriage used by the committee being draped in the American colors. It was the first demonstration of the kind made in honor of the little financier of the people, since the lectures had begun.

The evidences of his popularity were now to be seen on every hand. Many, however, had reserved their judgment to hear from him on the United States taking independent action, and all were anxious to listen to what he would say on that subject.

His appearance upon the platform was the signal for an ovation. He had grown immensely popular in those last five days.

He laid his silk hat on the table, and at once stepped to the middle of the platform. He raised his eyes to the audience; slowly turned his head to the right and left, and looked into the sea of faces that confronted him.

### INDEPENDENT FREE COINAGE

"In the midst of plenty, we are in want," he began.

"Helpless children and the best womanhood and manhood of America appeal to us for release from a bondage that is destructive of life and liberty. All the nations of the Western Hemisphere turn to their great sister republic for assistance in the emancipation of the people of at least one-half the world.

"The Orient, with its teeming millions of people, and France, the cradle of science and liberty in Europe, look to the United States to lead in the struggle to roll back the accumulated disasters of the last twenty-one years. What shall our answer be? [Applause.]

"If it is claimed we must adopt for our money the metal England selects, and can have no independent choice in the matter, let us make the test and find out if it is true. It is not American to give up without trying. If it is true, let us attach England to the United States and blot her name out from among the nations of the earth. [Applause.]

"A war with England would be the most popular ever waged on the face of the earth. [Applause.] If it is true that she can dictate the money of the world, and thereby create world-wide misery, it would be the most just war ever waged by man. [Applause.]

"But fortunately this is not necessary. Those who would have you think that we must wait for England, either have not studied this subject, or have the same interest in continuing the present conditions as England. It is a vain hope to expect her voluntarily to consent. England is the creditor nation of the globe, and collects hundreds of millions of dollars in interest annually in gold from the rest of the world. We are paying her two hundred millions yearly in interest. She demands it in gold; the contracts call for it in gold. Do you expect her to voluntarily release any part of it? It has a purchasing power twice what a bimetallic currency would have. She knows it.

"The men that control the legislation of England are citizens of that country with fixed incomes. They are interest gatherers to the

amount annually of over one thousand millions of dollars. The
men over there holding bimetallic conventions, and passing resolutions, have not one-fifth the influence with the law-making
power that the bimetallists in the United States have with our
Congress and President. No; nothing is to be expected from England.

"Whenever property interests and humanity have come in conflict, England has ever been the enemy of human liberty. All
reforms with those so unfortunate as to be in her power have
been won with the sword. She yields only to force. [Applause.]

"The money lenders in the United States, who own substantially all of our money, have a selfish interest in maintaining the
gold standard. They, too, will not yield. They believe that if the
gold standard can survive for a few years longer, the people will
get used to it—get used to their poverty—and quietly submit.

"To that end they organize international bimetallic committees
and say, 'Wait on England, she will be forced to give us bimetallism.' Vain hope! Deception on this subject has been practiced
long enough upon a patient and outraged people.

"With silver remonetized, and gold at a premium, not one-
tenth the hardships could result that now afflict us. Why? First: it
would double the value of all property. Second: only 4 per cent
of the business of the people of this nation is carried on with
foreign countries; and a part of this 4 per cent would be transactions with silver using nations; while 96 per cent of the business
of our people is domestic transactions, Home business. Is it not
better to legislate in the interest of 96 per cent of our business,
than the remaining 4 per cent?

.    .    .    .    .

"In the impending struggle for the mastery of the commerce of
the world, the financial combat between England and the United
States cannot be avoided if we are to retain our self-respect, and
our people their freedom and prosperity. [Applause.]

"The gold standard will give England the commerce and
wealth of the world. The bimetallic standard will make the

United States the most prosperous nation on the globe. [Applause.]

"To avoid the struggle means a surrender to England. It means more—it means a tomb raised to the memory of the republic. Delay is dangerous. At any moment an internecine war may break out among us. Wrongs and outrages will not be continuously endured. The people will strike at the laws that inflict them.

"To wait on England is purile and unnecessary. Her interests are not our interests. 'But,' you ask me, 'how are we to do it?' It will work itself. We have been frightened at a shadow. We have been as much deceived in this respect as we have about other matters connected with this subject.

"Free coinage by the United States will at once establish a parity between the two metals. Any nation that is big enough to take all the silver in the world, and give back merchandise and products in payment for it, will at once establish the parity between it and gold. [Applause.]

. . . . .

"When it is considered that we are giving two dollars worth of property now, in payment for one dollar in gold, you will realize that we are now paying 100 per cent premium on gold. [Applause.]

"And this applies not only to our foreign business, but to our home business.

"With silver remonetized, and a just and equitable standard of values, we can, if necessary, by act of Congress, reduce the number of grains in a gold dollar till it is of the same value as the silver dollar. [Applause.] We can legislate the premium out of gold. [Applause.] Who will say that this is not an effective remedy? I pause for a reply!"

Coin waited for a reply. No one answering him, he continued:

"Until an answer that will commend itself to an unbiased mind is given to this remedy, that guarantees a parity between the metals, write upon the character of every 'international bimetallist' the words *gold monometallist.*"

Pausing for a moment, as if still waiting for his position to be attacked, he proceeded:

"Give the people back their favored primary money! Give us two arms with which to transact business! Silver the right arm and gold the left arm! Silver the money of the people, and gold the money of the rich.

"Stop this legalized robbery that is transferring the property of the debtors to the possession of the creditors!

"Citizens! the integrity of the government has been violated. A Financial Trust has control of your money, and with it, is robbing you of your property. Vampires feed upon your commercial blood. The money in the banks is subject to the check of the money lenders. They expect you to quietly submit, and leave your fellow citizens at their mercy. Through the instrumentality of law they have committed a crime that overshadows all other crimes. And yet they appeal to law for their protection. If the starving workingman commits the crime of trespass, they appeal to the law they have contaminated, for his punishment. Drive these money-changers from our temples. Let them discover by your aspect, their masters—the people." [Applause.]

"The United States commands the situation, and can dictate bimetallism to the world at the ratio she is inclined to fix.

"Our foreign ministers sailing out of the New York harbor past the statue of "Liberty Enlightening the World" should go with instructions to educate the nations of the earth upon the American Financial Policy. We should negative the self-interested influence of England, and speak for industrial prosperity.

"We are now the ally of England in the most cruel and unjust persecution against the weak and defenseless people of the world that was ever waged by tyrants since the dawn of history. [Applause.]

"Our people are losing each year hundreds of millions of dollars; incalculable suffering exists throughout the land; we have begun the work of cutting each others throats; poor men crazed with hunger are daily shot down by the officers of the law; want, distress and anxiety pervades the entire Union.

"If we are to act let us act quickly.

"It has been truthfully said:

" 'It is at once the result and security of oppression that its victim soon becomes incapable of resistance. Submission to its first encroachments is followed by the fatal lethargy that destroys every noble ambition, and converts the people into cowardly poltroons and fawning sycophants, who hug their chains and lick the hand that smites them!'

"Oppression now seeks to enslave this fair land. Its name is greed. Surrounded by the comforts of life, it is unconscious of the condition of others. Despotism, whether in Russia marching its helpless victims to an eternal night of sorrow, or in Ireland where its humiliating influences are ever before the human eye, or elsewhere; it is the same.

"It is already with us. It has come in the same form that it has come everywhere—by regarding the interests of property as paramount to the interests of humanity. That influence extends from the highest to the lowest. The deputy sheriff regards the $4 a day he gets as more important to him than the life or cause of the workmen he shoots down.

"The Pullman Palace Car Company recently reduced the already low wages of its employés 33⅓ per cent. Unable to make a living, they laid down their tools. A few days later the company declared a quarterly dividend of 2 per cent on watered capital of $30,000,000. This quarterly dividend was $600,000.

"Had this company sent for the committee of the workmen and said, 'We were about to declare our regular quarterly dividend of 2 per cent; it amounts to $600,000; we have concluded to make it 1½ per cent; this will give us $475,000 for three months, or one quarter's profits, and we are going to use the other $125,000 to put back the wages of the men. There would have been no strike. The men would have hailed it as generosity, and the hearts of 4,000 workmen would have been made glad.

"It was not done. It was not to be thought of. These stockholders living in comfort with all their wants provided for, think more of their property interests than they do of humanity, and will see men starve or reduced to the condition of serfs rather than concede an equitable distribution of the profits of their business.

"This has occurred here in the city of your homes; in the World's Fair city; a city supposed to be as patriotic as any we have; if this is human nature here, what do you expect from the men in England who hold our bonds, notes and mortgages payable in gold.

"We are forced to take independent action. To hesitate is cowardly! Shall we wait while the cry of the helpless is heard on every hand? Shall we wait while our institutions are crumbling?" (Cries of "No—no—no!")

"This is a struggle for humanity. For our homes and firesides. For the purity and integrity of our government.

"That all the people of this country sufficiently intelligent to vote cannot understand that the reduction of our primary money to one half its former quantity reduces the value of property proportionately, is one of the inexplainable phenomena in human history.

"Those who do understand it should go among the people and awake them to the situation of peril, in which they are placed. Awake them as you would with startling cries at the coming of flood and fires.

"Arouse them as did Paul Revere as he rode through the streets shouting: 'The British are on our shores.'

"To let England dictate to us was not once the spirit of Americans."

·    ·    ·    ·    ·

**POPULIST ORATORY**

*Governor of Kansas, 1893–1895, Lewelling was a native of Iowa, born into a Quaker and abolitionist family in 1846. He was graduated from Whittier College and engaged in farming, teaching, newspaper publishing, and heading the Iowa State Reform School for Girls before moving in 1887 to Wichita, where he became a produce dealer, or "butter and egg peddler," as he put it. By 1890 he was Populist county chairman and in 1892 delivered a moving speech of welcome to the state convention that resulted in his nomination for governor by acclamation. Although the Populists won control of the state senate in 1892, a Republican majority controlled the house after a lengthy dispute over election returns. The division frustrated Lewelling's administration and it registered little positive achievement. Lewelling's speaking style was not that of the orotund spellbinder, so prevalent in the period, but was the more compelling for its warmth and sincerity. Here he speaks to a Populist meeting at Huron Place, Kansas City.*

–18–

# SPEECH AT HURON PLACE, JULY 26, 1894

## by Lorenzo Dow Lewelling

. . . I have been told that there are those in this great state that have from time to time suffered for the necessaries of life; I can't credit that statement, Mr. Chairman, from what I see here this evening, and yet, a good Republican friend of mine told me it was true and he surprised me further by telling me that the

SOURCE: "Speech of Governor Lewelling, at Populist Meeting at Huron Place, July 26th, 1894," typescript in the Kansas State Historical Society. Obvious typographical errors and misspellings have been corrected.

reason there were hungry people in Kansas and the United States, was because there was too much bread. He said the reason there were so many people going poorly clad, was because there was too much cloth and too many garments made for the people to wear. Now, I confess, I can't understand that philosophy, but he can, and he explained it and I leave you to find out from him what the theory is.

.     .     .     .     .

. . . What is government to me if it does not make it possible for me to live? and provide for my family! The trouble has been, we have so much regard for the rights of property that we have forgotten the liberties of the individual. We have had some illustration of that in the great strike at Chicago[1] and a number of other illustrations. I claim it is the business of the Government to make it possible for me to live and sustain the life of my family. If the Government don't do that, what better is the Government to me than a state of barbarism and everywhere we slay, and the slayer in turn is slain and so on the great theatre of life is one vast conspiracy all creatures from the worm to the man in turn rob their fellows. That my fellow citizens is the law of natural selection the survival of the fittest—not the survival of the fittest, but the survival of the strongest. It is time that man should rise above it.

.     .     .     .     .

Now, there are 350,000 able-bodied men in Kansas, and their average individual earnings last year and year before were $500. per man. That is what they earned on an average, but I might imagine some of you people here in this audience saying, "Well, I didn't get my share even of the $500." and I don't think you did. What has become of that $500. you were to get? It has gone where the wang-a-doodle mourneth for its first born. It went to

[1 The Pullman Strike of 1894. — Ed.]

pay excessive freight rates on commodities which we bought and sold, and then it went to pay interest on your mortgages. Why, I might tell, and I know something about it from experience, that the people of Kansas are paying 6%, 8%, 10% and some as high as 12 and 15% per annum. Then, what is to become of us, my fellow citizens? Where are we going to. Don't you see pretty clearly we are going into a hole every year?

Now our friends have told us that the only trouble about this country and our condition is a "lack of confidence." And I saw an old farmer the other day who said he had been to market with a load of wheat. He said he got $7.50 for the 30 bushels of wheat that he had taken to town, and he bought a couple of pairs of shoes for the children, and a calico dress for his wife, and then he felt confident he had gone dead broke. He said he felt all played out by the biggest confidence game that had ever been perpetrated on an unsuspecting public. And I sympathized with him because I believed it was true; still he had to pay his mortgage—and when his neighbor sold another load of wheat and still another load, and put his money in the bank and kept accumulating in order to pay off the mortgage and finally the bank broke and then he said he had lost his confidence, and his patience too, and swore by the Great Horn Spoon, that hereafter he would vote the populist ticket and vote for the kind of bank that never breaks and that is the Postal Savings Bank that is advocated by the Populist platform. . . .

. . . I have been asked why I was a Populist. I want to say to you, friends, that the same principles that made me a Republican in the early days, have today made me a populist, and I'll tell you what they are. I remember when I was a little boy my parents were the old line abolition kind of people that believed in equal rights to all and special privileges to none. God bless them for the sentiment, and don't you say so? Well, I remember in those days of the abolition question that we took a little paper called Uncle Lucas' Childs paper, and one side of the paper bore a motto about the size of a coin in the centre of a picture—a picture of an African slave with his hands uplifted and in chains, and around the rim of the coin a motto "Am I not a man and Brother?" That made a wonderful impression on my mind. I was taught thus in my infancy to stand for the man and woman who was down in the scale of life, and life's conflict. To stand for the weak against the strong, for God knows the strong can take care of themselves, and the weak are those that should be protected and provided for. And I say now, it is the duty of government to protect the weak, because the strong are able to protect themselves.

I say these are the reasons that made me a populist, and today my heart goes out to the working men and women of this nation as it went out to the black slave. I believe, and I say it freely, that the working men and women of this country, many of them, are simply today in the shackels of industrial slavery.

.    .    .    .    .

What kind of condition is it in which we live anyhow? You people of Kansas City are pretty well to-do and so are the people of Kansas generally, but they are not all over the country and there is some suffering here, we believe—we are so foolish as to believe that conditions might be improved by the government interfering and making it possible for the improvement of these conditions.

"We were talking about how you were going to pay your debts. About the interest there has accumulated. I want to say to you, I do not intend to discuss the currency question at length, but I want to say to you while we pass, that I do not believe it is possible, ever under the shining sun, while the present financial system continues, for the debt of the people of Kansas to be paid, I do not believe it is possible that the debt of the United States Government can be paid while the present financial condition exists. That time will come when the great ledger of civilization will be balanced in red, but God forbid that we may live to see that day. I say it will come, unless the financial conditions of this country are changed, and changed soon.

All we want is a little relief, a little remedy. I have in mind a remedy that might be applied right away. I will tell you what it is. Why, I would take the Colorado contingent of the Industrial

Army and set them out in Colorado to digging the silver from the native hills and making money out of it.[2] Why, my Republican friends say, these men are idlers, and vagabonds, they don't want to work, yet the fact remains that out in Colorado, they actually fought each other to obtain the picks and shovels with which to do work for the city in order that they might obtain a pittance to provide for themselves and families. When the mines shut down —they did shut down immediately after the repeal of the Sherman bill[3]—When the mines shut down there were 30,000 men thrown out of employment in ten days in Colorado. They didn't know what to do nor where to go. They began drifting across the country, they naturally tended towards the great centers of civilization and a great many of them brought up in Chicago and there they joined the immense multitude like the sands of the sea and they gathered themselves together on the lake shore. There were 5,000 assembled together discussing their ways and means. They said to the people, the passers by, to the authorities of Chicago, "Give us bread for we are starving, Give us work or give us bread" but instead of bread, they did not get the proverbial stone, but they were kicked out of the way by the heavy boots of the policeman, and next day the Chicago papers came out and said, "Oh, there's nothing like leather for dispersing a mob." The mob dispersed harmless and armless, without evil intentions to anyone, driven out of the way by the kicks of the police and that too under the shadow of the statue of Liberty which overlooks the lake shore. "Oh, Liberty how many crimes have been committed in thy name!"

. . . I ask you now, what can the poor man do today that comes to you and says, I have hands to work with, I have bodily strength, I am willing to give all those for a morsel of bread—but you say, "I have no work to give you." What is he to do then?

[2 A body of unemployed Cripple Creek silver miners, led by S. S. Sanders, had seiezd a train on the Missouri Pacific in May 1894 in an effort to reach Washington to petition for redress of grievances. One of many such "industrial armies" of the unemployed in that depression year, it never reached its destination. Its members were arrested by federal authorities in Kansas, and two hundred were convicted on charges of "interfering with the mails." — Ed.]

[3 The Sherman Silver Purchase Act of 1890, repealed in 1893. — Ed.]

Can he go and lie down on the street for rest? No, because there [are] laws against vagabondage. Can he go and crawl into a box car and take a nap there? No. Because he is trespassing upon the rights and privileges of others. Can he go to the door and ask for something to eat? No, because there [are] laws against begging. Can he go out into the fields and cultivate the fields? No, because the field belongs to somebody else. Can he draw a drink of water out of the spring or well in the field? No, because the spring or well belongs to the man who owns the field. What in the name of goodness is he to do? Answer me that question in the light of our present civilization and government. Don't you have some sympathy for the men in this position? Senator Ingalls[4] told us some two years ago, there are over a million men in the United States who are in that condition, and today the number is swelled to three million. Oh, is it any wonder there are common wealers? Is it then a wonder there are anarchists? There is no greater crime breeder in the world than poverty. Poverty is the mother of it all; and I came here this evening asking you to join with me in the organization of a great anti-poverty society. Will you do it? (Cheers, and cries of yes.). . . . They say I am a "Calamity howler," if that is so, I want to continue to howl until those conditions are improved. . . .

Excuse me, if I digress from my subject, but while I think about it, you remember as well as I do the Democratic party in its purity in times past has stood with giant force for the rights of individual states. They have been sticklers for the question of State's rights. They have been opposed to any encroachment of the Federal Government upon the power of the states. What do we see today? When labor is to be crucified between two thieves we see the President of the U. S. throwing an armed force across the border into Illinois, and other states, without so much as inquiring whether or not it will be agreeable to the authorities of the state itself. . . .[5]

[4 John James Ingalls (1833–1900), Republican senator from Kansas, 1873–1891. — Ed.]

[5 A reference to President Grover Cleveland's action in sending federal troops to Chicago during the Pullman Strike of 1894, against the wishes of Governor John Peter Altgeld. — Ed.]

When the president of the United States sends an armed force, when we have military all over the United States, when you are organizing military force right in your own city and calling for recruits—What are we to expect for the future, my fellow citizens. Something it will be for us to think about, anyhow. Now, excuse me for speaking about Kansas once more. While I have talked to you about the condition of the laborer, the condition of the farmer, is about the same all over Kansas, and I am specially glad to know the farmers to be in hearty sympathy with the cause of labor. Down in Arkansas City, they are bringing in supplies day by day to supply the men striking on the railroad. And I understand the same thing is done here. A friend of mine who is nominated for senator on the populist ticket had the audacity, my friends, to contribute to the striking laborers of that town. Today he is arraigned by the United States Court and summoned to Topeka and placed on trial for aiding and abetting the strikers against the government of the United States. Think of it!

And I find also that injunctions are already issued against working men to prevent them from expressing an opinion. It is not your right or privilege my fellow citizens, to make proselytes, anymore. I doubt whether you have the right to convert a man to the Christian religion because under the decision of the United States Court you have no right to convince a man to your opinion. You have no right to ask a man to quit work today, no matter what the cause. This is the position that some of the United States Courts have taken today. This is whither we are driven, my fellow citizens.

.    .    .    .    .

Well, I set out to tell you and I got off my subject, what the condition of the farmer is and that is about the same as that of the laborer. His earnings are naught. Add several ciphers together and you will have the sum of his profits this year and last. Take his wheat, which is worth twenty-five cents a bushel, and cost forty cents to raise it. How is he going to come out this year? I will tell you something: did you know that forty three per cent of

the homes of Kansas have already passed into the hands of landlords, who toil not neither do they spin? Nearly half the homes of
Kansas have already passed into the hands of landlords. . . . I
heard a man standing up in the pulpit with a black coat and a
white necktie and discoursing loud and long over the evictions of
the Irish tenants across the water and I will tell you, we have got
in the State of Kansas 10,000 people who are made homeless
every year by the foreclosure of mortgages and this has been
going on for several years.

. . . One of the means of contraction of the currency is the
holding of money in the bank's vaults. Why does the banker keep
it in the bank vaults? Because he is afraid to loan it to you and
me, because we may not pay it back. Why don't you put your
money in the bank? You say you are afraid the bank will break,
and so it is tweedle-dum and tweedle-dee. I don't blame either of
you because the conditions are the same, you are both "skeered."

.   .   .   .   .

I will tell you a little personal experience. . . . We were engaged in the butter and egg business, as some of my friends, the
enemy on the other side, said I was a butter and egg peddler
down in Wichita, and I plead guilty. We had these men employed. Now, we wanted to store some butter and eggs this summer for winter sale and we needed some money and went to a
banker and said we expect you to furnish us some money. They
said, "How much do you want?" We said, "We don't know, several thousand dollars." They said, "Go ahead with your business
and we will furnish you all the money you want." Then we went
to work and bought a car load of eggs, brought it to Kansas City
and put it in cold storage and . . . took our certificates of deposit
and went down to the bank and borrowed money on it and
bought another car load, and so on, *ad infinitum* I believe is what
we say. We were going on very satisfactorily until one day the
cashier of the bank said to us, "We will have to shut down on
you and can't let you have any more money." We asked him why,
he said because one of the banks failed and there is a run now,

and so we have to keep our money to meet our customers' demands. I says don't you know you promised us the money? They said yes, but it will ruin our business. Now, I don't blame the bank. I do not blame those gentlemen, that was the circumstance, and by the merest skin of our teeth, by the hardest kinds of shuffle we managed to tide ourselves over and we are in pretty good condition yet, thank you, and still doing business at the old stand. . . .

Still, under the present system you are tying up money in the vaults of the banks all the time. I won't take your time to discuss the question of increase of currency this evening, except to say that we are wanting silver money. . . . You have got a Greenback Dollar, the best money under the shining sun. Then you say, "What under the name of the shining sun are you roaring so about silver for?" I will tell you, my friends, I believe under free coinage of silver, I believe we will have work for those idle men, the contingent of the industrial army, at least of that portion in Colorado. They will find work digging the silver from the hills and coining it into money. It is not because silver is the ideal money, not because it is the best money. We are in the condition of the old maid now—excuse me, ladies, I meant the old maiden lady—who went out into the field to pray for a husband, and a big owl in a tree said, "Who, who," and she exclaimed, "Any body, Lord, so it is a man." Now, we say, "Anything, Lord, so it is enough to increase the amount in circulation." . . . If I had time I would turn here and confirm what I say by extracts from speeches of Senator Plumb[6] and other celebrated Republicans and I presume we can take it for granted, we do not have money enough in circulation. That is one trouble under which we are suffering today. And the trouble is, that we have been thinking only of the multitude, and we have had too little care for individual citizens. . . . We look at the city in a mass and we forget the individual sufferer. But these have gone on multiplying in Kansas until today one tenth of the entire population of the United States is brought face to face with poverty. Six million of people in this

[6 Preston B. Plumb (1837–1891), Republican senator from Kansas, 1877–1891. — Ed.]

land of plenty are today suffering for bread. And I ask you again, is it any wonder that there are common wealers? Is it any wonder that there are anarchists, and I want to say further, we are traveling in the line of past history, we are in the same condition as a nation as that [of] ancient Rome, when the currency of the people was contracted. . . . Remember when the currency contracts, your debts remain the same, only they get bigger, that is the law. A few years ago, a bushel of wheat would pay a dollar of your mortgage. Today it takes four bushel. . . .

.    .    .    .    .

Oh, relief will come. Yes, I have faith to believe that it will come. I will tell you my fellow citizens I believe it will come because I believe that beneath this serene and placid sleep of centuries sits human liberty. You ask me how? You ask me why? For my reason, if it must be given, I must reply, a just God sits on the throne in Heaven. So, relief will come, I believe this inspiration will be found in every heart. I believe the effort will be made by the people. Already great labor organizations are uniting themselves for battle, welded together in conduct and purpose and action. When the human soul becomes imbued with a great principal like that, when we are unified and stand together, then we become Godlike, and the might of the people rises like the tiny zephyr, to the impetuous whirlwind, like the murmuring rills of the surging torrent. Our path will be conflict, but it will also be conquest. It must be so! The demands of the people will be heard. They must be heard.

It seems to me, my friends, that the dead sea of civilization grows wider year by year. That the yawning gulf between Dives and Lazarus, becomes more and more impassible. On one side Gould and Vanderbilt—I have a list here of eighteen names ranging in wealth from twenty to a hundred and twenty five millions of dollars, and yet, I say to you my fellow citizens that no man in America ever had the genius or brain to earn a million dollars honestly. He can't do it while the sun shines.

Think of a man working at a dollar a day earning a million

dollars! How long do you suppose it would take him?

I say we have the Goulds and Vanderbilts and Rockefellers[7] on the one side—why, Vanderbilt once deposited $50,000,000 of government bonds. How much money was that? The interest amounted to $5000. About $3.50 a minute, fifty cents every time the clock ticked. . . .

. . . I simply say these men are arrayed on the one hand, and on the other, the industrial army, every man of which like the Saviour has not where to lay his head. 30,000 tenants annually ejected in New York City. One tenth of all who die buried in the potter's field. 10,000 farmers made homeless in Kansas every year, and ten shelterless girls struggling in vain for every position of employment that is vacant in your cities for one who is successful in obtaining work. What becomes of the other nine? Those who fail—mark my words!—are driven to seek shelter with her whose ways take hold of hell, and lead to the chambers of death. Yet, these are the conditions which prevail in our civilization and men are saying that this is the best government under the shining sun. It was in its original conception, and God forbid that it may go further astray than it has done at the present time. The great throbbing centers of civilization seem to me to be dead to the instincts of humanity and alike dead to the teachings of the man of Bethlehem. The night of despair seems to me to be upon us. Call me calamity howler if you will. I wish I had the voice and pen and reputation of Jeremiah that I might howl Calamity until the people all over this broad land should hear me. It seems to me that the night of despair is really at hand. And I ask you who is to be responsible for our civil government, if you please, by which we are turned into beasts by conditions that the government might and should prevent? The golden age of the 19th century! . . .

.    .    .    .    .

. . . The People's party has stepped into the breach between the

[7 The references are to Jay Gould (1836–1892), Cornelius Vanderbilt (1843–1899), and John Davison Rockefeller (1839–1937), all contemporary millionaires. — Ed.]

classes to demand justice for the poor as well as to the rich and for every man. The machinery of government has been arrayed against us. It seems to me that the Courts and Judges of this country have become the mere tools and vassals and jumping-jacks of the great corporations that pull the string while the courts and judges dance. That is the way it seems to me. So, these great corporations are forces against which we are to contend but I am willing, if you are willing, to place truth against the world. Truth is mighty and it will prevail.

We have come here today pleading for truth against error. Not for the individual. Men are nothing in a great contest of the people like this. It matters not who is the leader so that all the people stand together united for the great principles of humanity.

Now, my fellow citizens, I am about to close. I want to say to you in conclusion that I am with this people's party because I believe and have believed that it is feeling its way toward the sunlight of freedom for the toiling masses of this country and of other lands. I am with the people's party because it is feeling its way along the high walls of prejudice which shut out the sunlight of freedom, shut out relief from the outstretched hand of poverty. I am with the people's party because it aims at the defense and rescue of ten thousand children who die every year in this country from lack of food. I am with the people's party because it pleads for the 57,000 homeless children in the United States. I am with the People's party because it takes the side of 3,000,000 men who are out of employment at this very time and who in consequence are driven to desperation and crime. These, mark my friends, are only a few of the many reasons why the peoples' side in this great battle is the right side; and I believe that if there is a God in heaven, as I do believe, that he will hear the cry of his suffering children and the giant Despair will yet be slain by the great uprising of this nation. With these great principles of our common cause, we are going forth. We will be fearless as we go forth and we will be able to conquer. We will be able to subdue kingdoms and in time will stop the mouths of liars, out of weakness we will be made strong. We shall wax valiant in fight, and when November comes will put to flight the armies of the aliens. I thank you.

**COXEY'S ARMY**

*In the depression year of 1894 "General" Jacob S. Coxey of Massilon, Ohio, led the "Army of The Commonweal of Christ," the most celebrated among a number of ragged "industrial armies" of the unemployed, who marched on Washington to petition for redress of grievances. His "army" was not an official agency of the People's party, but Coxey was a Populist, drew the support of Populists, and presented an essentially Populist program that foretokened the relief and "pump-priming" policies of the New Deal. The movement reached a preposterous climax when Coxey was arrested for "walking on the grass" of the Capitol grounds. His protest was prepared for some such contingency, but Coxey was not allowed to deliver it. His program of inflation and public works is embodied in the two bills introduced in the House of Representatives.*


–19–

# ADDRESS OF PROTEST
## by Jacob S. Coxey

The Constitution of the United States guarantees to all citizens the right to peaceably assemble and petition for redress of grievances, and furthermore declares that the right of free speech shall not be abridged.

We stand here to-day to test these guaranties of our Constitution. We choose this place of assemblage because it is the property of the people, and if it be true that the right of the people to peacefully assemble upon their own premises and utter their petitions has been abridged by the passage of laws in direct violation

SOURCE: *Congressional Record,* 53d Cong., 2d Sess., p. 4512 (May 9, 1894).

of the Constitution, we are here to draw the eyes of the entire nation to this shameful fact. Here rather than at any other spot upon the continent it is fitting that we should come to mourn over our dead liberties and by our protest arouse the imperiled nation to such action as shall rescue the Constitution and resurrect our liberties.

Upon these steps where we stand has been spread a carpet for the royal feet of a foreign princess, the cost of whose lavish entertainment was taken from the public Treasury without the consent or the approval of the people. Up these steps the lobbyists of trusts and corporations have passed unchallenged on their way to committee rooms, access to which we, the representatives of the toiling wealth-producers, have been denied. We stand here to-day in behalf of millions of toilers whose petitions have been buried in committee rooms, whose prayers have been unresponded to, and whose opportunities for honest, remunerative, productive labor have been taken from them by unjust legislation, which protects idlers, speculators, and gamblers: we come to remind the Congress here assembled of the declaration of a United States Senator, "that for a quarter of a century the rich have been growing richer, the poor poorer, and that by the close of the present century the middle class will have disappeared as the struggle for existence becomes fierce and relentless."

We stand here to remind Congress of its promise of returning prosperity should the Sherman act be repealed. We stand here to declare by our march of over 400 miles through difficulties and distress, a march unstained by even the slightest act which would bring the blush of shame to any, that we are law-abiding citizens, and as men our actions speak louder than words. We are here to petition for legislation which will furnish employment for every man able and willing to work; for legislation which will bring universal prosperity and emancipate our beloved country from financial bondage to the descendants of King George. We have come to the only source which is competent to aid the people in their day of dire distress. We are here to tell our Representatives, who hold their seats by grace of our ballots, that the struggle for existence has become too fierce and relentless. We come and throw up our defenseless hands, and say, help, or we and our loved ones must perish. We are engaged in a bitter and cruel war with the enemies of all mankind—a war with hunger, wretchedness, and despair, and we ask Congress to heed our petitions and issue for the nation's good a sufficient volume of the same kind of money which carried the country through one awful war and saved the life of the nation.

In the name of justice, through whose impartial administration only the present civilization can be maintained and perpetuated, by the powers of the Constitution of our country upon which the liberties of the people must depend, and in the name of the commonweal of Christ, whose representatives we are, we enter a most solemn and earnest protest against this unnecessary and cruel usurpation and tyranny, and this enforced subjugation of the rights and privileges of American citizenship. We have assembled here in violation of no just laws to enjoy the privileges of every American citizen. We are now under the shadow of the Capitol of this great nation, and in the presence of our national legislators are refused that dearly bought privilege, and by force of arbitrary power prevented from carrying out the desire of our hearts which is plainly granted under the great magna-charta of our national liberties.

We have come here through toil and weary marches, through storms and tempests, over mountains, and amid the trials of poverty and distress, to lay our grievances at the doors of our National Legislature and ask them in the name of Him whose banners we bear, in the name of Him who plead for the poor and the oppressed, that they should heed the voice of despair and distress that is now coming up from every section of our country, that they should consider the conditions of the starving unemployed of our land, and enact such laws as will give them employment, bring happier conditions to the people, and the smile of contentment to our citizens.

Coming as we do with peace and good will to men, we shall submit to these laws, unjust as they are, and obey this mandate of authority of might which overrides and outrages the law of right.

In doing so, we appeal to every peace-loving citizen, every liberty-loving man or woman, every one in whose breast the fires of patriotism and love of country have not died out, to assist us in our efforts toward better laws and general benefits.

J. S. COXEY
*Commander of the Commonweal of Christ*

—20—

# COXEY'S BILLS

*THE GOOD ROADS BILL*

53RD CONGRESS, 2D SESSION, H. R. 7438, JUNE 12, 1894.

A bill to provide for the improvement of public roads, and for other purposes.

Be it enacted by the Senate and the House of Representatives of the United States of America in Congress assembled, That the Secretary of the Treasury of the United States is hereby authorized and instructed to have engraved and have printed, immediately after the passage of this bill, five hundred millions of dollars of Treasury notes, a legal tender for all debts, public and private, said notes to be in denominations of one, two, five, and ten dollars, and to be placed in a fund to be known as the "general county-road fund system of the United States," and to be expended solely for said purpose.

Sec. 2. That it shall be the duty of the Secretary of War to take charge of the construction of the said general county-road system of the United States, and said construction to commence as soon as the Secretary of Treasury shall inform the Secretary of War that the said fund is available, which shall not be later than

SOURCE: Jacob S. Coxey, *Cause and Cure*, II : 2, 5–6. The text is the form in which they were introduced in the House of Representatives, somewhat later than their introduction in the Senate by Senator Peffer.

sixty days from and after the passage of this bill, when it shall be the duty of the Secretary of War to inaugurate the work and expend the sum of twenty millions of dollars per month pro rata with the number of miles of road in each State and Territory in the United States.

Sec. 3. That all labor other than that of the office of the Secretary of War, "whose compensations are already fixed by law," shall be paid by the day, and that the rate be not less than one dollar and fifty cents per day for common labor and three dollars and fifty cents for team and labor, and that eight hours per day shall constitute a day's labor under the provisions of this bill, and that all citizens of the United States making application to labor shall be employed.

## THE NON-INTEREST-BEARING BOND BILL

53RD CONGRESS, 2D SESSION, H. R. 7463, JUNE 15, 1894.

A bill to provide for public improvements and employment of the citizens of the United States.

Be it enacted by the Senate and House of Representatives of the United States of America in Congress assembled, That whenever any State, Territory, county, township, municipality, or incorporated town or village deem it necessary to make any public improvements they shall deposit with the Secretary of the Treasury of the United States a non-interest-bearing twenty-five-year bond, not to exceed one-half of the assessed valuation of the property in said State, Territory, county, township, municipality, or incorporated town or village, and said bond to be retired at the rate of four per centum per annum.

Sec. 2. That whenever the foregoing section of this act has been complied with it shall be mandatory upon the Secretary of the Treasury of the United States to have engraved and printed Treasury notes in the denominations of one, two, five and ten dollars each, which shall be a full legal tender for all debts, public and private, to the face value of said bond and deliver to said State, Territory, county, township, municipality, or incorporated town or village ninety-nine per centum of said notes, and retain one per centum for expense of engraving and printing same.

Sec. 3. That after the passage of this act it shall be compulsory upon every incorporated town or village, municipality, township, county, State or Territory to give employment to any idle man applying for work, and that the rate be not less than one dollar and fifty cents per day for common labor and three dollars and fifty cents per day for team and labor, and that eight hours per day shall constitute a day's labor under the provisions of this act.

## TWO POPULIST PROCLAMATIONS

*Davis H. Waite was Populist governor of Colorado, elected in 1892 for a single term. In the "Tramp Circular," which was circulated to the boards of police commissioners in his state, Governor Lewelling of Kansas, previously introduced, defended the unemployed itinerants who came to symbolize the degradation of the masses in Populist rhetoric. "Bloody Bridles" was Waite's nickname, derived from his statement "It is better, infinitely better, that blood should flow to the horses' bridles rather than our national liberties should be destroyed." He gave free rein to his headstrong opinions in the "Thanksgiving Proclamation."*

–21–

# THE TRAMP CIRCULAR
## by Lorenzo Dow Lewelling

In the reign of Elizabeth, the highways were filled with the throngs of the unemployed poor, who were made to "move on," and were sometimes brutally whipped, sometimes summarily hanged, as "sturdy vagrants" or "incorrigible vagabonds." In France, just previous to the revolution, the punishment of being poor and out of work was, for the first offense, a term of years in the galleys, for the second offense, the galleys for life. In this country, the monopoly of labor saving machinery and its devotion to selfish instead of social use, have rendered more and more human beings superfluous, until we have a standing army of the unemployed numbering even in the most prosperous times not less than one million able bodied men; yet, until recently it was the prevailing notion, as it is yet the notion of all but the workpeople themselves and those of other classes given to thinking,

SOURCE: Topeka *Daily Capital,* December 5, 1893. Kansas State Historical Society.

166

and whosoever, being able bodied and willing to work can always find work to do, and section 571 of the general statutes of 1889 is a disgraceful reminder how savage even in Kansas has been our treatment of the most unhappy of our human brothers.

The man out of work and penniless is, by this legislation, classed with "confidence men." Under this statute and city ordinances of similar import, thousands of men, guilty of no crime but poverty, intent upon no crime but that of seeking employment, have languished in the city prisons of Kansas or performed unrequited toil on "rock piles" as municipal slaves, because ignorance of economic conditions had made us cruel. The victims have been the poor and humble for whom police courts are courts of last resort—they can not give bond and appeal. They have been unheeded and uncared for by the busy world which wastes no time visiting prisoners in jail. They have been too poor to litigate with their oppressors, and thus no voice from this underworld of human woe has ever reached the ear of the appellate court, because it was nobody's business to be his brother's keeper.

But those who sit in the seats of power are bound by the highest obligation to especially regard the cause of the oppressed and helpless poor. The first duty of the government is to the weak. Power becomes fiendish if it be not the protector and sure reliance of the friendless, to whose complaints all other ears are dull. It is my duty "to see that the laws are faithfully executed," and among those laws is the constitutional provision that no instrumentality of the state "shall deny to any person within its jurisdiction the equal protection of the laws." And who needs to be told that equal protection of the laws does not prevail where this inhuman vagrancy law is enforced? It separates men into two distinct classes, differentiated as those who are penniless and those who are not, and declare the former criminals. Only the latter are entitled to the liberty guaranteed by the constitution. To be found in a city "without some visible means of support or some legitimate business," is the involuntary condition of some millions at this moment, and we proceed to punish them for being victims of conditions which we, as a people, have forced upon them.

I have noticed in police court reports that "sleeping in a box car" is among the varieties of this heinous crime of being poor. Some police judges have usurped a sovereign power not permitted the highest functionaries of the states or of the nation, and victims of the industrial conditions have been peremptorily "ordered to leave town."

The right to go freely from place to place in search of employment, or even in obedience of a mere whim, is part of that personal liberty guaranteed by the Constitution of the United States to every human being on American soil. If voluntary idleness is not forbidden; if a Diogenes prefer poverty; if a Columbus choose hunger and the discovery of a new race, rather than seek personal comfort by engaging in "some legitimate business," I am aware of no power in the legislature or in city councils to deny him the right to seek happiness in his own way, so long as he harms no other, rich or poor; but let simple poverty cease to be a crime.

In some cities it is provided by ordinance that if police court fines are not paid or secured the culprit shall be compelled to work out the amount as a municipal slave; and "rock piles" and "bull pens" are provided for the enforcement of these ordinances. And so it appears that this slavery is not imposed as a punishment, but solely as a means of collecting a debt.

Such city ordinances are in flagrant violation of constitutional prohibition. The "rock-pile" and the "bull pen" have only been used in degrading the friendless and poor, and are relics of the departed auction-block era cease to disgrace the cities of Kansas.

And let the dawn of Christmas day find the "rock-pile," the "bull-pen" and the crime of being homeless and poor, obsolete in all the cities of Kansas governed by the metropolitan police act.

It is confidentially expected that their own regard for constitutional liberty and their human impulses will induce police commissioners to carry out the spirit as well as the letter of the foregoing suggestions.

L. D. LEWELLING
Governor

–22–

# THANKSGIVING PROCLAMATION
## by Davis H. Waite

WHEREAS, the President of the United States has designated Thursday, the 30th of the present month, as a day of thanksgiving and praise, I, Davis H. Waite, Governor of Colorado, do hereby appoint the same day as a day of thanksgiving for this State, and recommend to the good people thereof that they assemble on that day and render unto Almighty God praise and prayer for His blessings. No war, famine or pestilence has vexed the land during the past year, and the earth has yielded bountifully of her increase. But in this thanksgiving I invoke the people of Colorado to remember especially their "brethren in bonds"—the forty-five thousand miners of silver, who in a land of boundless natural resources, have been deprived of employment by tyranny and by corrupt and unconstitutional legislation, and, in many cases, have been compelled to abandon their homes;—the agriculturists of our State, whose crops cannot be marketed for the cost of production, and who find, as their products decrease in price, the value of the notes and mortgages which represent their indebtedness correspondingly increase; and the real estate owners and business men of Colorado, who, under a system of trust deeds and attachment laws, the most infamous since the days of Caligula, find their property, when incumbered, often sacrificed at a tithe of its value, and all this injustice is perpetrated to increase the inordinate riches of extortioners whose avarice and greed, aided by corrupt legislation, have grasped in the hands of thirty thousand people more than half of all the wealth in the United States, and is fast reducing to pauperism the common people of the world.

I implore the citizens of Colorado, on this day of prayer and

SOURCE: Reprinted from Joseph Columbus Manning, *Fadeout of Populism: Presenting, in Connection, the Political Combat Between the Pot and the Kettle* (New York: T. A. Hebbons, 1928), pp. 134–135.

praise, most fervently to petition Almighty God that He will arouse the public sentiment to a sense of the dangers which threaten not only our State and Nation, but civilization itself; and that in His mercy He will so order it, that "this government of the people, by the people, and for the people, may not perish from the earth."

Done at the Capitol, Denver, Colorado, Nov. 8, 1893.

DAVIS H. WAITE

Governor of Colorado

Attest:

(SEAL)                                            NELSON O. MCCLEES
                                                 Secy. of State

## A CONTEMPORARY ANALYSIS

*Frederick Emory Haynes, economist and historian, became an assist-*
*ant in economics at Harvard in 1896, the year in which he wrote this*
*piece, one of the best contemporary analyses of the Populist move-*
*ment. In his later career Haynes further pursued his interest in the*
*subject, producing a study of third-party movements, including Popu-*
*lism, and a biography of James Baird Weaver.*

## –23–
# THE NEW SECTIONALISM
## by Frederick Emory Haynes

At the present time we are hearing a good deal of a "new sectionalism" which is said to be arraying the West and South against
the East. The line of division between the sections is not definite:
an area of debatable ground is claimed by both sides. The states
beyond the Mississippi show most clearly the characteristics of
the new sectionalism. The South has been affected by local
peculiarities—notably by the presence of a large negro population—but its general attitude has been one of sympathy and co-
operation with the West. The states between the Mississippi, the
Ohio, and the Great Lakes form the debatable region. The East,
which is the chief object of Western and Southern hostility, includes the New England and Middle states, with New York as a
centre. Kansas, Nebraska, the Dakotas, Colorado, and Nevada
have been most distinctly committed to the new doctrines. These
states have been strongholds of the Populists. They have furnished most of the recruits for the industrial armies. They have

SOURCE: Frederick Emory Haynes, "The New Sectionalism," *Quarterly*
*Journal of Economics,* X (April 1896), 269–270, 280–295.

contributed the principal support to the demand for the free coinage of silver. In the South, Alabama and South Carolina, and more lately North Carolina, have been the chief seats of the movement. The new sectionalism, therefore, represents a cleavage among the states which divides the older and wealthier states of the East from the younger, less populous, and less wealthy states of the West and South. A line drawn from the source of the Mississippi to its junction with the Ohio, thence up the Ohio to the south-west corner of Pennsylvania, and along the southern boundary of Pennsylvania and of Maryland to the Atlantic, marks in a general way the boundary between the sections. Sixteen states, with a population of 32 millions, comprise the East, and twenty-eight states, with a population of 30 millions, the West and South—an almost equal division of the people between the sections. Such an estimate gives to the East the debatable ground contained in the five Central states. With the threefold division we should have the following: the East with eleven states and a population of over 18 millions; the doubtful states, five in number and with over 13 million people; and the West and South with twenty-eight states and 30 millions.

The chief characteristics of this new sectionalism have been: hostility to railways; belief in an irredeemable paper money issued by the federal government; demand for the free coinage of silver at a ratio of 16 to 1; hostility to banks of all kinds; opposition to the issue of bonds; and demand for an income tax to force the holders of great wealth to contribute, according to their ability, to the needs of the government. The attitude of the West and South has been made clear in their support of the income tax, and in their defeat of all the efforts of the present administration to obtain the consent of Congress to the issue of bonds. The chaotic condition of politics during recent years is chiefly explicable as a result of the disturbing effect of the new sectionalism. The purpose of this paper is to describe the new movement, to estimate its real strength, and to make some forecast as to its future.[1]

.    .    .    .    .

[1 A lengthy discussion of the rise of Populism and the evidences of sectionalism within the major parties has been omitted. — Ed.]

An examination of these figures[2] shows that in the Western states there is a majority for free coinage of silver; that, as represented in the Senate, these states were opposed two to one to the repeal of the silver purchase clause of the Sherman act; that they are unanimous for the levying of an income tax; and that they are against the issue of gold bonds more than five to one. The Southern states are even more strongly in favor of free coinage than the Western, slightly more opposed to repeal, almost unanimous for the income tax, and nearly three to one against gold bonds. The Central states have a small majority against free coinage, unanimously supported repeal, are almost unanimous for an income tax, and are apposed to the issue of gold bonds, though less strongly opposed than the West and the South. In the Eastern states we find almost complete unanimity against free coinage, in favor of repeal, great opposition to an income tax, and strong support of gold bonds. The sectional division is clear. The Eastern states are opposed to the West and South, while the Central states occupy an intermediate position. The Eastern states cast but one vote for free coinage in 1893, this one vote being cast by Congressman Sibley, of Pennsylvania, before referred to as a silver candidate for the Presidency. The same state gave the only Eastern vote against repeal. On the other hand, the West and South are practically unanimous for an income tax; while the East cast only five votes in its favor—three from Pennsylvania, one from Massachusetts, and one from Connecticut. The central states agree with the West and South in this respect as well as in regard to the issue of gold bonds, while as to free coinage and repeal they take sides with the East. The less thickly settled parts of the country favor free coinage and an income tax, and oppose repeal and gold bonds. The Senate has shown itself more friendly to the ideas of the new sectionalism than has the House, for the equal representation of the states in the former body gives to the less populous states an advantage there. Hence the long struggle in the Senate over repeal, and the repeated passage of free coinage bills by the same body. Wherever there are large centres of population, there is a noticeable hostility to free coinage and an

[2 Figures giving a sectional breakdown of votes in Congress, omitted here. — Ed.]

income tax. The two representatives from California who voted against free coinage in 1893 were from San Francisco and Oakland. The only votes from Missouri against free coinage came from St. Louis, and in Alabama the only opposition came from the district in which Mobile is situated.

Sectional ideas have broken through party lines. Questions of finance and taxation have been supported or opposed not according to party divisions, but according to sectional feeling. Both parties have suffered from these influences. Democrats in the East have voted in opposition to the majority of their party, while Republicans in the West have followed a similar course. In August, 1893, the Democratic vote was almost equally divided for and against free coinage; while a minority of Republicans joined with the Democrats in favor of free coinage. It was significant that one hundred and one Democratic votes were cast for an amendment opposed by a Democratic majority and by a Democratic President. On the vote for repeal in the Senate the Democratic vote was almost equally divided; while twenty-seven Republicans voted for repeal, and eleven against it. The vote on gold bonds in February, 1895, indicated an even more demoralized condition of parties. A majority of Democrats voted against a policy proposed by the Democratic administration, and known to be of the greatest importance to the national credit. The leader of the Republicans also failed to control his party, sixty-one Republicans voting against him.

Such facts as these throw light upon the present and recent demoralization of parties in Congress, and make more clear the reasons why so little has been accomplished by the legislative branch of the government. The questions before Congress have been questions upon which sectional feelings differ widely. The House contains a majority of representatives who favor Eastern views as to free coinage and repeal, while there is at the same time a majority for an income tax and in opposition to gold bonds. The Senate has a majority favorable to free coinage and an income tax, and opposed to repeal. The President is a strong representative of Eastern ideas. Briefly, the House is divided between representatives of the sections, the Senate is largely representative of the West and South, while the President represents the East. With such a balance of powers we need not be surprised that little progress is made. The same situation offers an explanation for the lack of harmony in the Democratic party. That party, relying as it does for much of its strength upon the South, feels very strongly the dividing influences of sectional feeling. The failure of the majority in the House and Senate to follow the lead of the administration is to be accounted for mainly by the growth of sectional differences. The new sectionalism is the key to an understanding of the existing political situation.

Now that we have completed our review of the influences that have been at work in the West and South during recent years, we are in a position to draw some general conclusions as to the nature of these movements. The first feature that attracts attention is the importance of the part played by the government in the development of the life and thought of the West. The free silver demand illustrates this. It comes from the issue of greenbacks by the government during the war. That act gave birth to the greenback party, the parent of the free silver party. Federal legislation, too, in regard to the West has tended to magnify the importance of government in the eyes of the people. From the beginning the government has done everything. The men who settled the West after the war settled on government lands, saw the great land grants to the railroads, saw, above all, the Union Pacific built by a government endowment of a land grant, and by a loan of $50,000,000 for construction. The great extension in the powers and influence of the federal government that began with the outbreak of the Civil War continued in the years following its close, and the development of this tendency has been contemporaneous with the life of the West. The tariff, currency, pensions, public improvements, have all contributed to the same end—the magnifying of the share of the state in the every-day life of the people. The policy of the government has therefore been responsible for the development of special movements and of special demands. It has also been responsible for the development of that attitude on the part of the people which makes them look to the government for everything—an attitude noticeable all over the country, but nowhere so marked as in the West and South.

Another set of influences that have been at work result from the industrial relations of the East and West. The West, as a new country, destitute of capital, has looked to the East for assistance. Its needs, coupled with the prospects of future profits, have led the West to agree to terms rather hard. The inevitable result has been some feeling of injustice when the terms of agreement are insisted upon. The conflict of interest came between the debtor and the creditor. The debtor felt the creditor was too insistent for his pound of flesh. The creditor became suspicious of the integrity of his debtor. Extend this relation from the individual to the community, and introduce a certain not inconsiderable element of corruption, and you have the present relations between the sections, with the recurrent cries of Wall Street conspiracy and the money power. Remember, too, that the beginnings of the indebtedness were made in a period of inflation, while the payments come after the return to a specie basis. Furthermore, the currencies of the world are in a state of confusion as a result of the decline in the price of silver. We need not be surprised at the appearance of a cleavage between the sections whose relations are mainly those of debtor and creditor.

Still another set of influences have been at work. These are the changes in the general economic conditions in the United States, as a result of the remarkable material development of the country. The settlement of the West has not gone on regularly throughout the past thirty years: it has advanced irregularly by fits and starts. A period of extraordinary activity has been followed by one of quiet. Population has gone West too fast, and has had to wait for the general movement to catch up with it. A boom has been followed by a collapse, the collapse usually leading to an outbreak such as the Granger movement. After each collapse there have remained still more lands to occupy, and the process has continued. Now, however, the settlement of the West is reaching a stage where no more lands are left to occupy. A more permanent condition of things is approaching. The West must face the conditions of a settled country. The margin of land is reduced to a minimum. The pinch of this new situation is beginning to be felt, and is making the movements resulting from the crop failures of 1887 to 1890 seem more serious. The same situation makes it probable that the unrest will be more lasting. The co-operation of the South with the West is easily understood, if we remember that the South, as well as the West, has been undergoing a rapid economic development since the end of the Civil War. The existence of slavery down to 1865 retarded the growth of that section, so that its transformation has been exceedingly rapid for the past generation. Manufactures have been established, railroads built, mineral resources developed. The aristocratic system of the Old South under slavery has given place to the democratic industrial system of the New South. The same difficulties, and even greater, have been encountered in the transition that have been experienced in the West. Hence the appearance of similar movements and of similar demands for the removal of grievances.

In the influence of the policy of the federal government, in the industrial relations of the East with the West and South, and in the economic changes that have come from the closer settlement of the West and the industrial transformation of the South, we have the principal influences that have produced the new sectionalism. But, in addition to these industrial and economic conditions, there are other causes that deserve attention. Among the more important of these are the corruption of the old parties, the rise of a new democracy, and the avoidance of live issues by the leading parties. The different political affiliations of the Populists in the West and South illustrate this aspect of the movement. In the West, where the Republicans have been for many years the majority party, the Populists have united usually with the Democrats; while in the South, where the Democrats have been the dominant party, the Populists have fused with the Republicans. In Kansas, Nebraska, and Iowa, strong Republican states ever since the Civil War, we find a fusion of the Democrats and Populists. In Alabama, Texas, and North Carolina, on the other hand, the Republicans and Populists have united. These attempts have had more success in the South than in the West. The greatest victory was won in North Carolina in 1894, when the fusionists carried the legislature, and elected two United States senators. The absorption of the Populists by the Democrats in South Carolina is hardly an exception; for the Tillmanite section of the Democratic party in that state is especially hostile to the older wing, which represents the power and prestige of the ruling aristocracy. The Tillman Democracy is really Populistic in its character: its political affiliations are produced by local conditions. Thus the Populists have been both in the West and in the South hostile to the party in power, responsible as it always must be for the corruption that creeps into a state in which one party has been for a long time dominant.

The rise of a new democracy requires some further comment. It is a very general opinion that we have had a perfectly democratic government ever since 1776. During the early years of the republic the government of the country was in the hands of the aristocracies of Virginia and New England, of which Washington, Jefferson, Madison, and the Adamses were the leaders. While theoretically sovereign, the people at large were "deferential" enough (to use a phrase of Bagehot's) to allow the control of affairs to remain in the hands of their superiors in birth and position. The first serious shock to this situation came with the advent to power in 1830 of Andrew Jackson. The great middle class, so called, the people with no pretension to birth and with no inherited wealth, were gradually roused to a point where they demanded a voice in public affairs. From 1830 to 1865 large classes, before indifferent or unable to exert an influence, began to take an effective part in governmental affairs. All property qualifications, such as existed in the early days of the republic, were swept away. Legally, there was a government of the people. Nevertheless, there remained large classes who were unable to exert any real influence upon politics. The years since 1865 have witnessed the gradual coming to political consciousness of these long silent classes. Economic and industrial changes, the results of popular education, and the growth to maturity of the children of the earlier immigrants from Europe, have all tended in the same direction. A similar development has been going on throughout the world. In the United States there are many indications that the great masses of the people, the working classes, are at length astir, and ready to take a real part in the control of the government. The true explanation of the so-called tidal waves of 1890, 1892, and 1894, is to be found in the participation of these classes, formerly without political influence. They show that the masses are now capable of forming opinions upon questions placed definitely before them, and have learned how to register those opinions at the polls. The passage of an unpopular tariff act was the chief cause of the tidal waves of 1890 and 1892, while in 1894 the people punished the Democrats for the disasters of 1893. The growth of labor organizations and the spread of socialistic agitation point in the same direction. The industrial armies of 1894 and the great strikes of recent years are results of the same cause. The Populist party derives its greatest strength from these very classes, hitherto unrepresented. Its rank and file are made up of the common people, and it is from their participation that it derives its great significance.

From another point of view the avoidance of live issues by the leading parties is responsible for the formation of independent movements. The great party organizations have long survived the issues they were formed to support. They have become mere machines for winning elections and keeping control of the offices. They refuse to risk anything by attempts to deal with pressing questions; and they prevent, by the very strength of their organization, the formation of new agencies. But the problems of the time become ever more insistent of attention. They will not down at the frown of party leaders. They must be dealt with, and machinery must be provided for their solution. The strength of the demand is shown by the many fruitless efforts to discover methods of solving them. In spite of great obstacles, independent organizations are formed to advocate all sorts of remedies. The refusal of the great party organizations and of well-known men to touch the problems has left the task to organizations and leaders incompetent or insufficiently equipped for the work. Because the Republicans and Democrats decline to take up the pressing industrial problems, their solution is left to the Populists. And the Populists will deserve credit if they accomplish nothing more than to lead the great parties and their leaders to face these questions. With all their faults, they have the one great merit of recognizing that industrial problems are the problems of the hour in the United States, as in the rest of the world.

This aspect of the movement leads us to the consideration of the new sectionalism as the American counterpart of socialism in Europe. There occurred in 1892 general elections in the three leading countries of Europe—England, France, and Germany. A significant feature in each of these elections was the important influence exerted by socialism. In Germany the Social-Democracy showed itself the strongest single party, returning sixty members to the Reichstag. In France the socialists first made their appearance as a leading party, with a strong representation in the Chamber of Deputies. In England the influence of the new socialism was first felt at a general election. The growing strength of socialism in Europe is thus an established fact. But in America it is generally supposed to have a slight hold. There is thought to be some natural opposition between socialism and the American spirit. We are said to be comparatively free from the great problems that vex the nations of the Old World. It is assumed that socialism has not yet entered the domain of practical politics. I believe that such a position is untenable, and that Populism or, to use the broader term, the new sectionalism, embodies ideas and demands essentially like those made by the socialists in Europe. In brief, a study of the present situation in this country leads inevitably, it seems to me, to the conclusion that Populism is the American counterpart of socialism in Europe. Socialism has entered the field of practical politics through the appearance of a new sectionalism.

The organized efforts to advance socialism in the United States can be very briefly enumerated. These have been the Socialist Labor party, the Single Tax League, Nationalism, and Christian Socialism. The Socialist Labor party has exercised a considerable influence upon the labor movement. The most important influence, however, has come from the Single Tax, which has been an entering wedge for more radical reforms, and has prepared the way for the adoption of purely socialistic proposals—and this in spite of the strong individualistic attitude of its leaders. Compared with the Single Tax, Nationalism has had a small effect. The relative importance of the two movements cannot be better indicated than by a comparison between the two books, *Progress and Poverty* and *Looking Backward,* which have respectively given rise to the movements. *Progress and Poverty* is an economic work which, after fifteen years of searching criticism, has taken its place upon the shelves of economists. *Looking Backward* is only one among the many Utopias that have been given to the world since the publication of the famous work of Sir Thomas More.

If these formal movements were all the influences at work in the United States in favor of socialism, the history would indeed be very brief; for there is little of a permanent character in any of them. As has been the case with Nationalism, an extremely rapid growth would be followed by as rapid a collapse. Such movements are, like the Coxey Army, mere surface manifestations of a social unrest which is making itself felt along the line of least resistance. In my opinion, the most important indication of the growth of socialism in the United States is the appearance in the West and South of an unconscious socialism in the shape of Populism.

The unconscious socialism of the West and South is essentially a home product, very slightly influenced by foreign movements. It is a product of conditions that have grown up since the Civil War, and appears most strongly in the West and South, because there the conditions have been more favorable to its growth. The characteristic feature of Populism, already pointed out, is the importance that is attached to the action of government. It looks to the government for everything—a feature of socialism wherever found. Populists may claim, as many of them do, that they are not socialists, and that they are opposed to socialism: the fact remains that their attitude is socialistic. Their demands are for government interference for the correction of evils. They believe the government can do better for individuals, in many cases, than the individuals can do for themselves. Furthermore, their proposals are the very ones advocated by socialists. The fact that they are undoubtedly the outgrowth of home conditions does not

change their character. The demand for the government ownership of railroads, due to the abuses of railroad management, is a
leading feature of the Populist platform. The hostility to banks,
and the demand for the abolition of private banks, point in the
same direction. The movement for the enlargement of the currency looks to the extension of governmental functions. Anti-
corporation feeling regards government ownership and control as
a panacea for all abuses. The reclamation of lands owned by
corporations, by speculators, and by aliens, is partial land nation-
alization. The Populist demand for income tax, adopted by the
Democrats, is an item of importance in German and English
socialistic programmes. The Coxey movement was merely one
form of the demand for the exercise of government activity, applied to the most pressing need of the moment—work for the
unemployed. The Populists believe (in the words of their platform of 1892) "that the powers of government—in other words,
of the people—should be expanded as rapidly and as far as the
good sense of an intelligent people and the teachings of experience shall justify, to the end that oppression, injustice, and poverty shall eventually cease in the land."

Whatever may be the course of socialistic development in the
United States in the future, and whether or no the Populist
movement proves more permanent than those which it has succeeded, the signs are not wanting that the lines are now being
drawn here, as elsewhere, in the conflict for economic emancipation which will fill the twentieth century, as the struggle for political freedom has filled the nineteenth. Every struggle between
capital and labor leaves the lines more sharply drawn; and every
severe outbreak, such as that of 1894, brings home to thoughtful
persons the conclusion that the pressing questions of the day are
industrial. Our statesmen and our men of leisure and education
must face these problems, and undertake their solution. The tariff
must give way to questions connected with transportation, with
monopolies, with the relations of employer and employed, and
the reform of taxation in such manner that accumulated wealth
may pay its share of the expenses of government. A proper understanding of Populism, as a movement with historical founda-

tions and allied to similar movements in other countries, will contribute to the desired end.

Finally, the question arises as to whether the new sectionalism is to be permanent, and what is to be its influence in our national life? I trust that I have made clear that it represents something more than the mere vagary of disordered and discontented minds, that it has its roots in the past, and that it has arisen because of real grievances. The West and South have passed through a period of rapid economic development, and in the course of this development certain evils have appeared. As a result, we have complaints and recriminations. The West and South are the debtors of the East, and regard that section as grasping and avaricious. The East, having suffered frequent loss, naturally looks at the West and South as debtors anxious to avoid payment of just debts. Hence arises the Western idea of the money power, in which England and the East are represented as grasping usurers, bent on the enslavement of the world. Contrasted with this idea is the equally mistaken Eastern view of the West and South as filled with persons possessed of wild and fanatical ideas on industry and government. The hope of the future lies in a clear understanding of one section by the other, and a cordial union between them for the reform of existing abuses. Under such a union Populism will disappear, and sectionalism will cease to disturb our politics. By such a course alone can the new sectionalism pass away peacefully, leaving none of the scars and burdens still remaining to us from the great conflict by which the older sectionalism of North and South was destroyed.

# V

# TWO OPPOSITION VIEWS

---

**LABOR'S DISSOCIATION**
*Although the Knights of Labor collaborated with the Alliances and the People's party, that organization was in decline. Gompers, president of the rising American Federation of Labor, followed a policy of disengagement in politics except, as he once put it, to reward labor's friends and punish its enemies. Here he explains why the federation was making no endorsement in the presidential campaign of 1892.*

## –24–

## ORGANIZED LABOR IN THE CAMPAIGN

### by Samuel Gompers

It is with some trepidation that I begin writing this article, for while it may be true that I have as good opportunities as any other man in the country of conjecturing the probable action of the workingmen of America, and particularly those affiliated with the American Federation of Labor in the coming Presidential campaign, I am certain that my article will please but very few. I have had to say and write some things in my more than twenty-five years' connection with the labor movement for which I have incurred the displeasure of some very earnest, though, in my opinion, mistaken men who differ with our movement and myself, as one of its representatives, as to methods, but not as to the ultimate end and aim of the social, economic and political struggle of the toiling masses.

SOURCE: Samuel Gompers, "Organized Labor in the Campaign," *North American Review*, CLV (July 1892), 91–96.

I feel sure that this production will in nowise tend to lessen this difference of opinion, but if it will tend to give a clearer understanding to a number of friends and foes as to what the trade unions really are; that their methods are within the range of reason; that their work is being crowned with success as far as conditions will permit; that they are the natural organization of the wage-earning masses; and that it is their mission to secure the amelioration as well as the emancipation of labor—then I shall feel my conscience eased, and be amply rewarded, in venturing to write an article upon the probable action of the American Federation of Labor in the coming Presidential campaign.

Why should its attitude be different in the coming Presidential campaign from what it has been in the past? In what way does the coming campaign differ from those of 1876, 1880, 1884 or 1888? Is there any particular principle involved in the party issues in which the wage-workers have a deep or keen interest? There is indeed none.

Was there any real improvement or deterioration in the condition of the working people, as a result of the changes, when Mr. Cleveland succeeded the late Mr. Arthur, or when Mr. Harrison succeeded Mr. Cleveland? I think not, and I feel satisfied that I will not lose my reputation as a "prophet" if I venture to predict that, so far as the wage-workers are concerned, it will matter little if President Harrison or some other Republican on the one side, or any member of the Democratic party on the other, should be elected to succeed the present incumbent, or even should the People's Party succeed (though I doubt that they even entertain the belief that they will succeed) in electing their candidate to the Presidency.

The members of the organizations affiliated with the Federation will no doubt, in a large measure, as citizens, vote for the candidate of the party of their own political predilections. But the number is ever on the increase who disenthral themselves from partisan voting and exercise their franchise to reward or chastise those parties and candidates, that deserve either their friendship or resentment. With us it is not a question of parties or men; it is a question of measures.

That there exists a feeling of dissatisfaction with, and bitter antagonism to, both the Republican and Democratic parties is not to be gainsaid. Broken promises to labor, insincere, halfhearted support and even antagonism of legislation in the interest of the toilers on the one hand, and the alacrity and devotion with which the interests of the corporations and the wealth-possessing class are nurtured, protected and advanced on the other, have had their effect, and the result is that many toilers have forever severed their connection with the old parties. That the number will continue to grow larger year by year I have not the slightest doubt. To me this party defection of the wageworkers is one of the signs of the dawn of a healthier public opinion, a sturdier manhood and independence, and a promise to maintain the liberties that the people now enjoy, as well as to ever struggle on to attain that happy goal towards which, throughout its entire history, the human family have been perpetually pushing forward.

But in leaving the old parties, to whom, to what shall former Democratic or Republican workmen turn? To the People's Party? Are such changes and improvements promised there that the workers can with any degree of assurance throw in their political fortunes with that party? Of course, acting upon the principle "of all evils choose the least," they will more generally coöperate with the People's Party than with any similar party heretofore gracing the Presidential political arena.

As a matter of fact, however, to support the People's Party under the belief that it is a *labor* party is to act under misapprehension. It is not and cannot, in the nature of its make-up, be a labor party, or even one in which the wageworkers will find their haven. Composed, as the People's Party is, mainly of *employing* farmers without any regard to the interests of the *employed* farmers of the country districts or the mechanics and laborers of the industrial centres, there must of necessity be a divergence of purposes, methods, and interests.

In speaking thus frankly of the composition of the People's Party there is no desire to belittle the efforts of its members, or even to withhold the sympathy due them in their agitation to remedy the wrongs which they suffer from corporate power and avarice; on the contrary, the fullest measure of sympathy and all possible encouragement should and will be given them; for they are doing excellent work in directing public attention to the dangers which threaten the body politic of the republic. But, returning to the consideration of the entire coöperation or amalgamation of the wage-workers' organizations with the People's Party, I am persuaded that all who are more than superficial observers, or who are keen students of the past struggles of the proletariat of all countries, will with one accord unite in declaring the union impossible, because it is unnatural. Let me add that, before there can be any hope of the unification of labor's forces of the field, farm, factory, and workshop, the people who work on and in them for wages must be organized to protect *their* interests against those who pay them wages for that work.

Then, if as an organization, the American Federation of Labor will take no official part in the coming Presidential campaign of a partizan character, it may, with a fair degree of reason, be asked what we will do? Some have asked whether we will have a candidate of our own in the field. I can answer both by saying that, apart from the acts already referred to above, we shall maintain as a body a masterly inactivity. As organized trade-unionists, we have had some experience with a Presidential candidate, and in campaigns of our own, the lessons of which have not been forgotten by us.

It may not be generally known that in 1872 the organized workingmen of the country placed a candidate in nomination for the Presidency of the United States. The National Labor Union, the immediate predecessor and parent of the Federation, at its convention of that year, held in Columbus, O., selected the late David Davis, of Illinois, as its standard bearer. So far as the nomination was concerned, quite a degree of success was attained. A candidate was placed in the field, but it was at the cost of the life of the organization. Another convention of the National Labor Union was never held after that. Indeed, so great was the reaction among the organized workingmen against this departure, and so thoroughly had they lost confidence in a general organization of a national character, that, despite all efforts to induce them to be represented in a national convention, defeat and disappointment were the result until 1881, when the Federation was called into existence.

Since its organization the American Federation of Labor has kept in mind two facts: first, the lamentable experience of its predecessor; and second, that, in the struggle for improved conditions and emancipation for the toilers, what is wanted is the organization of the wage-workers, not on "party" lines, but on the lines of their class interests.

As an organization, the American Federation of Labor is not in harmony either with the existing or projected political parties. So deep-seated is the conviction in this matter that, long ago, it was decided to hold the conventions of the Federation *after* the elections. Thus freed from party bias and campaign crimination, these gatherings have been in a position to declare for general principles, and to judge impartially upon the merits or demerits of each party, holding each to an accountability for its perfidy to the promises made to the working people, and at the same time keeping clear and distinct the economic character of the organization. By our non-political partisan character as an organization, we tacitly declare that political liberty with economic independence is illusory and deceptive, and that only in so far as we gain economic independence can our political liberty become tangible and important. This may sound like political heresy, but it is economic truth.

As time goes on we discern that the organized workingmen place less reliance upon the help offered by others, and it is a spark upon the altar of progress that they have learned to more firmly depend upon their own efforts to secure those changes and improvements which are theirs by right.

Of course it must not be imagined that we have no interest in the political affairs of our country; on the contrary, we believe that it is our mission to gather the vast numbers of the wealth-producers, agricultural, industrial, and commercial, into a grand army of organized labor, and, by our struggles for improved conditions and emancipation, instil into the minds of the workers a keener appreciation of their true position in society and of their economic, political and social duties and rights as citizens and workers. Every advantage gained in the economic condition of the wage-workers must necessarily have its political and social effect, not only upon themselves but upon the whole people. Hence for the present, at least, nearly all our efforts are concentrated upon the field as indicated above.

Many may find fault in our refraining from directly entering the political arena by the nomination of candidates for national and State offices and will point to results in England and other countries for our emulation. In considering this question it must be borne in mind that the *bona-fide* labor movement, as expressed in the trades-unions of America, is much younger, both in years and experience, than it is abroad, and that the element of time is an important factor for the rank and file to mature that confidence in the wisdom and honesty of their leaders, which is as necessary a pre-requisite to the party entering the field of politics, as it has been in that of economics.

Whatever has been gained for the toilers in our country has been the achievement of the trades-unions, and it would be most unwise, not to say anything harsher, to abandon the organization, position and methods of past success to fly "to others we know not of." More than half of the battle of labor has already been won. No really intelligent man to-day disputes the claims of labor. The stage of ridicule is happily past; the era of reason has taken its place; and what is now needed is the means and the power to enforce our claim. To that end we are marshalling our forces, and we will demonstrate to the world that the demands and struggles of the toiling masses, while ostensibly and immediately concerned with their own improvement and emancipation, will develop the possibilities, grandeur and true nobility of the human family.

Having mapped out our course, the members of the American Federation of Labor can look on the coming Presidential campaign with a degree of equanimity not often attained by the average citizen. The excitement and turmoil, criminations and recriminations will not rend our organization asunder, as it has done so many others; and during it all, and when the blare of trumpets has died away, and the "spell-binders" have received their rewards, the American Federation of Labor will still be found plodding along, doing noble battle in the struggle for the uplifting of the toiling masses.

**UPPER-CLASS SCORN**

*William Allen White, editor of the Emporia (Kansas) Gazette, first received national attention because of his 1896 editorial castigating the Populists. Later a progressive Republican, White in his autobiography recanted his extreme opposition. "I was a young fool," he said, ". . . writing reactionary editorials about Sound Economics which I had learned from . . . college textbooks. . . ." But the tone of his editorial was characteristic of the hostility expressed in many metropolitan and small-town journals at the time. White here tells how the editorial came to be written and reproduces the text.*

–25–

# WHAT'S THE MATTER
# WITH KANSAS?

## by *William Allen White*

. . . When I came home from the convention Sallie was ill, and the doctors had told her that there was a spot on her lungs. Passes being easy to get, we went to Colorado, where my Aunt Kate was running a hotel. She took Sallie in. I returned to Emporia and sat at a telegraph desk while the story was going through of that great day in Chicago when William Jennings Bryan was nominated by the Democratic party as its Presidential candidate. That story, even on the wire, thrilled the nation. Here was a new figure. Here was a young man. Here was an intrepid advocate of a cause which he proclaimed as that of the downtrodden. It was the first time in my life and in the life of a generation in which

SOURCE: William Allen White, *The Autobiography of William Allen White* (New York: The Macmillan Company, 1946), 278–283. Reprinted by permission of The Macmillan Company.

any man large enough to lead a national party had boldly and unashamedly made his cause that of the poor and the oppressed. The story coming through in bulletins, even detached and sometimes overlapping and out of chronological order, pictured a scene that some day will be a part of a great drama. It was the emergence into middle-class respectability of the revolution that had been smoldering for a quarter of a century in American politics.

I saw the story in no such perspective as I do today. I was moved by fear and rage as the story came in. I had never heard of Bryan. To me, he was an incarnation of demagogy, the apotheosis of riot, destruction, and carnage. A little group of us were standing around the ticker as the story came in, and I can remember someone—and oh, if I could only remember his name—cried out as the drama climaxed in Bryan's nomination:

"Marat, Marat, Marat has won!"

It was with those words echoing in my heart that I entered the campaign of 1896, full of wrath and inspired with a fear that became consternation as the campaign deepened. It seemed to me that rude hands were trying to tear down the tabernacle of our national life, to taint our currency with fiat. So, swallowing protection as a necessary evil and McKinley's candidacy as the price of national security, I went into the campaign with more zeal than intelligence, with more ardor than wisdom. The ardor of Kansas was more than a fever. It was a consuming flame. After the nomination of Bryan, which seemed like the swinging of a firebrand in a powder mill, people argued on the streets. The Republicans cried, "Socialists," which would have been a reasonable indictment if they had not immediately followed by calling the Democrats nihilists and anarchists. In offices, on the front porches of the town homes, everywhere the clamor of politics filled the air. I remember one day in July going to Topeka, where in Eugene Ware's office I sat with delight and heard him deliver a diatribe which rang the changes of what ails Kansas or what's wrong with our state.[1] I sat chuckling at his poetic eloquence and

[1 Eugene Fitch Ware (1841–1911), Kansas poet, lawyer, and minor Republican politician. — Ed.]

told him that I was going to use that in an editorial sometime. He waved his hand and cried:

"Go to it, young man, with my blessing!"

At home I could not walk up Commercial Street without being pulled and hauled by the Populists. I hated wrangling. I never debated anything orally. My answer to argument all my life has been a grin or a giggle or a cocked eye, anything to avoid an acrimonious discussion. Anyway, I have always had to work too hard to bother with the futilities of debate for its own sake.

The Gazette kept me at work twelve hours a day. I was writing the editorials, a good share of the local items, soliciting the advertising, and looking after the subscription books. Subscriptions, in spite of the Populist boycott which had been clamped on early in the summer, were growing. The Republicans were rallying to the Gazette. The other paper, Lieutenant Governor Eskridge's Emporia Republican, had been a protagonist of free silver. The Governor,[2] being a man in his sixties, could not take his political medicine without a wry face. All summer he was sputtering and spitting out, and the Republicans did not like his attitude. He was on the losing side. The Populists remembered his years of abuse. And, anyway, the young bull was strutting through the party herd with the old bull on the fringes thereof. In mid-August the proofs came to me for the book of short stories, "The Real Issue." When I opened the package, I was inordinately proud. I remember that I stopped in the midst of my work to look at the type and examine the make-up and form of the title page. It was most exciting. Being what I was, there was no alternative. I must take those proofs right out to Sallie Lindsay, and we must read them together. So came Saturday, August 13. I had decided to take the evening train to Colorado with the proof sheets. I hurried through my morning work. I got up some editorial for Monday, clipped out some editorials from other Republican papers, wrote the day's local stories, and broke it to Lew Schmucker that he would have to run the paper for four or five days. Early that afternoon I went to the post office for the mail. It was before the

[2 Edmund Needham Morrill (1834–1909). — Ed.]

days of mail delivery in the town. I remember that I had on my crash suit, which my mother had washed and ironed as she had so many times laundered my father's nankeens. I was dressed to go to Sallie in my best bib and tucker, and I probably looked like a large white egg as I waddled down the street to the post office, and came back with my arms full of newspaper exchanges. A block from the office a crowd of Populists tackled me. I was impatient and wanted to be on the way. They surrounded me. They were older men—men in their forties and fifties and sixties —and I was twenty-eight. They were shabbily dressed, and it was no pose with them. They were struggling with poverty and I was rather spick-and-span, particularly offensive in the gaudy neckties for which I have had an unfortunate weakness. Anyway, they ganged me—hooting, jeering, nagging me about some editorial utterances I had made. I was froggy in the meadow and couldn't get out, and they were taking a little stick and poking me about. And my wrath must have flamed through my face. Finally I broke through the cordon and stalked, as well as a fat man who toddles can stalk, down the street to the office. I slapped the bundle of mail on Lew Schmucker's desk and sat down to write for Monday's paper an editorial, and I headed it, "What's the Matter with Kansas?" And I remembered what Eugene Ware said and added frill for frill to his ironic diatribe, and it came out pure vitriol:

## WHAT'S THE MATTER WITH KANSAS?

Today the Kansas Department of Agriculture sent out a statement which indicates that Kansas has gained less than two thousand people in the past year. There are about two hundred and twenty-five thousand families in this state, and there were ten thousand babies born in Kansas, and yet so many people have left the state that the natural increase is cut down to less than two thousand net.

This has been going on for eight years.

If there had been a high brick wall around the state eight years ago, and not a soul had been admitted or permitted to leave,

Kansas would be a half million souls better off than she is today. And yet the nation has increased in population. In five years ten million people have been added to the national population, yet instead of gaining a share of this—say, half a million—Kansas has apparently been a plague spot and, in the very garden of the world, has lost population by ten thousands every year.

Not only has she lost population, but she has lost money. Every moneyed man in the state who could get out without loss has gone. Every month in every community sees someone who has a little money pack up and leave the state. This has been going on for eight years. Money has been drained out all the time. In towns where ten years ago there were three or four or half a dozen money-lending concerns, stimulating industry by furnishing capital, there is now none, or one or two that are looking after the interests and principal already outstanding.

No one brings any money into Kansas any more. What community knows over one or two men who have moved in with more than $5,000 in the past three years? And what community cannot count half a score of men in that time who have left, taking all the money they could scrape together?

Yet the nation has grown rich; other states have increased in population and wealth—other neighboring states. Missouri has gained over two million, while Kansas has been losing half a million. Nebraska has gained in wealth and population while Kansas has gone downhill. Colorado has gained every way, while Kansas has lost every way since 1888.

What's the matter with Kansas?

There is no substantial city in the state. Every big town save one has lost in population. Yet Kansas City, Omaha, Lincoln, St. Louis, Denver, Colorado Springs, Sedalia, the cities of the Dakotas, St. Paul and Minneapolis and Des Moines—all cities and towns in the West—have steadily grown.

Take up the government blue book and you will see that Kansas is virtually off the map. Two or three little scrubby consular places in yellow-fever-stricken communities that do not aggregate ten thousand dollars a year is all the recognition that Kansas has. Nebraska draws about one hundred thousand dollars;

little old North Dakota draws about fifty thousand dollars; Oklahoma doubles Kansas; Missouri leaves her a thousand miles behind; Colorado is almost seven times greater than Kansas—the whole west is ahead of Kansas.

Take it by any standard you please, Kansas is not in it.

Go east and you hear them laugh at Kansas; go west and they sneer at her; go south and they "cuss" her; go north and they have forgotten her. Go into any crowd of intelligent people gathered anywhere on the globe, and you will find the Kansas man on the defensive. The newspaper columns and magazines once devoted to praise of her, to boastful facts and startling figures concerning her resources, are now filled with cartoons, jibes and Pefferian speeches. Kansas just naturally isn't in it. She has traded places with Arkansas and Timbuctoo.

What's the matter with Kansas?

We all know; yet here we are at it again. We have an old mossback Jacksonian who snorts and howls because there is a bathtub in the State House; we are running that old jay for Governor.[3] We have another shabby, wild-eyed, rattlebrained fanatic who has said openly in a dozen speeches that "the rights of the user are paramount to the rights of the owner": we are running him for Chief Justice, so that capital will come tumbling over itself to get into the state. We have raked the old ash heap of failure in the state and found an old human hoop skirt who has failed as a businessman, who has failed as an editor, who has failed as a preacher, and we are going to run him for Congressman-at-Large. He will help the looks of the Kansas delegation at Washington. Then we have discovered a kid without a law practice and have decided to run him for Attorney General. Then, for fear some hint that the state had become respectable might percolate through the civilized portions of the nation, we have decided to send three or four harpies out lecturing, telling the people that Kansas is raising hell and letting the corn go to weed.

Oh, this is a state to be proud of! We are a people who can

[3 White was referring to John W. Leedy (1849–1935), the successful Populist candidate on a state ticket endorsed also by the Democrats. — Ed.]

hold up our heads! What we need is not more money, but less capital, fewer white shirts and brains, fewer men with business judgment, and more of those fellows who boast that they are "just ordinary clodhoppers, but they know more in a minute about finance than John Sherman"; we need more men who are "posted," who can bellow about the crime of '73, who hate prosperity, and who think, because a man believes in national honor, he is a tool of Wall Street. We have had a few of them—some hundred fifty thousand—but we need more.

We need several thousand gibbering idiots to scream about the "Great Red Dragon" of Lombard Street. We don't need population, we don't need wealth, we don't need well-dressed men on the streets, we don't need cities on the fertile prairies; you bet we don't! What we are after is the money power. Because we have become poorer and ornerier and meaner than a spavined, distempered mule, we, the people of Kansas, propose to kick; we don't care to build up, we wish to tear down.

"There are two ideas of government," said our noble Bryan at Chicago. "There are those who believe that if you legislate to make the well-to-do prosperous, this prosperity will leak through on those below. The Democratic idea has been that if you legislate to make the masses prosperous their prosperity will find its way up and through every class and rest upon them."

That's the stuff! Give the prosperous man the dickens! Legislate the thriftless man into ease, whack the stuffing out of the creditors and tell the debtors who borrowed the money five years ago when money "per capita" was greater than it is now, that the contraction of currency gives him a right to repudiate.

Whoop it up for the ragged trousers; put the lazy, greasy fizzle, who can't pay his debts, on the altar, and bow down and worship him. Let the state ideal be high. What we need is not the respect of our fellow men, but the chance to get something for nothing.

Oh, yes, Kansas is a great state. Here are people fleeing from it by the score every day, capital going out of the state by the hundreds of dollars; and every industry but farming paralyzed, and that crippled, because its products have to go across the ocean before they can find a laboring man at work who can afford to buy them. Let's don't stop this year. Let's drive all the decent, self-respecting men out of the state. Let's keep the old clodhoppers who know it all. Let's encourage the man who is "posted." He can talk, and what we need is not mill hands to eat our meat, nor factory hands to eat our wheat, nor cities to oppress the farmer by consuming his butter and eggs and chickens and produce. What Kansas needs is men who can talk, who have large leisure to argue the currency question while their wives wait at home for that nickel's worth of bluing.

What's the matter with Kansas?

Nothing under the shining sun. She is losing her wealth, population and standing. She has got her statesmen, and the money power is afraid of her. Kansas is all right. She has started in to raise hell, as Mrs. Lease[4] advised, and she seems to have an over-production. But that doesn't matter. Kansas never did believe in diversified crops. Kansas is all right. There is absolutely nothing wrong with Kansas. "Every prospect pleases and only man is vile."


I remember even across these years that I slammed the editorial above on the copy spike with a passionate satisfaction that I had answered those farmer hooligans. I was happy and turned to something else for the afternoon. Before I left I had read the proof on it, which meant that I probably revised it two or three or four times, as I always do even now when I have for the paper an editorial that I am proud of. And so, late that afternoon I gathered up my proofs, a book or two that had come, the magazines of the week, and took the train for Colorado to lay my treasures before the feet of my lady love, fancying myself a romantic figure. And so there at the little red-stone depot of Manitou, where she came running down the platform to meet me, and I hurried with all my treasures for her, the book of our pride, the papers and magazines which would bring us together so happily, a journey ended in lovers' meeting.

[4 Mrs. Mary Elizabeth Lease (1853–1933), Kansas Populist orator, reported to have advised farmers to raise less corn and more hell. — Ed.]

# VI
# BRYAN AND FUSION

---

**THE SILVER DEMOCRATS**

*In the campaign of 1896 the silver Democrats seized control of their party and nominated Bryan, thereby staking out a claim to the issue that had become the Populists' most important appeal to the electorate. On March 4, 1895, a group of the silver Democrats, led by Bryan and Richard P. Bland, issued an appeal for silverites to organize for the next campaign. With the "Cross of Gold Speech" in support of the proposed silver plank in the platform Bryan stampeded the Democratic National Convention and assured his nomination.*

## –26–
## ADDRESS TO THE SILVER DEMOCRATS

### *by Richard P. Bland and*
### *William Jennings Bryan*

To the Democrats of the United States:

We, the undersigned Democrats, present for your consideration the following statement:

We believe that the establishment of gold as the only monetary standard and the elimination of silver as a full legal tender money, will increase the purchasing power of each dollar, add to the burden of all debts, decrease the market value of all other forms of property, continue and intensify business depression, and, finally, reduce the majority of the people to financial bondage.

SOURCE: William Jennings Bryan, *The First Battle: A Story of the Campaign of 1896* (Chicago: W. B. Conkey Co., 1896), pp. 156–157.

We believe that no party can hope for enduring success in the United States so long as it advocates a single gold standard, and that the advocacy of such a financial policy would be especially fatal to a party which, like the Democratic party, derives its voting strength from those who may without reproach be called the common people; and we point to the overwhelming defeat of the party in 1894, to the opposition aroused by the veto of the seigniorage bill and to the still more unanimous protest against the issue of gold bonds, as proof that the Democratic party cannot be brought to the support of the gold standard policy.

We believe that the money question will be the paramount issue in 1896, and will so remain until it is settled by the intelligence and patriotism of the American voters.

We believe that a large majority of the Democrats of the United States favor bimetallism, and realize that it can only be secured by the restoration of the free and unlimited coinage of gold and silver at the present ratio, and we assert that the majority have, and should exercise, the right to control the policy of the party and retain the party name.

We believe that it is the duty of the majority, and within their power, to take charge of the party organization and make the Democratic party an effective instrument in the accomplishment of needed reforms. It is not necessary that Democrats should surrender their convictions on other questions in order to take an active part in the settlement of the question which at this time surpasses all others in importance.

We believe that the rank and file of the Democratic party should at once assert themselves in the Democratic party and place the party on record in favor of the immediate restoration of the free and unlimited coinage of gold and silver at the present legal ratio of 16 to 1, as such coinage existed prior to 1873, without waiting for the aid or consent of any other nation, such gold and silver coin to be a full legal tender for all debts public and private.

We urge all Democrats who favor the financial policy above set forth to associate themselves together and impress their views upon the party organization; we urge all newspapers in harmony with the above financial policy to place it at the head of the editorial column and assist in the immediate restoration of bimetallism.

## –27–
# CROSS OF GOLD SPEECH*
## by William Jennings Bryan

Mr. Chairman and Gentlemen of the Convention: I would be presumptuous, indeed, to present myself against the distinguished gentlemen to whom you have listened if this were a mere measuring of abilities; but this is not a contest between persons. The humblest citizen in all the land, when clad in the armor of a righteous cause, is stronger than all the hosts of error. I come to speak to you in defense of a cause as holy as the cause of liberty —the cause of humanity.

When this debate is concluded, a motion will be made to lay upon the table the resolution offered in commendation of the administration, and also the resolution offered in condemnation of the administration. We object to bringing this question down to the level of persons. The individual is but an atom; he is born, he acts, he dies; but principles are eternal; and this has been a contest over a principle.

Never before in the history of this country has there been witnessed such a contest as that through which we have just passed. Never before in the history of American politics has a great issue been fought out as this issue has been, by the voters of a great party. On the fourth of March, 1895, a few Democrats, most of them members of Congress, issued an address to the

SOURCE: William Jennings Bryan, *The First Battle: A Story of the Campaign of 1896* (Chicago: W. B. Conkey Co., 1896), pp. 199–206.

Democrats of the nation, asserting that the money question was the paramount issue of the hour; declaring that a majority of the Democratic party had the right to control the action of the party on this paramount issue; and concluding with the request that the believers in the free coinage of silver in the Democratic party should organize, take charge of, and control the policy of the Democratic party. Three months later, at Memphis, an organization was perfected, and the silver Democrats went forth openly and courageously proclaiming their belief, and declaring that, if successful, they would crystallize into a platform the declaration which they had made. Then began the conflict. With a zeal approaching the zeal which inspired the crusaders who followed Peter the Hermit, our silver Democrats went forth from victory unto victory until they are now assembled, not to discuss, not to debate, but to enter up the judgment already rendered by the plain people of this country. In this contest brother has been arrayed against brother, father against son. The warmest ties of love, acquaintance and association have been disregarded; old leaders have been cast aside when they have refused to give expression to the sentiments of those whom they would lead, and new leaders have sprung up to give direction to this cause of truth. Thus has the contest been waged, and we have assembled here under as binding and solemn instructions as were ever imposed upon representatives of the people.

We do not come as individuals. As individuals we might have been glad to compliment the gentleman from New York (Senator Hill), but we know that the people for whom we speak would never be willing to put him in a position where he could thwart the will of the Democratic party. I say it was not a question of persons; it was a question of principle, and it is not with gladness, my friends, that we find ourselves brought into conflict with those who are now arrayed on the other side.

The gentleman who preceded me (ex-Governor Russell) spoke of the State of Massachusetts; let me assure him that not one present in all this convention entertains the least hostility to the people of the State of Massachusetts, but we stand here representing people who are the equals, before the law, of the greatest citizens in the State of Massachusetts. When you (turning to the gold delegates) come before us and tell us that we are about to disturb your business interests, we reply that you have disturbed our business interests by your course.

We say to you that you have made the definition of a business man too limited in its application. The man who is employed for wages is as much a business man as his employer; the attorney in a country town is as much a business man as the corporation counsel in a great metropolis; the merchant at the cross-roads store is as much a business man as the merchant of New York; the farmer who goes forth in the morning and toils all day—who begins in the spring and toils all summer—and who by the application of brain and muscle to the natural resources of the country creates wealth, is as much a business man as the man who goes upon the board of trade and bets upon the price of grain; the miners who go down a thousand feet into the earth, or climb two thousand feet upon the cliffs, and bring forth from their hiding places the precious metals to be poured into the channels of trade are as much business men as the few financial magnates who, in a back room, corner the money of the world. We come to speak for this broader class of business men.

Ah, my friends, we say not one word against those who live upon the Atlantic coast, but the hardy pioneers who have braved all the dangers of the wilderness, who have made the desert to blossom as the rose—the pioneers away out there (pointing to the West), who rear their children near to Nature's heart, where they can mingle their voices with the voices of the birds—out there where they have erected schoolhouses for the education of their young, churches where they praise their Creator, and cemeteries where rest the ashes of their dead—these people, we say, are as deserving of the consideration of our party as any people in this country. It is for these that we speak. We do not come as aggressors. Our war is not a war of conquest; we are fighting in the defense of our homes, our families, and posterity. We have petitioned, and our petitions have been scorned; we have entreated, and our entreaties have been disregarded; we have begged, and they have mocked when our calamity came. We beg no longer;

we entreat no more; we petition no more. We defy them.

The gentleman from Wisconsin has said that he fears a Robespierre. My friends, in this land of the free you need not fear that a tyrant will spring up from among the people. What we need is an Andrew Jackson to stand, as Jackson stood, against the encroachments of organized wealth.

They tell us that this platform was made to catch votes. We reply to them that changing conditions make new issues; that the principles upon which Democracy rests are as everlasting as the hills, but that they must be applied to new conditions as they arise. Conditions have arisen, and we are here to meet those conditions. They tell us that the income tax ought not to be brought in here; that it is a new idea. They criticise us for our criticism of the Supreme Court of the United States. My friends, we have not criticised; we have simply called attention to what you already know. If you want criticisms, read the dissenting opinions of the court. There you will find criticisms. They say that we passed an unconstitutional law; we deny it. The income tax law was not unconstitutional when it was passed; it was not unconstitutional when it went before the Supreme Court for the first time; it did not become unconstitutional until one of the judges changed his mind, and we cannot be expected to know when a judge will change his mind. The income tax is just. It simply intends to put the burdens of government justly upon the backs of the people. I am in favor of an income tax. When I find a man who is not willing to bear his share of the burdens of the government which protects him, I find a man who is unworthy to enjoy the blessings of a government like ours.

They say that we are opposing national bank currency; it is true. If you will read what Thomas Benton said, you will find he said that, in searching history, he could find but one parallel to Andrew Jackson; that was Cicero, who destroyed the conspiracy of Cataline and saved Rome. Benton said that Cicero only did for Rome what Jackson did for us when he destroyed the bank conspiracy and saved America. We say in our platform that we believe that the right to coin and issue money is a function of government. We believe it. We believe that it is a part of sovereignty, and can no more with safety be delegated to private individuals than we could afford to delegate to private individuals the power to make penal statutes or levy taxes. Mr. Jefferson, who was once regarded as good Democratic authority, seems to have differed in opinion from the gentleman who has addressed us on the part of the minority. Those who are opposed to this proposition tell us that the issue of paper money is a function of the bank, and that the Government ought to go out of the banking business. I stand with Jefferson rather than with them, and tell them, as he did, that the issue of money is a function of government, and that the banks ought to go out of the governing business.

They complain about the plank which declares against life tenure in office. They have tried to strain it to mean that which it does not mean. What we oppose by that plank is the life tenure which is being built up in Washington, and which excludes from participation in official benefits the humbler members of society.

Let me call your attention to two or three important things. The gentleman from New York says that he will propose an amendment to the platform providing that the proposed change in our monetary system shall not affect contracts already made. Let me remind you that there is no intention of affecting those contracts which according to present laws are made payable in gold; but if he means to say that we cannot change our monetary system without protecting those who have loaned money before the change was made, I desire to ask him where, in law or in morals, he can find justification for not protecting the debtors when the act of 1873 was passed, if he now insists that we must protect the creditors.

He says he will also propose an amendment which will provide for the suspension of free coinage if we fail to maintain the parity within a year. We reply that when we advocate a policy which we believe will be successful, we are not compelled to raise a doubt as to our own sincerity by suggesting what we shall do if we fail. I ask him, if he would apply his logic to us, why he does not apply it to himself. He says he wants this country to try to secure an international agreement. Why does he not tell us what he is going to do if he fails to secure an international agreement? There is more reason for him to do that than there is for us to provide against the failure to maintain the parity. Our opponents have tried for twenty years to secure an international agreement, and those are waiting for it most patiently who do not want it at all.

And now, my friends, let me come to the paramount issue. If they ask us why it is that we say more on the money question than we say upon the tariff question, I reply that, if protection has slain its thousands, the gold standard has slain its tens of thousands. If they ask us why we do not embody in our platform all the things that we believe in, we reply that when we have restored the money of the Constitution all other necessary reforms will be possible; but that until this is done there is no other reform that can be accomplished.

Why is it that within three months such a change has come over the country? Three months ago, when it was confidently asserted that those who believe in the gold standard would frame our platform and nominate our candidates, even the advocates of the gold standard did not think that we could elect a president. And they had good reason for their doubt, because there is scarcely a State here today asking for the gold standard which is not in the absolute control of the Republican party. But note the change. Mr. McKinley was nominated at St. Louis upon a platform which declared for the maintenance of the gold standard until it can be changed into bimetallism by international agreement. Mr. McKinley was the most popular man among the Republicans, and three months ago everybody in the Republican party prophesied his election. How is today? Why, the man who was once pleased to think that he looked like Napoleon—that man shudders today when he remembers that he was nominated on the anniversary of the battle of Waterloo. Not only that, but as he listens he can hear with ever-increasing distinctness the sound of the waves as they beat upon the lonely shores of St. Helena.

Why this change? Ah, my friends, is not the reason for the change evident to any one who will look at the matter? No private character, however pure, no personal popularity, however great, can protect from the avenging wrath of an indignant people a man who will declare that he is in favor of fastening the gold standard upon this country, or who is willing to surrender the right of self-government and place the legislative control of our affairs in the hands of foreign potentates and powers.

We go forth confident that we shall win. Why? Because upon the paramount issue of this campaign there is not a spot of ground upon which the enemy will dare to challenge battle. If they tell us that the gold standard is a good thing, we shall point to their platform and tell them that their platform pledges the party to get rid of the gold standard and substitute bimetallism. If the gold standard is a good thing, why try to get rid of it? I call your attention to the fact that some of the very people who are in this convention today and who tell us that we ought to declare in favor of international bimetallism—thereby declaring that the gold standard is wrong and that the principle of bimetallism is better—these very people four months ago were open and avowed advocates of the gold standard, and were then telling us that we could not legislate two metals together, even with the aid of all the world. If the gold standard is a good thing, we ought to declare in favor of its retention and not in favor of abandoning it; and if the gold standard is a bad thing why should we wait until other nations are willing to help us to let go? Here is the line of battle, and we care not upon which issue they force the fight; we are prepared to meet them on either issue or on both. If they tell us that the gold standard is the standard of civilization, we reply to them that this, the most enlightened of all the nations of the earth, has never declared for a gold standard and that both the great parties this year are declaring against it. If the gold standard is the standard of civilization, why, my friends, should we not have it? If they come to meet us on that issue we can present the history of our nation. More than that; we can tell them that they will search the pages of history in vain to find a single instance where the common people of any land have ever declared themselves in favor of the gold standard. They can find where the holders of fixed investments have declared for a gold standard, but not where the masses have.

Mr. Carlisle said in 1878 that this was a struggle between "the idle holders of idle capital" and "the struggling masses, who produce the wealth and pay the taxes of the country;" and, my friends, the question we are to decide is: Upon which side will the Democratic party fight; upon the side of "the idle holders of idle capital" or upon the side of "the struggling masses?" That is the question which the party must answer first, and then it must be answered by each individual hereafter. The sympathies of the Democratic party, as shown by the platform, are on the side of the struggling masses who have ever been the foundation of the Democratic party. There are two ideas of government. There are those who believe that, if you will only legislate to make the well-to-do prosperous, their prosperity will leak through on those below. The Democratic idea, however, has been that if you legislate to make the masses prosperous, their prosperity will find its way up through every class which rests upon them.

You come to us and tell us that the great cities are in favor of the gold standard; we reply that the great cities rest upon our broad and fertile prairies. Burn down your cities and leave our farms, and your cities will spring up again as if by magic; but destroy our farms and the grass will grow in the streets of every city in the country.

My friends, we declare that this nation is able to legislate for its own people on every question, without waiting for the aid or consent of any other nation on earth; and upon that issue we expect to carry every State in the Union. I shall not slander the inhabitants of the fair State of Massachusetts nor the inhabitants of the State of New York by saying that, when they are confronted with the proposition, they will declare that this nation is not able to attend to its own business. It is the issue of 1776 over again. Our ancestors, when but three millions in number, had the courage to declare their political independence of every other nation; shall we, their descendants, when we have grown to seventy millions, declare that we are less independent than our forefathers? No, my friends, that will never be the verdict of our people. Therefore, we care not upon what lines the battle is fought. If they say bimetallism is good, but that we cannot have it until other nations help us, we reply that, instead of having a gold standard because England has, we will restore bimetallism, and then let England have bimetallism because the United States has it. If they dare to come out in the open field and defend the gold standard as a good thing, we will fight them to the uttermost. Having behind us the producing masses of this nation and the world, supported by the commercial interests, the laboring interests, and the toilers everywhere, we will answer their demand for a gold standard by saying to them: You shall not press down upon the brow of labor this crown of thorns, you shall not crucify mankind upon a cross of gold.

**A MINORITY VIEW**

*Journalist, author, and foe of monopoly, Lloyd saw in the People's Party an opportunity to develop a mass farmer-labor coalition of the left. He ran for Congress in 1894 on the Populist ticket in a Chicago district, but he quit the party after its decision to endorse Bryan in 1896. Lloyd called free silver "the cow-bird of the Reform movement. It waited until the nest had been built by the sacrifices and labour of others, and then laid its eggs in it, pushing out the others which lie smashed on the ground." This is his account of the 1896 Populist convention.*

–28–

# THE POPULISTS AT ST. LOUIS
## by Henry Demarest Lloyd

The People's Party has "shot the chutes" of fusion and landed in the deep waters of Democracy as the Independent Republican movement of 1872 did. Nearly all the reform parties of the last generation have had the same fate. Democracy is that bourne from which no reform party returns—as yet. The Independent Republicans organized as a protest against corruption in the administration of the national government and to secure tariff reform on free trade lines. Unlike the People's Party, theirs began its career under the leadership of some of the most distinguished men in the nation. Among them were Hon. David A. Wells, who had been United States Commissioner of Internal Revenue; Ex-Governor Hoadley of Ohio; E. L. Godkin, editor of the New York *Nation;* Horace White, then of the Chicago *Tribune;* Ex-Gover-

source: Henry Demarest Lloyd, "The Populists at St. Louis," *Review of Reviews,* XIV (September 1896), 278–283.

nor Randolph of New Jersey; the Hon. J. D. Cox, who had been Secretary of the Interior; Edward Atkinson of Boston; the Hon. Carl Schurz. It was the expectation of most of these gentlemen and their followers that the Cincinnati convention would nominate Charles Francis Adams of Massachusetts, our great War Minister at the Court of St. James, for President, and that with his election and a Congress pledged to civil service reform and revenue tariff the country would enter upon a new era of purity and prosperity. The revulsion when their free trade egg hatched out Horace Greeley was comparable only to that of the gold and machine Democrats at Chicago at the nomination of Bryan and the adoption of the anti-Cleveland and pro-silver platform. The People's Party had no men of national prestige to give its birth *éclat*. It has been from the beginning what its name implies—a party of the people.

One of the principal sources was the Farmers' Alliance. To President Polk[1] of that body more than to any other single individual it owes its existence. The agrarian element has been predominant throughout its career. One of its best representatives in this convention was the temporary chairman—the Hon. Marion Butler, the handsome young farmer of North Carolina. Too young to be a candidate for President or Vice-President, he has worked his way up from his fields through the Farmers' Alliance into a seat in the United States Senate. But in addition to the revolting agrarians, nearly every other reform force—except the Socialists—has been swept into it. Its first national convention of 1892 was attended by veterans of the old Greenback movement like General James B. Weaver, by rotten-egging whom, in the campaign that followed, the Southern Democrats made tens of thousands of Populists; by anti-monopolists like Ignatius Donnelly, whose Shakespeare cryptogram has made him one of the best known writers of his day; by leaders like Powderly. It was no easy thing to find common ground for men so dissimilar to meet upon. The delicate work of preparing a platform was accom-

[1] Leonidas LaFayette Polk (1837–1892), founder of the Raleigh (N. C.) *Progressive Farmer*, president of the Southern Farmers' Alliance, 1890–1892. — Ed.]

plished, thanks mainly to the skillful pen of Ignatius Donnelly.
The convention went wild with joy when it became known that
the Committee on Platform had succeeded in coming to an agreement and unification was assured. For over an hour the thousand
members of the convention sang, cheered, danced and gave
thanks. It was one of the most thrilling scenes in the panorama of
American political conventions. Singularly enough, it was in the
Democratic convention, this year, not that of the People's Party,
that the forces of enthusiasm and revolutionary fervor flamed the
brightest.

The Populist gathering of this year lacked the drill and distinction and wealth of the Republican convention held the month
before in the same building. It had not the ebullient aggressive-
ness of the revolutionary Democratic assembly at Chicago, nor
the brilliant drivers who rode the storm there. Every one com-
mented on the number of gray heads—heads many of them
grown white in previous independent party movements. The delegates were poor men. One of the "smart" reporters of the
cosmopolitan press dilated with the wit of the boulevardier upon
finding some of them sitting with their shoes off,—to rest their
feet and save their shoes, as they confessed to him. Perhaps even
his merry pen would have withheld its shafts if he had realized
that these delegates had probably had to walk many weary miles
to get to the convention, and that they had done their political
duty at such sacrifice only for conscience sake. Cases are well
known of delegates who walked because too poor to pay their
railroad fare. It was one day discovered that certain members of
one of the most important delegations were actually suffering for
food. They had had no regular sleeping place, having had to save
what money they had for their nickel meals at the lunch counter.
The unexpected length of the proceedings had exhausted their
little store of money. Among these men, who were heroically
enduring without complaint such hardships in order to attend to
political duties which so many of those who laugh at them think
beneath their notice, were some of the blacklisted members of the
American Railway Union. They were there in the hope that they
might have the opportunity of helping to make their leader,

Eugene V. Debs, a candidate for President. But Mr. Debs, though he had a large following, refused to allow his name to be put before the convention, urging that every one should unite in favor of Bryan, as there seemed a chance of his election, and through him the people might at least hold their ground until ready for a more decisive advance.

In the South, the Democracy represents the classes, the People's Party, the masses. The most eloquent speeches made were those of whites and blacks explaining to the convention what the rule of the Democrats meant in the South. A delegate from Georgia, a coal-black negro, told how the People's Party alone gave full fellowship to his race, when it had been abandoned by the Republicans and cheated and betrayed by the Democrats. It was to this recognition of the colored men a distinguished political manager referred when he said recently in an interview that the Populists of the South could go where they belonged—"with the negroes." With thrilling passion the white Populists of the South pleaded that the convention should not leave them to the tender mercies of the Democrats, by accepting the Democratic nominees without the pledges or conditions which would save the Populists from going under the chariot wheels of southern Democracy. "Cyclone" Davis, spokesman of the Texas delegation, tall and thin as a southern pine, with eyes kindled with the fire of the prophet, a voice of far reach and pathos, and a vocabulary almost every other word of which seemed drawn from the Gospels or the denunciatory Psalms, wrestled and prayed with the convention to save the Populists of Texas from the fate that awaited them if they were sent back, unprotected, to their old enemies. The Democrats, the "classes," hate with a hatred like that of the Old Regime of France for the Sans Culottes of St. Antoine the new people who have dared to question the immemorial supremacy of their aristocratic rule, and who have put into actual association, as not even the Republicans have done, political brotherhood with the despised negro. This is the secret of the bolt of the Texas Populist, just announced. They have gone over to gold with the sound money men of both the old parties, because more than silver, more than anti-monopoly, the issue with them is the elementary right to political manhood. The issue in many parts of the South is even more elementary—the right to life itself, so bitter is the feeling of the Old Democracy against these upstarts from the despised masses of the whites. The line between the old Democracy and Populism in the South is largely a line of bloody graves. When the convention decided to indorse Bryan without asking for any pledge from the Democrats for the protection of the southern Populists one of its most distinguished members, a member of Congress, well known throughout the country, turned to me and said: "This may cost me my life. I can return home only at that risk. The feeling of the Democracy against us is one of murderous hate. I have been shot at many times. Grand juries will not indict our assailants. Courts give us no protection."

The People's Party convention was dated to follow the conventions of the two other parties by its managers in the pessimistic belief that the Democratic party as well as the Republican would be under the thumb of the trusts and the "gold bugs." The People's Party would then have the easy task of gathering into its ranks the bolting silver and anti-monopolist Republicans and Democrats, and increasing its two millions of votes to the five and a half millions that would put it in possession of the White House for four years. It was a simple plan. That its lead would be taken from it by one of the old parties, least of all that this would be done by the party of President Cleveland and Secretary Olney, those in charge of the People's Party did not dream. The Democracy had not forgotten how they were forced to accept Horace Greeley in 1872, because the independent Republicans had had their convention first. Its progressive elements with a leader of surpassing shrewdness and dash, Altgeld, who unites a William Lloyd Garrison's love of justice with the political astuteness of a Zach Chandler or a Samuel J. Tilden, took advantage of the tactical error of the People's Party managers in postponing its convention. The delegates as they betook themselves to St. Louis thought they saw a most promising resemblance between the prospects of the People's Party in 1896 and those of the Republican party in 1856. The by-elections since 1892 showed that its membership roll was rising and was well on the way to two millions. It was the party whose position was the most advanced on the question of social control of privileged social power, which, if contemporary literature is any guide, is the question of the times. But as the end of four years' work since the young party startled the old politicians in 1892 by showing up over a million votes in its first presidential election, the party is going this year to vote for President for one who is willing to take its votes but not its nomination. He will be its nominee but not its candidate. Such are the perplexities of the situation that it is even extremely doubtful whether the nominee will receive an official notification of his nomination or a request that he will consent to be a candida ∴. It is urged by influential members of the party that as a Democrat he would be "embarrassed" by such a notification and request, and that the "crisis" is so grave that they must sacrifice their party to their patriotism, and save their country by voting for the Democratic candidate without his knowledge "officially"—on the sly, as it were. Until their convention met these millions had hoped that theirs would be the main body of a victorious army. This hope ends in their reduction to the position of an irregular force of guerillas fighting outside the regular ranks, the fruit of the victory, if won, to be appropriated by a general who would not recognize them. Even more interesting is it that this is cheerfully accepted by most of the rank and file of the People's Party. No protest of sufficient importance to cause a halt was made at the first, when the shock was greatest, and the noise of dissent has grown fainter as the excitement of the campaign rises. The party is composed altogether of men who had already had the self-discipline of giving up party for the sake of principle. Every one in it had been originally either a Democrat or a Republican, and had severed all his old political ties to unite with those who, like himself, cared more for reform than old party comforts. To men who had already made one such sacrifice, another was not difficult. The People's Party is bivertebrate as well as bimetallic. It was built up of the old Greenback and Anti-monopoly elements, reinforced by castaways of the Union Labor, National, and other third party enterprises. Its members had become well acquainted with the adversities of fusion and amalgamation, and used to being "traded" out of existence.

One of the plainest looks on the face of the St. Louis convention was anxiety—anxiety of the managers who for years had been planning to get by fusion—with Republicans or Democrats —the substance if not the name of victory, and saw in the gathering many resolute "middle of the road" opponents[2]; anxiety of the mass of the delegates lest they were being sold out; anxiety, most surprising of all, among the radicals, lest by insisting too much upon their own radicalism they might explode a coalescence which, if left to gather headway, might later be invaluable to them. The predominant anxiety found its most striking expression in the preparation and adoption of the platform. In the committee room every suggestion for the utterance of any novelty in principle or application was ruthlessly put down. When the platform was reported to the convention, the previous question was at once moved, and the platform adopted without a word of debate. Even in the Democratic convention half a day was given to discussing the articles of political faith. No motion to reconsider this closure and secure a discussion of the principles of the movement was made. Even the radicals sat silent. In the proceedings of the convention the creed of the party was therefore practically not considered. In a large view the only subject which engrossed the gathering was whether the party should keep on in its own path or merge for this campaign with the Democracy. The solicitude to do nothing which should hinder the Rising of the People, if that had really begun, was the motive that led to the indorsement of Bryan. Most of the three hundred, over one hundred of them from Texas alone, who refused to unite in this, would have joined its one thousand supporters had the protection they prayed for against the old Democracy been given them by the exaction of guarantees from the Democratic candidate and campaign managers. It was not that they loved Bryan less. A determination that the People's Party and that for which it stood should not be lost if this year's battle was lost by its ally, Democracy, accounts for the nomination of Watson. The majority which

[2 "Middle-of-the-road" Populists were those who opposed fusion. — Ed.]

insisted that all the precedents should be violated and the Vice-President nominated before the President, and which rejected Sewall and took Thomas E. Watson of Georgia—a second Alexander H. Stephens in delicacy of physique and robustness of eloquence and loyalty to the people—was composed, as the result showed, mostly of the same men who afterward joined in the nomination of Bryan. It is true there was a strong opposition to Sewall, because he was national bank president, railroad director and corporation man. But the nomination speeches and the talk of the delegates showed convincingly that the same men who meant to support Bryan were equally well minded that there should not be an absolute surrender to the Democracy. The Democracy must yield something in return for the much greater concession the People's Party was to give.

Contrary to expectation and to the plan by which the two conventions had been brought to St. Louis on the same dates, the silver convention exercised no influence on that of the Populists.[3] The delegates of the latter listened with unconcealed impatience to every reference to the silver body, and refused to allow its members any rights upon the floor. The report of the Conference Committee was listened to without interest. The tumultuous refusal of the convention to allow Senator Stewart of the silver convention an extension of time when he was addressing them, was one of the many signs that the convention cared less for silver than did the Democratic convention.[4] Most of the Democrats really believe free silver is a great reform. That is as far as they have got. But it was hard to find among the Populists any who would not privately admit that they knew silver was only the most trifling installment of reform, and many—a great many— did not conceal their belief that it was no reform at all. The members of the People's Party have had most of their education on the money question from the Greenbackers among them—

[3 The National Silver Party Convention met in St. Louis at the same time as the Populists. The party was launched in January 1896 by a joint effort of the American Bimetallic League, the National Bimetallic Union, and the National Executive Silver Committee, which also formed a nonpolitical American Bimetallic Union. — Ed.]

[4 William Morris Stewart (1827–1909) of Nevada. — Ed.]

men like the only candidate who contended with Bryan for the nomination before the convention—Colonel S. F. Norton,[5] author of the "Ten Men of Money Island," of which hundreds of thousands of copies have been sold, who for twenty years has been giving his means and his life energy to agitating for an ideal currency. The People's Party believes really in a currency redeemable in all the products of human labor, and not in gold alone, nor in gold and silver. A party which hates Democracy accepted the Democratic nominee, and a party which has no faith in silver as a panacea accepted silver practically as the sole issue of the campaign. Peter Cooper, the venerable philanthropist, candidate for President on the Greenback ticket in 1876—whose never absent air cushion Nast by one of his finest strokes of caricature converted into a crown for General Butler when running as Greenback and Labor candidate for Governor of Massachusetts—presided over the first days of the convention from within the frame of a very poorly painted portrait. But later, by accident or design, about the time when it thus became plain that the convention would make only a platonic declaration of its paper money doctrines, and would put forward only "Free Silver" for actual campaign use, the face of the old leader disappeared and was seen no more with its homely inspiration above the chairman's head.

The solution of the paradoxical action of the convention as to Democracy and money was the craving for a union of reform forces which burned with all the fires of hope and fear in the breasts of the delegates, and overcame all their academic differences of economic doctrine and all their old political prejudices. The radicals had men who were eager to raise the convention against the stultification they thought it was perpetrating. If the issue had been made there was an even chance, good arithmeticians among the observers thought, that the convention could have been carried by them, and a "stalwart" ticket put into the field on a platform far in advance of that adopted in Omaha in

[5 Seymour F. Norton, of Chicago, author of *Ten Men of Money Island* (Chicago, 1891), editor of the *Monthly Sentinel,* and advocate of greenback currency in opposition to the silver panacea. — Ed.]

1892, one demanding, for instance, the public ownership of all monopolies. This contingent felt that the social question is more than the money question, the money question more than the silver question, and the silver question more than the candidacy of any one person. If the money question was to be the issue it wanted it to be the whole money question—the question how an honest dollar can be made instead of being only stumbled on in placers or bonanzas, and how it can be made as elastic as the creative will of the people and as expansive as civilization itself. Certainly the strongest single body of believers in the convention was this of anti-monopoly in everything, including the currency. These men would much rather have declared for the demonetization of gold then the remonetization of silver. That their strength was formidable—formidable enough to have split the convention near the middle, if not to have carried it—no one could deny who studied on the ground of feelings and beliefs of the delegates. But those who might have called this force into activity were quiescent, for Col. Norton's candidacy was unsought, impromptu and without organization. The leaders did not lead, and their followers did not clamor to be led. "General" J. S. Coxey of the Commonweal Army, who has left large property interests to suffer while he has devoted himself to educating the people of his "Good Roads" plan of internal improvements, to be paid for by non-interest bearing bonds, was present, and made no resistance outside of the Committee of Resolutions. Ex-Governor Waite of Colorado, whose name will be cheered in any assembly of labor men or Populists, as the only Governor who has called out the militia to protect the workingmen against violence at the hands of their employers, for the sake of harmony forbore to press his claims at the head of a contesting delegation from Colorado. Senator Peffer, who has shown an ample courage in every emergency at Washington, sat silent, though he was bitterly opposed to the methods of the managers. The fear ruled that unless the reform forces united this time they would never again have the opportunity to unite. It was in the air that there must be union. The footfall of the hour for action was heard approaching. It was a psychological moment of *rapprochement* against an appalling danger which for thirty years now had been seen rising in the sky. If the radicals made a mistake, it was a patriotic mistake. The delegates knew perfectly well that the silver miners were spending a great deal of money and politics to get them to do just what they were doing. They knew what the Democratic politicians were doing with the same object. They knew that with some of their own politicians the anxiety to return to the old political home was not dissociated from visions of possible fatted calf. But though they knew all this, they went on by an overwhelming majority to do what the mine owners and the Democrats and the traders wanted them to do, and the acquiescence of the mass of the party in their action is now beyond question. We can comprehend this better when we see men like Edward Bellamy, the head of the Nationalists, and Henry George of the Single Taxers, and the Rev. W. D. P. Bliss of the Christian Socialists also taking the same attitude and for precisely the same reason that the real issue is "between men and money," in Bellamy's phrase; and they cannot afford to side with money against men.

## A MAJORITY VIEW

*Temporary chairman of the Populist national convention of 1896, Marion Butler was also senator from North Carolina. He published the Raleigh (N.C.) Caucasian, a Populist organ, and had served as president of the North Carolina and Southern Alliances. In his keynote speech Butler undertook to lay the foundation for a policy of supporting Bryan while retaining the separate identity of the People's party. His purpose was to build a reform coalition on the silver issue, yet to maintain the new party for the sake of developing broader issues in the future and to serve as a safeguard against the recapture of the Democracy by its Cleveland or Bourbon wing. Butler's viewpoint was more characteristic of Populist opinion than Lloyd's. His policy was adopted by the convention and, as national chairman, Butler subsequently sought to put it into effect. After the defeat of 1896, however, the People's Party was left in disarray and declined rapidly.*

-29-

# KEYNOTE SPEECH, 1896
## by Marion Butler

Fellow Citizens: All history teaches that there come great crises in the affairs of men, and all history teaches that humanity is blest and raised to a high level or temporarily cursed, according as the men upon whose shoulders rest the responsiblity are able to meet the crisis with wisdom and patriotism and to use it for the betterment of humanity. Two political parties have held national conventions this year. Both have had their say, made their promises, and put forward their leaders.

Another political party, young, but a growing giant in strength,

source: William Jennings Bryan, *The First Battle: A Story of the Campaign of 1896* (Chicago: W. B. Conkey Co., 1896), pp. 259–264.

has assembled to speak to the American people at this important and critical hour.

We are here because there is need for us to be here. The two parties that have already spoken have between them had charge of the machinery of a great representative government, in which kind of government there are the greatest possibilities for good and for evil—the kind of government where the prosperity of the people or their misery can be affected to the greatest degree. The two parties have between them had charge of your government for over twenty-five years, and during that time a great and prosperous people, a people laboring to carry out the injunction to make two blades of grass grow where one grew before, have performed their duty in the eyes of God and man, and have made this country blossom like a rose, as far as creating wealth was concerned, yet during this time of unexampled creation of wealth, of unexampled industry and economy on the part of the people, these two parties have succeeded in bringing this great nation to the verge of ruin.

Did they know better, or did they not know better? Were they honestly mistaken, or did they do it on purpose? In either event their leadership is a discredit to the existence of the party and the necessity of this organization is proven. Every candidate put before the American people since the war by both of these parties has been a man whose nomination and election has carried joy to the hearts of aggregated capital and combined greed. They have selected the men who have stood in touch with, and been the allied agents of, the powers that have brought this country to the verge of bankruptcy, and these powers, which have destroyed every republic in the past, will destroy this one unless checked. My friends, these two great parties, under false leadership, have during this period succeeded in keeping from the people the greatest issue in American politics; they have managed to array the great masses of the American voters with frenzied zeal on two sides of great national campaigns, when the issue was a sham put up for the purpose of dividing the people. It made no difference which side won, the people lost.

Wall street in the United States and Lombard street in England won. While these things were going on the great American heart was wrapped in party prejudice. It was not until they had awakened from this condition and aroused themselves that they began to think upon these questions. Then it was that the great middle classes began to put their heads together for their common good; and when that small cloud appeared upon the horizon, the hearts of the people of the country went forth, and the light of this doctrine spread throughout the land. It was at that time that God raised up a Moses to lead us out of the land of darkness. It was then that Col. L. L. Polk came to the rescue, and with that foresight and wisdom that seem to have been prompted by Providence, he foresaw that unless sectional feeling engendered by the issues of the war could be allayed, no progress could be made. He foresaw that as long as the people were arrayed against each other by passion and prejudice, so long would the enemies of mankind combine to use the great weapon of sectional prejudices to the detriment of the people and destroy their prosperity and property. Then it was that that grand patriot left his home and gave his life to his country. Then it was that he went with a message to the north and to the east and to the west; then it was that he came back to the south with a message from our northern friends.

At this hour there stands at Raleigh an enduring monument; and the proudest inscription to be put on that monument will be, "Here lies the man who broke down Mason and Dixon's line."

My friends, the minute that all bitterness is laid aside and the hearts of the people beat as one, that very minute the American people begin to act for themselves. Then it was that the people who had been trodden into the dust and loaded with great burdens knew that their interests were the same as the people of the north and the east. That very moment they placed themselves upon the same platform of principles founded by Thomas Jefferson and Abraham Lincoln. In 1892 we went down to defeat, but our principles grew and flourished because they could not be trampled down. They were eternal; they were right, and from that hour to this they have continued to grow throughout this broad land.

A few weeks ago the great Republican party met in this city. The politicians again wanted to straddle the great issue that was before the people but the People's party had exposed the straddling treachery. The logic of events caused them to express themselves clearly upon the question of the day, and consequently they went over, bag and baggage, to the great money kings of Wall street and of Europe.

A few weeks after that there came another evidence of this great movement. The great Democratic party met in Chicago and was forced there to take a position, for they could not evade the issue longer; they were frightened; they were so alarmed, and some of them, no doubt, so conscience-stricken, that they formally decided to deliberately commit petty and grand larceny by stealing the People's party platform almost entire. They almost tried to get into our party. I am reminded of the old fellow who had his Bible stolen. He said: "Faith, and I hope it will cure the disease."

My friends, I hope it will cure the disease. My only surprise is that when they were stealing, they did not steal all the platform. If they had been frightened a little worse, I think they would. By the time this money question is settled and before, too, if we don't hurry up, the great transportation question—that great question which stands side by side with the money question—will be upon you.

A delegate: "What will they do with the transportation question?"

Senator Butler: "They will straddle it."

My friends, the great transportation question with the great financial question, are the two questions that must be solved before you can ever destroy these trusts and combines. The Standard Oil Trust could not exist in this land if it were not for its co-partnership with the transportation companies of the United States. The old parties of trusts and combines must turn their eyes to the thing that produces trusts and combines. When they do that, then they will strike the tap root of all the evil that has afflicted them—the evils of finance and transportation.

My friends, by the time you get this great financial question settled, this transportation question will be a burning question—a question as demoralizing to the old parties and as potent in awakening the American people to their condition as the great financial question has been; and if it had been as strong in the hearts of the people, the Democratic party would have declared for it in its convention. The People's party came into existence to perform a great mission. There was a necessity for it, and it is going to stay here as long as there is any necessity for it.

As long as the American people need an organization that is true, and one that will stand by them under all circumstances and give them the rights to which they are entitled, this party will continue to exist. If the People's party were to go out of existence tomorrow, the next Democratic National Convention would repudiate the platform it recently adopted at Chicago, and Mr. Bryan would stand no more chance four years hence of being nominated by that party than Thomas Jefferson would if he were alive.

Now, my friends, we have done a good deal. No young party has ever accomplished so much in the same length of time as we have done. We have endured the bitterness of denunciation and the abuse and malignity of party feeling. Right here comes upon us the greatest responsibility that has ever rested upon any party. We have raised an issue so universal, so great, so important, that we have split both of the old parties in two. Now we have either to save that issue or to renounce what we have gained and lay it down in defeat. No greater responsibility ever rested upon any convention.

Fellow citizens, shall it ever be said—remember we are making history, and prosperity or misery—shall it ever be said in the future that this great band of patriots who have had the nerve and the courage to leave the parties of a lifetime—this great band of patriots who have broken every tie that bound us and our fathers and our grandfathers in political organization—shall it ever be said that, after we have forced this issue to the front, we at this trying and critical hour shall ourselves be controlled more by party prejudice than by patriotism?

The only way to build up this party is by appealing to the best element of the old parties and appealing to their patriotism by telling them that this issue is greater than party. That is the only way we have ever taken a single man out of the old parties who was worth having. And it is the only way we shall ever take any man out of them in the future who is worth having. In this solemn hour let us drop the bitter feelings that may have been engendered since we came here. Let us stop believing that in one small head all wisdom and patriotism are contained. I have seen since I have been here one set of patriots going to one extreme, almost, it seemed, with more enthusiasm and madness than with reason. I have seen another set of patriots equally honest, equally devoted to truth and right, equally desirous of seeing the greatest good done for the greatest number, going to the opposite extreme. I have seen one extreme impugn the motives of the other, and the other extreme return the compliment. I have even heard a few thoughtless men charge that Hanna was running one, and others charge that the Democracy was running the other. My friends, I have seen enough faith in the faces before me, and enough faith in the God above me, to believe that this convention will not turn itself into a Democratic annex. I have too much faith in its patriotism and in its sense to believe that it will turn itself into a Republican annex. There is your danger. There stands one danger and here stands another, and one is as big as the other. It has been a part of my experience that, whenever you see some good men going to one extreme and other good men going to the other extreme, the path of truth lies between them. At this hour we need a Benjamin Franklin to rise over this body as he did when the warring factions were framing our Constitution. This great patriot and Christian arose when the crisis had come, and, raising his hand, said: "Let us all follow in prayer."

A great stillness came over the meeting, they prayed, asking for inspiration and wisdom from on high, and from that hour on history tells us that that great convention ceased to wrangle, and became a deliberative body, and every man reasoned and had patience with his brother. It was that seeming grace that gave us our great Constitution. And if this convention today rises to the height of patriotism that is necessary to save this country, it must be controlled by the same feeling and with the same inspiration from on high.

At this point Delegate Doggett, of California, cried out, "Nominate a Populist, without any reference to what the other parties have done heretofore."

My friend, there, has an honest belief. I am mighty apt to hear from another man over here on the other side if I wait a little. Both think they are right. But if this party lives (and God grant that it shall never die) and rises to the mission that it was born to accomplish, it must at this critical hour have the patriotism, the unselfishness of party pride to do just what we have been preaching for the last four years. If this convention won't follow its own teachings, it is unworthy to represent the people at home.

We have two extremes here, but it won't do to ruin this convention. We have to reason. What must we do? It is proper and right; it is fitting for a great party that had its birth on the broad cornfields and cottonfields of the South and the broad wheatfields of the West to have the wisdom and the patriotism to winnow the chaff from the wheat. What should we do? (A voice, "Nominate Bryan.")

My friends, we are told that whom the Gods would destroy they first make mad. I want to counsel our good and enthusiastic friends that every time they shout out here and interrupt, they are hurting our cause. This convention is not going to be ruled by any wild sentiment by either side, I believe. This convention has not been crushed by the other parties and it will not be stampeded by the moon. What is our duty? It is to indorse and approve what is right and condemn what is wrong. Any other course is not true Populism. The mission of the People's party has been to strike out what is wrong and to uphold what is right. And we have appealed to patriotism to rise above the party to do this and our appeal has brought forth two millions of patriots, and there are two million more patriots coming swooping into our camp. Listen, and I will tell you what you will find when you get home. I have been down on the old plantation at home where I was raised; I lived with a band of farmers representing all three political parties, and they were at the train and shook my hand when I left. The way those men felt is about the way the great American heart feels today. They said: "Butler, let us rise to that patriotic position that will make us have the confidence and respect of every honest man in the old parties."

If ever we gain another vote, we must gain it by being consistent now. One man who is a Populist said: "Butler, I will never go back to the Democratic party. I have no confidence in its leaders. I am willing to acknowledge what good they do, as far as they go, but no further." A Republican said to me: "I have been taught to hate the Democratic party. I have been taught to believe that the Republican party contained all the patriotism and unselfishness in the country, and at this hour I stand free and foot-loose, ready to obey the dictates of conscience and to lead in the way that will bring the best American victory to the American people." Now, my friends, if this is not Populism, if this is not the doctrine that you have taught in your home and in your township and in your county to build up the People's party, then your Populists are not like those in my section. The doctrine I am now preaching is the doctrine we built the party on, and I tell you today if you waver from your position of consistency, from this high patriotic position your party is built on, you talk no better than the old parties that you rose up to destroy.

There is not a man in this hall who, if he will go to his room tonight and get down on his knees, and pray to Almighty God to take all the prejudice and all the partisan feeling out of his heart, and ask His aid to do as a true Populist ought to do, but will rise saying: "It is my duty to stand by what I have taught in the past and let it lead where it may."

My friends, there is not a man in the People's party that loves it more and has more cause to be revenged against the old parties than I. There is danger of those patriotic enough to leave the old parties becoming prejudiced to such an extent as to be controlled by their feelings instead of their hearts and reasons. I believe that this convention is going to do what is wisest. I believe it is going to stand together. It is not going to split. How can it? We split both of the old parties and we split them on a principle. We cannot split, because we all stand for the same principles. And of course a party that has raised up a great principle and split the two old parties is not going to be foolish enough to allow itself to split on method and detail. We will stand together. We will go home from here a united band of brothers. We will strip our coats for the fray and see the millions of organized capital and gold monopoly stricken down in this country. We will do more than that. We will show you that this young giant, the People's party, comes out of that campaign stronger than it went into it. Mark you, the old parties will make mistakes in the future as they have in the past. This party is going to stand ready to hit them and take in their honest men at every mistake they make. We are willing to approve everything right they do, and we will condemn them when they blunder, or when they betray us as they have in the past. Remember that you are People's party men; that you have accomplished more in four years than the old parties have accomplished in a hundred. Remember that if we do our duty at this hour, the time is not far distant when we will be the majority party in America.